Praise for *I'm God's*

"It is with anticipation that I will recommend this study as an adjunct to psycho-therapy. Anticipation that God will use it as an offering of hope, empowerment, guidance, and recognition of value and nurturance to those whom will seek His face as a means of release from discouragement and depression."

—*Dr. Laura Roberts, Cornerstone Clinical Services, Portland, Oregon*

"I believe that God led me to your study, as it was exactly what I had been searching for and needed to help in my recovery from depression. I now see that having faith in God and turning to Scripture is the only way to get better and live a meaningful life. You have helped me and no doubt countless of others who are struggling."

—*Leanne K.*

"I liked the bite-sized bits of material because I could 'chew' on one idea at a time. Like a loudspeaker getting people's attention, getting them involved, and rescuing the hiding, hurting people."

—*Kat M.*

"I love it! This devotional is practical, down to earth, and enhances spiritual growth.

—*Adele Hooker, minister, retired*

"I can feel the light, and the reading has opened up such trust and hope in Father God."

—*Janice F.*

"It helped me a great deal to have someone bring the Bible to me and to draw out the relevant teachings and verses. Very helpful."

—*Elaine S.*

I'm *God's Girl*?

Why Can't I *Feel* It?

Kathleen,
Romans 15:13 —
Kimberly

by KIMBERLY DAVIDSON

DAILY BIBLICAL ENCOURAGEMENT TO
Defeat Depression & the Blues

I'm *God's Girl*?
Why Can't I *Feel* It?

TATE PUBLISHING *& Enterprises*

Published by Tate Publishing & Enterprises, LLC
127 E. Trade Center Terrace | Mustang, Oklahoma 73064 USA
1.888.361.9473 | www.tatepublishing.com

Tate Publishing is committed to excellence in the publishing industry. The company reflects the philosophy established by the founders, based on Psalm 68:11,
"The Lord gave the word and great was the company of those who published it."

Book design copyright © 2008 by Tate Publishing, LLC. All rights reserved.
Cover design by Lynly D. Grider
Interior design by Janae J. Glass

Published in the United States of America

ISBN: 978-1-60604-643-2
1. Christian Living: Practical Life: Women
2. Inspiration: Motivational: Devotionals
08.11.05

Table of Contents

Important Note

This devotional study is not intended to take the place of medical or psychological care. It is intended to be part of the spiritual component of your comprehensive care plan. If you are seeking outside help, a good place to start is to consult with your pastor and/or family physician.

If you are *suicidal,* seek professional help *immediately*. Call 1–800–273–8255 or 911 and ask for help. A professional will provide a safe place for you to talk and tend to your immediate needs.

The women's stories in this book are true, but their names and any identifying information have been changed to protect them. In some cases, I have combined similar stories into one narrative.

"When God opens a door, no one can close it…" (Revelation 3:7)

What if the Perfect Depression Medication Wasn't a Medication at All?

Another book on depression! But this book is different. It is *not* about how depression affects you, or about anti-depressants, or how to help or live with a depressed person. In this book we will explore in a series of daily teachings the different paths some amazing, and surprising, women took to get out of their personal dark dungeons.

Most books on depression are designed to be read in a short period of time, assuming one can focus long enough to read the material. More than likely, depression didn't devour your life over night. Presumably you have been carrying this burden for a while, and therefore change will not likely happen in a few weeks. The purpose of the daily format is to provide small, consistent doses of God's medicine. It's all about a relationship with God, not merely about changing your behavior or circumstances. It's about knowing the one who has the power to transform you into his special God's Girl. Only God knows how to heal and rejuvenate a soul.

This journey is about claiming the same hope that many extraordinary women of the Bible found, and the same joy many of our contemporaries are presently experiencing. You may wonder if God still performs miracles and healing today. Be assured that the same God who walked with Mary of Nazareth, Mary Magdalene, Moses, David, Hannah, the disciples, and Paul lives within you. This is the same God who gave them victory over seemingly invincible enemies, who provided for them when their resources were insufficient, and who guided their decisions. He is prepared to work powerfully in your life today.

If there is anything that ought to characterize the life of a Christian, it is joy. Step by step, day by day, we will follow a treasure map that can lead to significant changes in your life. This book is a God-tool for women who truly want to change and take charge of their lives.

Every woman has, for a time, felt down in the dumps and experienced loss of some kind. Adversity is a normal part of life. Even a life filled with success invites occasional disappointments. Yet sometimes we sink in quicksand and we can't get out. We can't pull ourselves out because life feels too hard. Loneliness is rampant in America today. Dr. Robert McGee, author of *Search for Significance*, wrote:

> Loneliness has already reached epidemic proportions ... Ninety-two percent of Christians attending a Bible conference admitted that feelings of loneliness are a major problem in their lives. All shared a basic symptom: a sense of despair at feeling unloved and fear of being unwanted or unaccepted.[1]

What a tragic commentary. A study published in the journal *The Archives of General Psychiatry* suggested that about one in four people diagnosed with depression might instead be struggling with emotions associated with the loss of a loved one or a job or some other event in the person's life—*the blues.* Many people describe themselves as depressed when they are really discouraged or unhappy or lonely.

Sadness can be a symptom of clinical or major depression. Dr. James Potash, an associate professor of psychiatry at John Hopkins, explains, "When psychiatrists think of depression, we think of what is called a syndrome—meaning a collection of signs (what other people can see) and symptoms (what a person feels) that occur together."[2]

Depression can be brought on by biochemistry as well as the loss of a loved one, unemployment, or even a bout of ill health. When we lose the ability to enjoy things or feel badly about ourselves, believing we do not deserve to be happy, or feel guilty for no reason or blame ourselves for something we had no part in, this is when we are likely to experience depression. Depression goes beyond the blues. Depression is generally a result of anger turned inward and/or a deep sense of loss.[3]

One in four women will experience at least one episode of depression in her lifetime. Some women experience many episodes.[4] Consider the words of one of America's greatest presidents, Abraham Lincoln, "I am now the most miserable man living. If what I feel were equally distributed to the whole human family there would not be one cheerful face on the earth."[5] We all develop elaborate defense mechanisms to block pain, dulling our sense of purpose.

You may have the blues or be genuinely depressed. In either case, lost in your feelings you are clinging to a thread of hope that something or someone will break through the fog of despair because we all have the desire to have joy in our lives.

Depression: A Spiritual Crisis

What is your chief concern in life right now? Most likely you answered, "To have happiness or joy." There is a difference between happiness and joy. The word "joy" is used 224 times in the Bible (NIV), whereas the words "happy" and "happiness" combined are used only thirty times. That is not a coincidence. Joy is not the same as happy or happiness. Joy is a deeply rooted confidence based upon knowledge that God loves you and that he cares for you. Joy is knowing, without a shadow of a doubt, that God is always there for you. It is dependant on a relationship with God.

Whereas, happiness is dependant on circumstances or on happenings, like a job promotion or getting married or finding out you are pregnant. A resolve to be happy is to set our own conditions to the events of each day.

Many see depression today as more a spiritual crisis when the issue becomes: What am I here for? Where is joy and laughter in life? What's my purpose?

Before lasting peace and joy can be found, we must answer these questions.

Christian psychotherapist Dr. Les Carter agrees that a modest amount of depression can be a sign of a hungry spirit.[6] He wrote, "Life is a journey, and our efforts to relate appropriately are meaningless if we do not stay focused on where we come from and where we are going."[7]

We're all spiritual beings. It is when our spirit unites with God's that we find true peace, joy, and fulfillment. Depression can even produce insight and wisdom that can be had in no other way.

From his years of experience caring for the depressed, Dr. Walter Johnson wrote, "Although I am convinced, and indeed scientific evidence is very strong in this area, that in many cases biological factors are a predominant cause of depression, I am very insistent that spiritual counseling is of the utmost importance in treating depressed individuals in conjunction, when necessary, with antidepressant medications."[8]

Dr. Daniel G. Amen, a pioneer in the field of brain imaging, states in *Healing the Hardware of the Soul*:

> How we live our life matters. The condition of our soul and the spiritual connections we make have a strong impact on the physiology of the brain. It is a reciprocal relationship. I have seen that sin (doing things that you know are wrong) disrupts healthy brain function and leads to anxiety, fear, and depression, while living with integrity and having a positive relationship with God and others actually improves brain function.
>
> A number of research studies have demonstrated that people of faith suffer less from anxiety disorders and depression and they recover seventy percent faster from these illnesses than those without a strong religious faith. The suicide rate and even mortality rate is lower for religious people than the non-religious.[9]

If we don't have union with God, life holds no hope. Recovery simply means recovering God's plan for our life. It takes courage to step forward and say, "I want help to be free from my burdens." This journey requires we follow God willingly and trust him to lead us safely through the pain and around unseen obstacles. He knows the safest and best route. The word journey is repeated to convey that change doesn't happen overnight. God doesn't always work in the way that seems most logical to us. Instead of guiding the Israelites along the most direct route from Egypt to the Promised Land, he took them on a longer route.

However, every day you can enjoy the place where you are while you travel down this road. Nothing is as heartbreaking as wasted grief. We can be determined to learn from it rather than be bound by it. Along the way you will find out who you really are—God's Girl. If you relate to what you've just read, this book is for you. Make a commitment, no matter how difficult, to focus and find energy. Make a promise to yourself today to meet God every day on these pages. Say yes to the incredible journey he has in store for you. To navigate this book, you will need a Bible and a journal or notebook. I quote from the New International Version (NIV) unless otherwise specified.

This is your day: "Arise, shine, for your light has come" (Isaiah 60:1).

Before We Begin ~ Pray With Me

Father, Jesus spoke often to his disciples about his joy being full in them. They were filled with joy as they realized who they were: your children. You say I, too, am created in your image, that your spirit resides in me, and I am a co-heir with your son. But Father, life seems so bleak right now. I don't have energy or hope. Even as I pray, I don't sense your presence. I am thirsty for an encounter with you.

Father, your Word says you know the plans you have for me, plans to prosper me and not harm me, plans for my future. Thank you for giving me incredible gifts and talents to accomplish your specific and unique purpose for me. But I am really feeling down on myself and everyone around me. Help me to pick up this book daily. Help me to recognize the voice of the enemy and all perpetrators.

Father, all I can do is affirm the goodness of life and try to hold on until the darkness is replaced by your light and love. Jesus did not pray that I'd be merely happy or even that I'd escape grief. He prayed that I'd have the same joy you had given him, a divine joy, a joy that comes from a deep and unwavering relationship with you.

Speak to me, touch me, and teach me; fill me with your joy using the Holy Bible and the material in this book to renew my mind. Help me to smile and laugh, even if just for a moment. Be my strength and salvation. I ask you to restore me and make me whole. I want to find and use my gifts and talents, set goals, and develop your plan for my life.

I am asking for wisdom or understanding, everything necessary to reach the finish line. Help me to set my heart and mind on you every minute of each day, and use your Word as a lamp to my feet and to light my path. Thank you, Father, for ensuring victory in my life today. In Jesus' name. Amen.

Part One

God's Exceptional Girls

Encouraged by God's Word

"Shout for joy, O heavens; rejoice, O earth; burst into song, O mountains! For the LORD comforts his people and will have compassion on his afflicted ones." (Isaiah 49:13)

Day 1: Extraordinary Women

Thank God there is hope—always hope. We have the same hope many women of the Bible had. As we study their lives, we will find they each have one thing in common with us: God's hand on them when life looked dark and they felt desperate. Although they lived in settings quite different than we are accustomed to, they faced many of the same challenges we face. Like you and I, they were unremarkable in and of themselves. They were common, ordinary, and in some cases, low-caste women. The one exception was Eve, God's first girl, who began life "perfect." Eve ruined her life by sinning. The biblical writers gave words to their emotions. They cried out to God, and sometimes against God…and God listened. God was their power.

As we study each woman's portrait, we are instructed in God's ways and find wholeness for our own lives. We will also meet some contemporary women who have been where we are right now. Look up from the bottom of your pit and feel them urging you to climb out. Their stories are stepping stones for us to ascend. Take their hands. Learn from them. Their faith infuses our faith, which must be nourished by the Word of God every single day because it provides indispensable guidance for living. Times may change, but the affect of God's presence remains the same.

Faith is our choice to believe that God will respond to our cries and prayers. To believe is more than intellectual agreement that Jesus is God. It means we put our trust and confidence in him, in the fact that *he alone* has the power to change us.

Reflection: What women, past or present, are heroes and represent hope for you?

~ *God loves you even when you're depressed.* ~

Dr. Gregory Jantz[10]

Day 2: God's Girls
Chosen and Special Daughters

God has the same personal message for you as he did for the women we will get to know: "Out of all the peoples on the face of the earth, I have *chosen you* to be my treasured possession" (Deuteronomy 14:2, author's emphasis). What a personal promise!

All the women cited in this book are God's Girls not because of any natural qualities they have created on their own, but because the Lord God, whom they put their trust and faith in, changed and refined them. Why would he use such improbable women? To display his mighty power of transformation. When we witness his work in our broken lives, our eyes turn upward. The Bible says, "For he *chose us* in him before the creation of the world" (Ephesians 1:4, author's emphasis). God orchestrated this moment long ago, to call every believer into a very special relationship with himself. This is an expression of the very heart of God. *Chosen people are special people.*

Each woman reminds us of our fallen, helpless condition. *But* through faith in Jesus, we have the ability to be filled with joy and victory because God says, *"I have chosen you and have not rejected you"* (Isaiah 41:9).

God's Girl is not the description of one woman but a portrait of different godly women, all with a direct connection to Jesus Christ. These women are influential not because of their beauty or career path or how smart their kids are. They *became* who they were created to be—women of influence and faith. They exemplify moral and spiritual qualities, not status, wealth, or beauty. The best part is we can learn from these women because they were, and are, just like you and I.

Reflect on the hope and these incredible promises from God.

~ *This day is a gift. Whatever it brings, I want to be present for it.* ~

Anonymous

Day 3: A Story
Ms. Jekyll, Monster Hyde

For decades I lived a secret, double life. By day I was Ms. Jekyll, a woman who worked very hard at making the outside sparkle. Look closely. Something was wrong. By night I morphed into the Monster Hyde—retreating into a dark, depressing dungeon where I fought the battles with my demons. I held a secret no one could know about. I was sick: a bulimic, an alcoholic, soaring on a rollercoaster ride with depression. Deep shame and a sense of worthlessness got greater and greater as the years passed.

I chose to medicate my pervasive anxiety with food, alcohol, and men; destructive, compulsive behaviors that I covertly hoped could cover the pain. The bulimia and alcohol provided a sense of emotional numbness, offering an escape from feelings of grief, shame, guilt, and loneliness. For years I couldn't stop the promiscuity, which only deepened the wounds of shame, humiliation, and abandonment.

I managed to keep my outside looking clean and polished. Addiction merely dressed my inadequacies and low self-image. There was no joy, only fear. As my self-esteem deteriorated, I isolated myself more, withdrawing into this monster's cave, turning to substances for comfort, and never realizing I was perpetuating the spiral of despair.

The problem is this kind of lifestyle promotes independence. It isolates and separates you from those who could help and encourage. It's painful because God designed us for interdependence. I yearned to return to the past to recover what I had lost—good health and secure relationships. Instead I found myself battling an empty, dark present.

Reflection: How do you relate to this story?

~ Feeling rejected became a default mode in times of stress or loneliness, triggering feelings of depression whenever my "circuits" felt overloaded. ~

Jane Johnson Struck[11]

Day 4: The Wrong Pursuit of Happiness

"Why me? Why do I do this? Why am I even here on earth?"

My responses pointed back to something I did wrong, or something that was wrong with me. I had high expectations for myself and what I assumed my life was "supposed to look like." I became depressed at my failure to meet these high standards.

At the time I'd never considered myself depressed. Depressed people sleep all day and ... *That's not me! And who wants that label?* I doubted everything about myself. Negative self-talk was normal-talk for me. I was too ashamed to ask for help, so I just sank deeper and deeper into the murky quicksand.

In my angst I would cry out to God or read a self-help or philosophy books, following treatment advice given to someone else, but these means failed because I wasn't asking the right person for help. Then in the midst of it all because of the promiscuity and drinking, I got pregnant and chose to have an abortion.

There was no joy, no hope. I couldn't take living that way anymore. *Help me!* Then something happened on my way to hell. I got saved. I needed someone to point me to Jesus Christ, and God sent that person. I made a choice to follow and commit my life to Jesus, and life started turning around.

Reflection: My story turned from despair to hope when Jesus entered. What ray of hope do you see in your life today?

> ~ *Hope does not disappoint us, because God has poured out his love into our hearts by the Holy Spirit, whom he has given us.* ~

The Apostle Paul (Romans 5:5)

Day 5: That Dark Place *Again*

Today is my forty-something birthday. As with many of my contemporaries, I stopped celebrating after number twenty-nine. The day began like any other work day…until I was called into my boss's office. I knew in my gut I would be the next lay-off casualty. Happy birthday to me! Another loss. I was in that dark place again.

Distressed, I turned to God, but this time something felt different. What I didn't know before was that I had to give God absolute control over my life, which I hadn't done. Clearly I was still in bondage, my soul still rooted in shame and pride. I still depended on others to bring me value. Instead of reading the Bible, I was reading *Cosmo* and *People*. I was more concerned about pursuing *my* image, rather than following God. God said, "All day long I have held out my hands to an obstinate people, who walk in ways not good, pursuing their own imaginations" (Isaiah 65:2).

All my life I could hardly stand *not* to be in control. Now I had to give Jesus all control. It was a struggle. I had to ask myself: what are my spiritual and emotional needs? To be a good person? Give my money to charity? Be the perfect wife? No. The answer was Jesus. I knew *about* God, but I didn't *know* him. We have two choices: do nothing, or make the decision to change with the help of the Almighty God. Our lives don't change. We change when we ask Jesus to come live with us.

Reflection: What specifically has happened to make you feel stressed and out of control? Pray for an answer if it is not clear. This is your bondage. Jesus is at your door with his hand held out. Now give it to him. Let go and trust him only.

~ Here I am! I stand at the door and knock.
If anyone hears my voice and opens the door, I will come in. ~

Jesus (Revelation 3:20)

Day 6: Spiritual Nourishment

Tears can be as heavy as words. God collects each tear we cry and will lead us to springs of living water (Isaiah 25:8, Revelation 7:17). Isn't that a soothing picture?

God never gave up on me. He promised that *nothing* would separate him from me. "As long as a tiny spark remains, a fire can be started and fanned into a roaring blaze" (Romans 8:39).

My story is of God's unconditional and merciful love. I wasn't giving him anything, yet he gave me the hope and miracle of healing. He gave me the hope of a new and better future. I was free to pursue my dreams! I was transformed because I was exposed to a higher standard. Before Jesus, my life was out of control and indulgent. I didn't realize how much until I met him. I learned to talk to God. He listens. My voice matters to him. He waited . . . and waited . . . patiently for me to give back, and that has been the real blessing in my life—my relationship with God. He takes me seriously.

Someone once said that it takes an act of faith to walk the path God blazes. In his book, *When God Interrupts,* M. Craig Barnes writes: "When we are abandoned by the things we value, when we discover that no matter how much we have gathered we do not have enough, when we realize that even in the currency we value we are very poor, we are ready to start talking to God. Not before. Faith means betting our lives on the grace of God."[12] You can talk to God because you matter a great deal to him.

Reflection: What other similarities or parallels do you see in this story and your life? Today name what your hope is. Naming our hope sets us free.

~ *Remember, your encounter with God is the only thing that will set you free.* ~

Anonymous

Day 7: Trials of Faith

Life's difficulties, your struggles, are trials of faith.

God uses pain to get our attention. He gives us the gift of faith, and then our faith is tried while navigating through the pain. With the Lord's leading I stepped out, allowed him to use the pain and faith as part of my transformation process. Ms. Jekyll and the Monster Hyde died. The Bible says that "if anyone is in Christ, she is a new creation; the old has gone, the new has come" (2 Corinthians 5:17). God did not intend for me to live undefeated, having sin and evil continually rob me of joy and peace.

For the first time, I completely surrendered my will to God. Peace flooded my soul. Surrender means I can't do it by myself any longer. It is a difficult and painful process, yet it is extremely rewarding. I finally understood and really believed that apart from God, I could do nothing. I accepted myself as his valued child. I no longer felt the urge to escape through bingeing and purging, drinking excessively, or seeking counterfeit intimacy. I claimed victory!

By faith I put my trust in God and started talking (praying) to him every day. I committed to start taking care of my body and reading the Bible. That was the genuine start of my personal relationship with him. Together we started on an incredible journey to clean up the emotional damage that had led to my depression and destructive behaviors. God never leaves anything incomplete. What a promise!

Reflect on what surrender and trust in God means to *you* personally.

> ~ *The Lord may, and most likely will, allow our faith to be tested.*
> *If our faith is real, it will survive. And, after the experience passes,*
> *we will have even more faith than before.* ~

Stanley Baldwin[13]

Day 8: Real Transformation

I'm God's Girl! God blesses and restores the years the locusts have eaten. The hurt and depression were replaced with landscapes of grace. All strongholds—old ideas, toxic moods, and negative worldly thoughts were being broken down, demolished. God recovered his plan for my life and delivered it to me on a solid gold plate.

This is victory! Winning the battle means seeing myself as I really am: a woman of nobility, created in the image of God with a crown on my head. Not a cuffed prisoner but a victor. I am the apple of God's eye! I am royalty!

When I chose Jesus, the Holy Bible became my weapon to resist and fight the enemy. God's Word led me to change my thinking, which meant victory! There's a saying, "You accomplish victory **step by step**, not by leaps and bounds." I am a champion today because I sought guidance from God and pressed through the grief and hopelessness step by step. God knew the pain that my sin brought on and longed to rescue me. I love God more than anything else in the world. I eventually could feel love and love others and, more importantly, love me.

The same comfort and love I received from God enables me to come alongside others as a special friend. Jesus taught me also what it means to honor—to honor God, my marriage, and my family. As I grew more and more into God's Girl, I found security and my focus changed from myself to others. I reached out as God's beloved daughter.

Reflection: How does this story of transformation give you hope today?

> ~ *I came to Christ bankrupt. My capacity to blunder drove me to*
> *His feet, and to my happy astonishment He took me, forgave me,*
> *and sent my happy soul singing its way down the years.* ~
>
> E. Stanley Jones[14]

Day 9: A Kaleidoscope

I am not perfect. But I have a perfect, gracious God. As long as I continue practicing his principles (which I will be sharing with you), I am at least headed in the right direction. In many ways I will always be broken because I am human and in need of Jesus. Some of us are more broken than others, and it is the job of the less broken to help the more broken. With healing comes a brokenness that makes us God's Girl, allowing God to persistently continue his transforming work. I am constantly working toward being the woman God created me to be. It is my desire to take you with me for a while. We will navigate through God's Word and purpose every day.

We never start a relationship with God, we respond to him. One way we respond to God is by opening up our Bible and seeking out his Word. If we don't, we'll never find our purpose, which is to glorify God wherever he has placed us.

Like you, I want to be a ray of light in this broken world, to reflect the light of Jesus. I would never have looked into my crystal ball and predicted I would actually be God's Girl, a disciple of Jesus Christ, illuminating his light. When life is good … it's good! Amen!

We are each like a kaleidoscope made up of bits of broken, colored glass, which are constantly and forever changing. Inside each kaleidoscope is a mirror that reflects the beauty of each piece of broken, colored glass. As the pieces come together, a magnificent and beautiful vision is created. You are that beautiful vision!

Reflect on *your* unique image of the kaleidoscope. What colors are in the glass? What do the pieces look like? Envision them coming together.

~ *I never realized that broken glass could shine so brightly.* ~

Henri J.W. Nouwen[15]

Day 10: MileStone

Jesus said, "Don't be anxious about tomorrow. God will take care of your tomorrow too. Live one day at a time" (Matthew 6:34, TLB). Our journey requires baby steps taken one day at a time. Dispersed along the way are *MileStones* designed to move you further ahead and acknowledge your progress: (1) Move Forward, (2) Challenge the Old Way of Thinking, (3) Prayer and Meditation, and (4) Self-Soother. The acronym *Stone* stands for: **S**teps **T**o **O**vercome **N**egative **E**motions.

Move Forward

Minister and civil rights leader Martin Luther King Jr. said, "If you can't fly, run. If you can't run, walk. If you can't walk, crawl. But by all means, keep moving."

With God we are safe and can reveal our painful secrets. His healing journey encourages us to seek him, which is to discover the truth enabling us to move forward. Look at what Jesus does to the wounded and broken people. The blind can see. The deaf can hear. The lame walk. The mysterious woman stops bleeding.

If you haven't bought a Bible or journal yet, do so, because you cannot move forward without either.

Challenge the Old Way of Thinking

I believe the most content people in the world are the ones who know God. Turmoil takes on a new meaning when they leave the consequences to him. Oswald Chambers said it best, "Never quench the Spirit, and do not despise Him when He says to you: Don't be blind on this point anymore; you are not where you thought you were. Up to the present I have not been able to reveal it to you, but I reveal it now."[16]

Day 11: Pray and Meditate

I felt the presence of God surround me. The weight had been lifted off. I knew God had heard my prayer. There is nothing more mysterious than prayer because it moves us to call upon a being we cannot see. Prayer asks God to change what we can see. Let me assure you that there is no "one size fits all" way to pray. We each have different spiritual temperaments, and God wants our worship according to the way he made each one of us.

Prayer means we talk to God, then we meditate. Meditation means slowing down, quieting ourselves, so we can hear what God's gentle voice is trying to tell us. We allow his words to penetrate our soul. Some days it is difficult to pray, especially when you are down or tired, but it's important to commit to a routine.

A second way to begin breaking through our wall is through journaling. Journaling is about putting our thoughts onto paper. It is a tool that enhances emotional growth because we have an opportunity to release pent-up emotions.

What will it take for you to make a ten- to twenty-minute commitment to prayer and journaling each day? Martin Luther wrote, "Prayer is the most important thing in my life. If I should neglect prayer for a single day, I should lose a great deal of the fire of faith."[17]

Self-Soother

An important part of our journey involves self-soothing because it helps to relieve stress. It is important to schedule these self-soothers because they help us begin to move away from the pain of depression to the awareness of joy and happiness.

Take a hot bubble bath and meditate on what you have learned this week.

Part Two

The Gift of Change

Encouraged by God's Word

"May the God of hope fill you with all joy and peace as you trust in him, so that you may overflow with hope by the power of the Holy Spirit." (Romans 15:13)

Day 12: God's Girl Sara

"I'd always been one of those people who had it all together. But simple tasks like getting showered and dressed were crippling." The doctors diagnosed Sara with major clinical depression. She tried every form of treatment and dozens of medications. Then her diagnosis was changed to refractory depression, or non-responsive depression.

Long story short, Sara later learned that her depression was not of a biochemical or emotional nature as everyone assumed. It was spiritual. She started to see a Christian counselor, went to church and began praying. Sara elaborated, "I discovered a series of lies I believed my entire life, which greatly affected my personality ... so much deception and destruction. I always believed that I was a loser and never good enough."

Dr. Valerie Whiffen, author of *A Secret Sadness* asserts:

> Depression is different from sadness, because it changes the way we feel about ourselves. We feel we aren't good enough, or we're to blame for our problems. When sadness changes the way we feel about ourselves, we are on the road to depression.[18]

God's quiet voice broke through, "I have a plan of hope for you, Sara!" He promised, "You will seek me and find me when you seek me with all your heart. I will be found by you and will bring you back from captivity" (Jeremiah 29:11–14). Sara started studying the Bible and praying. Within three months her depression subsided.

Reflection: What can you take away from Sara's story that gives you hope?

~ *Lead me from death to life, from falsehood to truth. Lead*
me from despair to hope, from fear to trust. ~

Christopher Herbert[19]

Day 13: Soul Searching

Put these two gems into your treasure chest: every miracle in the Bible started as a problem; and even in the midst of your storm, God still has a plan and purpose for your life. The Bible is our ultimate authority, and we need to become good students of it so we can understand the character and will of God, and ultimately, our purpose.

Consider this: you are standing outside on a bright, sunny day, but you cannot see the sun. Then you notice you've been standing under an umbrella. If an umbrella can block out the magnificence of the sun, how easy it is for our fears, doubts, and feelings of unworthiness to block us from God. As the sun continues to shine with an umbrella over our head, God is always ready to have a relationship with us in the midst of our despair.

Our hearts are heavy. We're tired of carrying this pain. That's not God. He pursues his children, patiently waiting for us to respond to him. We can wait until circumstances get really out of control. Or we can choose to grab a hold of his hand right now. It's never too late to make friends with God.

"Restore us, O God; make your face shine upon us" (Psalms 80:3). Your heavenly Father has the ability to give you a supernatural heart and mind transplant, and give you your life back. Not the tarnished, abused, or neglected one, but the one he designed while you were being knitted together in your mother's womb.

Reflection: What do you want God to do for you through this book specifically? Where does your spirituality fall in your plan for healing?

~ *Depression is neither a sign of weakness, nor of*
moral decay, nor a punishment of God. ~

Dr. Binford W. Gilbert[20]

Day 14: Come Just As You Are

I never planned my life to take the turn it did. Why can't we just dump the past and move on to sunnier pastures? Because we each have invisible bonds from our past that still connect us to people or circumstances. If not dealt with God's way, they continue to influence our present.

In order to experience joy, we have to embrace memories, both good and bad. Don't be afraid. God has already made the same promise to you that he did Sara: "to prosper you and not to harm you, plans to give you hope and a future" (Jeremiah 29:11).

For this to become reality, we choose to look forward to what God has in mind. We can be personally transformed—but only with the help of Almighty God. All you need is a sincere desire to change and a willing heart and mind. That may seem like an unmovable mountain at the moment, but not if we ask our wonderful counselor to lead us. You may have to revisit a hurt or trauma in order to develop healthier ways of living. You don't have to prove anything to anyone or pass a moral test. You don't have to explain yourself. You don't have to be any more worthy or deserving or trustworthy or upstanding than you are now. You have only one decision to make—to take back the joy in life and really seek Jesus Christ himself and make him number one in your life. The goal is to replace powerlessness, or fear of victimization, with personal empowerment. When there is joy, we cannot feel hopeless, insecure, ashamed, unworthy, unsafe, or guilty. When there is joy, we say we never knew life could be this good!

Reflection: In your own words define joy.

> ~ *Take the first step in faith. You don't have to see the*
> *whole staircase, just take the first step.* ~
>
> Martin Luther King Jr.[21]

Day 15: The Pain of Changing

There are two kinds of pain in the world: the pain of never changing, and the pain of changing. When we are not living the kind of life God intended, change is called for. If we want to keep doing it our way, God will step aside and let us wear ourselves out. Or, we can learn to trust him with our life. The Bible says, "Cast your cares on the LORD and he will sustain you" (Psalms 55:22). We can chose to act like a kid, bent on self-will and scream, "I'll do it myself!" or we can step out in faith and take God's hand and let him do all the hard work. We must initiate that change.

Sometimes change feels good; other times it feels bad; but no matter how tough the opposition may seem, we have hope because we ask God for wisdom, perseverance, and courage. "Be strong and take heart, all you who hope in the LORD" (Psalms 31:24).

I won't lie to you; whether you struggle with the blues or are seriously depressed, change will not happen overnight. Change requires time, the encouragement of others, the truth and application of God's Word, and the power of God's Spirit. I know that if you walk with the Lord in faith and trust him on a day by day basis, you will be changed positively in some way. The process of change is built on a foundation of truth, which we will explore. Truth is our medicine and is often painful, but it is not the enemy. Pain is a sign that life is beginning again!

Reflection: Make the decision today to take God's hand and walk into the storm (the pain) holding tightly onto him. Give him permission to shine his light on your thoughts, feelings, and actions.

~ Problems do not go away. They must be worked through or else they remain forever a barrier to the growth and development of the spirit. ~

Dr. M. Scott Peck[22]

Day 16: Band Aid or Deep Cleansing?

Years ago I read an article written by a woman who described three benefits of not having children. One, the couple without children has both financial and spatial flexibility. They can do whatever they want, whenever they want. Two, the couple are not prisoners to years of emotional highs and lows. Three, if you are the woman, you don't have to endure the pain and those ugly stretch marks ... and that dreaded baby fat that, for some women, never goes away.

My husband and I didn't have children. I read this article with glee. But then I thought it had to be the author's attempt to cover the pain and sadness of not experiencing the joy of parenthood. At that time in my life, this article was a nice, pretty Band-Aid that I could put over my feelings of sadness and inadequacy. Her three points helped me emotionally justify my position and deny my feelings.

That's what we often do; put a neat Band-Aid over the wound instead of deep cleaning it so it will mend properly. The writer of Hebrews says, "Let us draw near to God with a sincere heart in full assurance of faith, having our hearts sprinkled to cleanse us from a guilty conscience and having our bodies washed with pure water. Let us hold unswervingly to the hope we profess, for he who promised is faithful" (10:22–24).

God knew I was stuck in the quicksand. He knew I couldn't get out on my own and needed to give me a push up from the bottom of the pit. This should be good news because he can do the same for you!

Reflection: What situations or people are you putting a Band-Aid on?

~ *God promises a safe landing, not a calm passage.* ~

Anonymous

Day 17: Do You Really Want to Change?

Years ago I met a woman who walked with a pronounced limp. I asked if doctors could restore her. She replied, "Yes, but … it would be horrible. They would have to break my leg all over again. I'd be in a cast and a wheelchair for two months then on crutches with a brace for a couple of months, followed by nine months of grueling physical therapy. No way! I can manage just fine the way I am."

Puzzled, I asked, "Are you saying you don't want to restore your leg … get well?" There was dead silence. She looked away and murmured, "Maybe I don't." I probed further, "Don't you think it's worth the hard work and pain to be able to walk and run and dance again for the rest of your life?" Her fear crippled her decision.

Do you want to get well—be restored? Some people believe change is motivated primarily by the avoidance of discomfort. Or if you can just make people feel bad enough, they will change. These are fallacies. In John 5:6, when Jesus saw the lame man around the pool and learned he had been in this condition for a long time, he asked him the same question. The question was meant to encourage an expression of the man's desire. The invalid responded by making excuses. Then Jesus commanded him, "Get up! Pick up your mat and walk" (John 5:8–9). At once the man was cured; he picked up his mat and walked. With Jesus' command came enablement. He doesn't ask us to do something that is impossible without enabling us to do it.

Reflection: If Jesus said that to you, how would you respond? No one is comfortable with voluntary pain. Would you say no for fear of revisiting the old pain?

~ Some of us get so comfortable in our depression that we
really don't want to get out of it. ~

Dr. Maxwell Maltz[23]

Day 18: The Gift of Restoration

"Come back to me and live" (Amos 5:4).

These are God's words. Restoration is a gift from God. Forests burn down and are able to grow back. Broken bones heal. Even grief is not a permanent condition. Restoration is part of the healing process.

In the Old Testament, leprosy, like AIDS today, was a terrifying disease because there was no known cure. If a person contracted leprosy, a priest declared him a leper and banished him from his home and city. He was sent to live in a community with other lepers until he either got better or died. Yet when a leper begged Jesus to heal him, Jesus reached out and touched his diseased body (Matthew 8:1–4).

When we hurt we find ourselves weighing perceived benefits against the perceived disadvantages. Our tears are our advantage. They can be seeds that will grow into a harvest of joy, because God is able to bring beauty out of dust and ashes. When burdened by sorrow, know your times of grief will end. We must be patient as we wait. As we wait on the Lord, we will find new strength. We will eventually "fly high on wings like eagles" (Isaiah 40:31).

Perceived advantage: God's great harvest of joy is coming!

Reflection: Pray as David did, "When I walk into the thick of trouble, keep me alive in the angry turmoil. With one hand strike my foes, With your other hand save me. Finish what you started in me, God. Your love is eternal—don't quit on me now" (Psalm 138:7–8, Msg).

~ *Troubles are often the tools by which God fashions us for better things.* ~

Henry Ward Beecher

Day 19: Our Mighty Physician

Someone once said that insanity is doing the same thing over and over again, expecting a different result. We've become very comfortable procrastinating or making excuses in order to avoid confronting the skeletons in our closet. Whether we have a loss that seems irreparable, or a life-threatening diagnosis, or a child that's just entered teenager-ville, we'll always have hope as long as we rely on God.

You may know about God, but not know him personally. That is one of the objectives of this book, for you to know God intimately. God said, "I am the LORD, who heals you" (Exodus 15:26).

The first step toward healing is not running away from the pain but to run toward it. We access God's power by requesting it from him based on our belief and faith in his character. How? Our antidote is to mediate on the record of God's goodness to his children, which we find in the Bible. This is the source of victory.

God's Word is that healing agent, just as medicine is a healing agent: "He sent forth his word and healed them ... I have heard your prayer and seen your tears; I will heal you ... I will add fifteen years to your life" (Psalm 107:20; 2 Kings 20:4–6).

This is hope for those of us who have wasted too much time in the land of funk! "You restored me to health and let me live. Surely it was for my benefit that I suffered such anguish. In your love you kept me from the pit of destruction; you have put all my sins behind your back" (Isaiah 38:16–17).

Reflection: Come to God just as you are. Ask him to begin to walk with you through your present circumstances.

~ *The distance is nothing; it is only the first step that is difficult.* ~

Marie de Vichy-Chamrond

Day 20: Our Mighty Counselor

God has provided you with your own personal Counselor! Jesus said to his disciples, "I will ask the Father, and he will give you another Counselor to be with you forever—the Spirit of truth ... for he lives with you and will be in you" (John 14:16–17).

The following is an excerpt from *Answers to Life's Problems* by Billy Graham.[24]

> Question: I have some emotional problems and my family doctor says I need to see a psychiatrist. My friend says I just have to have enough faith. What do you think?
>
> Billy Graham: "I would be the first to say that faith in God is very, very important. It is essential for our eternal salvation, and it is crucial for our everyday lives. But at the same time I do not agree with your friend, because God may choose to use an able psychiatrist to help you with some of the problems you are facing.
>
> You see, when you have faith in God, you actually trust a problem into his hands. You are saying, "Lord, I don't know how to deal with this, but I have faith that You do. I trust that You will lead me and give me wisdom, so I will know what is right. I trust You to show me the right answer to this situation."

I have met hundreds of women who have put their faith in God and have been healed. Some were guided to excellent counselors, some to gifted physicians, and some to rehabilitation facilities, and a few have even been miraculously healed.

Reflection: How will your faith in God be critical for your next 24, 48, 72 hours?

~ *Faith does not necessarily mean that we sit back and fold our hands,*
assuming God will work without ever using human tool. ~

Billy Graham

Day 21: MileStone

Steps To Overcome Negative Emotions

Move Forward

Taking Your Medicine

Medicine must be taken according to directions to be effective. To take it *after* meals when the directions say to take it *before* meals will reduce its effectiveness. To take it once in a while when the directions say three times a day will produce limited results, if any. No matter how good the medicine is, it must be taken according to the directions or it won't work. So it is with God's medicine.

The directions for taking God's medicine are found in Proverbs 4:20–21: "Listen closely to my words. Do not let them out of your sight, keep them within your heart; for they are life to those who find them and health to a man's whole body."

Tears Are Medicine Too

Most people say they feel better after a good cry, which is no surprise. It's not the purification act that spells relief; it's most likely the actual chemical composition of tears. When you cry, it appears stress hormones released by the brain are flushed out of your system. You begin to feel calmer, maybe even refreshed. [25]

Go ahead and have yourself a good cry. It's good for you!

> ~ *What a relief it is to weep for the hurt child within us, or cry over a painful situation. Tears water the soul.* ~

> Anonymous

Day 22: Challenge the Old Way of Thinking

Old thinking says: *I can do it by myself!* Or we may use Scarlett O'Hara's (*Gone with the Wind*) method of dealing with reality: "I'll think about that tomorrow." God is challenging us not to go this alone. We need him and other people. Think and pray about beginning to connect with friends and a church if you aren't doing so. A small fellowship group or Bible study is an excellent resource for sharing, encouragement, and comfort. God wants all of us to be in an environment where we can experience his love through our relationships with other believers.

Secondly, you may feel now is the time to talk to a professional therapist. A special notation if you are coping with sexual abuse: you may believe because the abuse happened decades ago, there is nothing you can do about it now. Ignoring painful feelings may have been adaptive at the time the abuse happened (a child lacks control over the abuse). However, continuing to avoid bad feelings as an adult can lead women to stay in painful situations. Ignoring the abuse can put you at further risk for depression.

Guidelines for finding a counselor: [26]
Seek a counselor that is Christian, or who offers a spirituality component. Locate a counselor who takes the opportunity to take you to the Word of God, to teach you about the character and ways of God, to help you see the necessity of total surrender to Jesus Christ as Lord. Dr. Charles Stanley said, "If it's [psychotherapy] not based on the Word of God, all you have is just somebody's opinion, you have some ways or some steps, but apart from God, they're still depending upon themselves.[27]

Ask for a personal referral. Ideally try to get a recommendation from a therapist's client. If you can't find that, ask your doctor or pastor for a few names. Look for a licensed psychologist, social worker, or family therapist who shares your values and faith (psychiatrists typically don't do much counseling).

Evaluate. After your first visit, ask yourself: did I feel heard and valued? Did I feel comfortable? If you answer no to these, keep searching for the right fit. It may be a good idea to give a therapist a second chance if you feel hurt or upset.

Finances and logistics. Is this counselor covered by your insurance policy? Is the cost doable? Typically psychologists are most expensive, followed by social workers and family therapists. Is the office location convenient for you?

Pray and Meditate

I love GOD because he listened to me, listened as I begged for mercy. He listened so intently as I laid out my case before him. Death stared me in the face, hell was hard on my heels. Up against it, I didn't know which way to turn; then I called out to GOD for help: "Please, GOD!" I cried out. "Save my life!" (Psalm 116:1–4)

. . . and He did!

Self-Soother

Either rent or take out of your collection an old funny movie and watch it tonight.

Part Three

The Power

Encouraged by God's Word

"For everything that was written in the past was written to teach us, so that through endurance and the encouragement of the Scriptures we might have hope." (Romans 15:4)

Day 23: I Love You!

Does your heart cry, "God has forgotten me. I'm not worthy of God's grace and mercy"? Nothing could be further from the truth! God assures you, "Can a mother forget the baby at her breast and have no compassion on the child she has borne? Though she may forget (some mothers do forget), I will not forget you! I have engraved you on the palms of my hands" (Isaiah 49:15–16). Close your eyes. Picture your name imprinted into your Father's immense hand. (Your name), beloved daughter of God.

God is talking to you. "That's how much you mean to me! That's how much I love you! I'd sell off the whole world to get you back, trade the creation just for you" (Isaiah 43:4). When we are plugged into God, we are plugged into love. It flows through us like a current, energizing our sluggish hearts and minds. We can read all kinds of self-help books, watch talk shows, attend seminars, but if we lack a connection with God, we will continue to struggle. God has a purpose for each one of us *if* we allow him to be Lord of our life and are willing to let go of the past, the grief, fear, bitterness, and loss. It isn't enough to have good intentions; you must have the desire to let him reside within you and take control of *everything*. Restoration is possible if we do it God's way.

A professor of mine once said that we all have two lines—a lifeline and a purpose line. If the purpose line drops, then the lifeline drops. If we don't feel we have a purpose, a meaningful reason to live on this earth, we lose our lifeline.

Reflection: In your journal write what the Isaiah verses say to you personally.

~ While not fun, depression can generate a longing to come to terms with life's purpose, and it can force you to contemplate the role of spirituality in life's journey. ~

Dr. Les Carter [28]

Day 24: Our Instruction Manual

Wouldn't it be nice to pull out an instruction manual with easy directions that would solve all our problems? Good news: the Holy Bible is that instruction manual. The Bible is the instrument God uses to change our thinking. *I'm God's Girl? Why Can't I Feel It?* uses the Bible for a reason. It is a tool to help you get closer to God and resist the enemy. The literal written content won't set you free. It is Jesus Christ who sets you free. The Bible speaks truth and has special meaning and instruction for each one of us today. Your response to what you read, in faith, will determine the outcome.

The apostle Paul said, "I can do nothing by myself, but I can do all things through Christ which strengthens me" (Philippians 4:13). A few verses earlier, Paul says, "I have learned to be content whatever the circumstances" (4:11).

With the infusing of Jesus Christ's strength, we can learn (Paul said "learned") to be content with our circumstances and ourselves. We learn to believe the saying, "God doesn't make junk!"

Whether we are aware of it or not, daily we are in a battle to become what we were created to be. You deserve to have all of your aspirations realized, no matter what has happened. If you want to change and get your life back, you need a Bible.

Reflection: I challenge you to set time aside each day to leave this world and beam into God's world, the Bible. If you don't have a Bible yet, make plans to purchase or borrow one today.

~ *The Bible was not given to increase our knowledge, but to change lives.* ~

D.L. Moody

Day 25: God's Word Transforms

I love stories packed with drama, with both good and bad characters, and plots with an exciting resolution. That is a description of the Bible, and there's even a collection of poems. It is the living voice of God and the way he communicates to us. The Bible describes God's Word as living and active, sharper than any two-edged sword (Hebrews 4:12) and promises not to return empty (Isaiah 55:11). It has a beginning and an end. Each story is in the Bible for a reason, and we can learn from each person.

The more time you spend reading God's Word, the more you will be changed—guaranteed. The Bible gives us hope. It is power. God tells us he is the only one who can set the captive free. He is the only one who will bind up the brokenhearted. He is the only one who can make us new creations in Christ. He is the only one who can transform our hearts and minds from a sinner into a saint, from despair to joy.

If you're not happy, go directly to God and seek his face. Just like a child who is unhappy because someone took her doll away, she runs to the safety of her parent. He is our safety net, our joy, happiness, and peace. Someone once said, "The miracle is not in the healing—it's in the asking."

Jesus said numerous times, "Follow me." Ask God to assist your study of the Scriptures within the Bible. Ask him to speak to you through his Word so you might understand his truth and will for your life.

Reflection: Are you ready to follow Jesus? If not, what are your concerns?

~ If this book had not been the book of God, men would have destroyed it long ago. Emperors and popes, kings and priests, princes and rulers have all tried their hand at it; they died and the book still lives. ~

H. L. Hastings

Day 26: Our Image of God

Before we move forward, it is vital we talk about the one we are placing our future in. Who is God to you? What image do you have of him? I believe we each have an intellectual understanding of God, which is what we were taught in Sunday school, catechism, Bible studies, and sermons, plus a personal and emotional experience of God. Christians should have a God concept that is characterized by love, peace, strength, and wisdom, but many do not. Why?

We all need to feel secure, so we pattern relationships after what we learned about relationships from our parents. If we felt we had to be perfect to please our parents, then we feel we have to be perfect to please God. Conversely, if we feel we can make mistakes and be accepted by our parents, then we can make mistakes and be accepted by God. This is not unusual because the Bible says that our parents are made in God's image. So we believe our earthly dad has the same power and influence that we perceive our heavenly Father has.

If our earthly dad didn't validate us or show us love, or he hurt us in some way, then we might expect the same from our heavenly Father. Our culture rewards the self-made man, so you may have received the message that God won't help you, therefore you don't need, or can't depend on, God. Perhaps you were told you were bad, an evil sinner, therefore God is the source of your pain! These perceptions are simply not true.

Reflection: What are your present perceptions of God? What about your earthly father? Compare your list and circle any common perceptions.

~ *We are intrinsically lovable.* ~

C.S. Lewis [29]

Day 27: What The World Needs Now is His Love

When I was a teenager, one of my favorite songs was, "What the World Needs Now (Is Love Sweet Love)." Billions of people in this world are desperate for love. Maybe you're one of them. There is an awesome God who wants to love you deeply!

It's easy for us to define God in terms of our own expectations and history with our own earthly father. In doing so, we make God man-like. God is infinitely greater than man is. You may not be experiencing his almighty love because you have an unloving God image. One reason we hold false perceptions of God is our tendency to project onto God the unloving characteristics of the people we look up to.

God's Girl develops her image of God from the Bible, not from false or painful relationships. Our negative images of God are often rooted in our emotional hurts from our past. Maybe, like me, you have been running after that mirage called "acceptance."

Perhaps a parent or teacher told you that she or he didn't like you, that you'd never amount to anything, or you were just plain looking. Have you been blaming yourself? Our desire for approval never dies with age, and it affects our self-image.

The good news is that God can root out and replace the negative and painful with hope and love. God so desires for us to know his character that he went to extraordinary lengths to let us see and feel it through his son, Jesus. Jesus would never hurt us. God is looking for a heart that recognizes the need for him.

Reflection: Is your heart turned toward God? What do you want to say to him right now?

> ~ *Gods says, "I am God, and not man—the Holy One*
> *among you. I will not come in wrath." ~*

Hosea (Hosea 11:9)

Day 28: Negative God Images

We have been reflecting about our image of God. Do you see yourself in any of these God-image scenarios? [30]

1. A little girl has known only rejection and abuse from her father whom she loves. Then in Sunday school she is taught that God is her heavenly Father. Based on her experience with her natural father, she now sees God as a rejecting and abusing person she cannot trust.

2. If your father was distant, impersonal, and uncaring, and wouldn't intervene for you, you may see God the same way. Therefore you feel unworthy of God's love and involvement in your life. You find it difficult to draw close to God because you see him as disinterested in you.

3. Maybe your father was pushy and controlling, inconsiderate, or violated and used you. You may see God in the same way. You think you are probably worthless in God's eyes, and perhaps that you deserve to be taken advantage of. You may think God will force you to do things you don't want to do.

4. If your father was like a drill sergeant, demanding, never expressing approval, or intolerant of mistakes, you may have cast God in his image. You likely feel God will not accept you unless you meet his demands, which seem unattainable. This perception may have driven you to become a perfectionist.

5. If your father was weak and you couldn't depend on him to help you or defend you, your image of God may be that of a weakling. You may feel unworthy of God's comfort and support, or that he is unable to help you.

6. Maybe your father was overly critical and was hard on you. Maybe he didn't believe in you or your capabilities and discouraged you from trying. If so you may perceive God the same way. You don't feel you're worth God's respect or trust. You may even see yourself as a continual failure, deserving criticism.

Reflection: Think about the ways your image of your father possibly may have affected your perception of God, which in turn affects your own self-image today.

~ *God loves you just the way you are, but he refuses to leave you that way.* ~

Max Lucado [31]

Day 29: The Loving Daddy

Yesterday may have been an eye opener for you. In contrast to the negative perceptions many women have about God, there are positive character qualities. Do you see yourself in any of these God-image scenarios?

1. If your father was patient, you are more likely to see God as patient and available for you. You feel you are worth God's time and concern. You feel important to God, and he is personally involved in every aspect of your life.

2. If your father was kind, you probably see God acting kindly and graciously on your behalf. You feel you are worth God's help and intervention. You feel his love for you deeply and are convinced he wants to relate to you personally.

3. If your father was a giving man, you may perceive God as someone who gives to you and supports you. You feel you are worthwhile to God. You believe God will give you what is best for you, and you respond by giving of yourself to others.

4. If your father accepted you, you tend to see God accepting you regardless of what you do. God doesn't dump on you or reject you when you struggle, but understands and encourages you. You are able to accept yourself even when you blow it or don't perform up to your potential.

5. If your father protected you, you probably perceive God as your protector in life. You feel you are worthy of being under his care, and you rest in his security.[32]

Reflection: If you found your father on this list, you are further ahead than many other women. Thank God right now for that precious gift, and pray for your sisters that will be working toward changing their negative and wrong perceptions.

~ *The greatest gift I ever had came from God. I call him Dad!* ~

Anonymous

Day 30: God Has Huge Plans for Your Life

"Why did God create me? What does he want from me?" It is not a coincidence you are reading this. God's Word says he went out of his way to choose *you*. You have the opportunity to accept or reject his offer. He loves you immensely, but he will not force you to follow him. That is your choice.

Above everything else, God wants a personal relationship with you. Maybe you've never been told you can have personal relationship with God through his Son Jesus Christ. God loved *you* so much that he stepped out of eternity and became a perfect man in the person of Jesus Christ and then willingly died in your place to purchase a pardon for your sins. The Bible goes on to say that after Jesus was buried, he rose from the dead. It is that event that makes a relationship with God possible for all of us!

The Bible tells us that God created us in his image. He made us to reflect him in the very essence of our being and life. We were created for a specific reason. The disciples lived and walked with Jesus every day, and we can do the same. We can know Jesus better and his plans for us more deeply and fully because his Spirit dwells inside of us when we ask him into our lives. God is fully committed to helping you become the person he intended for you to be—God's Girl.

Reflection: How would you characterize your relationship with God right now?

~ Your relationship with God will be fulfilling yet challenging. It will be purifying because He will expose areas of your life that need to be cleansed. You will become wiser and more disciplined. He will also give you the desires of your heart as you delight yourself in Him. ~

Dr. Charles Stanley, InTouch Ministries [33]

Day 31: Why Doesn't God Answer All My Prayers?

When God doesn't do what we want, it's not easy. It has been said that to demand God to answer all our prayers is to ask for his omnipotence (power) without having the benefit of his omniscience (knowledge). Looking back, I'm grateful God said no to some of my prayers. God knows more than we do about our life. The mystery of faith calls us to love and serve a God whom we don't always understand, which is why it's called faith.

Prayer is more than simply talking to God. It means trusting him with our day-to-day concerns and circumstances. When we focus on knowing God and we spend time with him, we begin to understand the way he thinks. Then something happens in our hearts and minds. Over time we discover that our point of view begins to shift. We trust God with our problems. We also think about ourselves less. Instead we place greater priority on God and the concerns of others.

Reflection: We are realizing we are not self-sufficient and need to ask God for everything. Just be yourself before God and present your troubles. Prayer need not be impressive and eloquent. Jesus taught that it should involve approaching God with a reverential attitude, placing our will alongside his, and asking humbly for God to meet our daily needs, forgive our sins, and keep us from sinful situations.

~ *Prayer is the mortar that holds our house together.* ~

Mother Teresa

Day 32: MileStone

Steps To Overcome Negative Emotions

Moving Forward

Someone once said, "A ship in harbor is safe, but that is not what ships are built for." Moving forward involves risking what is unknown. Moving out of an old, familiar rut requires that we have courage and that we trust in the one who knows and cares. To move on, we must act.

Yesterday is gone. Endings, though, give us the chance to begin again. We may not be able to see the new beginning that lies ahead, but we can trust God that it will be there for us when we are ready. Moving forward means we cannot bring everyone with us on this journey (as much as we would like). We don't have to wait for those we love to decide to change as well. We are not being disloyal by allowing ourselves to move forward.

Challenge the Old Way of Thinking

As you begin to move in the direction of becoming the woman God created you to be (a very special, unique, and one-of-a-kind God's girl), it is important to surround yourself with what you want to become and begin to change that old way of thinking.

Moving forward requires us to begin to identify sources of negativity and affirm ourselves with the truth. Our mind is like a computer virus, full of negative thoughts that we need to identify, quarantine, and replace with truth. We reboot often! Andrew Carnegie said that anything in life worth having is worth working for.

Day 33: Pray and Meditate

St. Theresa's Prayer

May today there be peace within.

May you trust God that you are exactly where you are meant to be.

May you not forget the infinite possibilities that are born of faith.

May you use those gifts that you have received, and
pass on the love that has been given to you.

May you be content knowing you are a child of God.

Let this presence settle into your bones, and allow your soul the freedom
to sing, dance, praise and love. It is there for each and every one of us.

Self-Soother

Take a short walk. If it's cold or rainy, put warm clothing on and grab an umbrella. Use all your senses and take in God's creative work.

Part Four

Breaking Out of a Prison of Pain

Encouraged by God's Word

"I, the LORD, have called you in righteousness; I will take hold of your hand. I will keep you and will make you to be a covenant for the people and a light for the Gentiles, to open eyes that are blind, to free captives from prison and to release from the dungeon those who sit in darkness." (Isaiah 42:6–7)

Day 34: Why Do We Endure Pain?

All around us the world seethes and festers with painful ailments and injustices that are beyond our control. Pain is a gift (yes, a gift) because it shows us that we have the capacity to feel, whether it is physical or spiritual. Physical pain demonstrates our capacity to experience the hurtful, negative part of our world. The function of pain is put into perspective in this story.

Ashlyn Blocker's parents and kindergarten teachers all describe her the same way: fearless. They nervously watch her plunge full-tilt into a childhood deprived of natural alarms. In the school cafeteria, teachers put ice in Ashlyn's chili. If her lunch is scalding hot, she'll gulp it down anyway. On the playground a teacher's aide watches Ashlyn from within fifteen feet, keeping her off the jungle gym and giving chase when she runs. If she takes a hard fall, Ashlyn won't cry. Ashlyn is among a tiny number of people in the world known to have congenital insensitivity to pain with anhidrosis, or CIPA.[34]

Pain is there for a reason. It lets your body know something's wrong and needs to be fixed. Our nerves give us messages, warning us of danger, as well as delights. What is true of the body is true of the soul. Amidst our pain God loves us, gives himself to us, and eagerly waits our response. No one understands God's ways, but we *choose* to keep walking toward him in the darkness. His peace is available if we *choose* to take it.

Reflection: Will you choose God's will even if it means experiencing pain?

~ A commitment to Christ and obedience to his commands stretch us
beyond ourselves, and that hurts. But this is a very different pain from that
inflicted by torture or punishment. Growth pain is the kind we don't
regret; it leads to health and not disease or neurosi. ~

Eugene H. Peterson [35]

Day 35: Jesus' Pain

In the Bible the garden of Gethsemane is known as the site of agony, where our Lord was taken prisoner by the Jews and suffered intense anguish. The Bible reads:

> "He [Jesus] began to be sorrowful and troubled. Then he said to them, "My soul is overwhelmed with sorrow to the point of death" (Matthew 26:36–38).

> "An angel from heaven appeared to him and strengthened him. And being in anguish, he prayed more earnestly, and his sweat was like drops of blood falling to the ground" (Luke 22:43–44).

This angel appeared to Jesus and strengthened him against the loss of hope. The effect was surprising—Jesus cried harder, so hard that his sweat became like drops of blood. The "sweat of blood," called haematodrosis, though rare and abnormal, is neither impossible nor out of the ordinary course of nature. Jesus actually feels our hurt. Matthew said, "He had compassion on them" (Matthew 14:14).

The Greek word for compassion is *splanchnizomai:* to be moved as to one's inwards (splanchna).[36] It is to be moved with compassion in your gut and is frequently recorded of Christ toward the multitude and individual sufferers. Jesus *felt* the limp of the crippled, the pain of the diseased, the aloneness of the leper, the shame of the adulteress woman, and the humiliation of the sinful. Our hope becomes the richest in our deepest suffering. Jesus' message: *I feel your pain. Do not lose hope.*

Reflection: How has this story strengthened or changed your definition of hope?

> ~ *Yet it was our grief he bore, our sorrows that weighed him down. And we thought his troubles were a punishment from God, for his own sins!* ~
>
> Isaiah (Isaiah 53:4, TLB)

Day 36: Job's Pain

Are not my few days almost over? Turn away from me so I can have a moment's joy before I go to the place of no return, to the land of gloom and deep shadow, to the land of deepest night, of deep shadow and disorder, where even the light is like darkness.

Do these words (Job 19–22) describe your experience?

The book of Job describes intense pain and suffering. Job was a good man who suddenly lost everything of value, including his children. The light in Job's life quickly turned to darkness. Job wanted to know what he had done to deserve such torment. God eventually speaks to Job. God doesn't answer the "whys." *He reveals himself.*

Why doesn't God show us the entire picture? Perhaps because enlightenment might not help us. Perhaps because we are incapable of comprehending the answer. When I was a kid and challenged my dad, he'd say, "Because I said so." In other words, "Just trust me!" We can't possibly understand the view from above. What I find comforting is that Job shows us that emotional turmoil is part of the human condition.

Reflection: Can you be satisfied knowing you may not be given complete answers from God? Talk (or write in your journal) with God about your attitude toward suffering.

~ God wants us to choose to love him freely, even when that choice involves pain, because we are committed to him, not to our own good feelings and rewards. He wants us to cleave to him, as Job did, even when we have every reason to deny him hotly. ... Job did not see the Giver because of his gifts; when all gifts were removed, he still sought the Giver. ~

Philip Yancey [37]

Day 37: Our Pain

God has been honest with us: we will experience trouble and pain in this life. The psalmist wrote, "I know, O LORD that your laws are righteous, and in faithfulness you have afflicted me" (Psalms 119:75).

As we tackle life's difficulties, we come face to face with our own suffering and we make a choice how to react. Lewis Smedes points out, "We have to feel pain we do not want to feel, carry burdens we do not want to carry, put up with misery we do not want to put up with, cry tears we do not want to shed. If we feel no hurt now, we will, when it is all said and done, be the most miserable of people ... In the end it will be all right with us only if we have felt some of life's wrongness."[38]

Have these words spoken of you? Job was a man of upright character, a man of God, yet God allowed Satan to destroy everything of value. You may feel that God is callous, unfair, and even silent, allowing Satan access to your life. I wondered why a loving God allowed me to wallow in the pain of addiction. Why did he wait seventeen years before showing up? While God may allow us to suffer in his crucible for a reason beyond our understanding, he is always aware of our pain ... and is equally compassionate. Just because the devil shows up, that doesn't mean we panic or lose hope. We can seek answers from all the wrong sources or choose to believe the truth that God is absolutely in control and our pain has merit.

Meditate on this truth: God is always sovereign. Everyone else, including Satan, is under God's authority, power, and control.

~ *Crises and difficult circumstances can potentially elicit the best in a person.* ~

Marian Eberly [39]

Day 38: True Freedom

Is it possible to become comfortable in our bondage? Yes. It's human nature to want to live in the familiar. Freedom for the Hebrew slaves meant Pharaoh would be angry and attack them. Freedom wasn't worth it. Even today many slaves and prisoners upon release do not want freedom. They prefer the reassurance of the known.

I am privileged to volunteer at a women's correctional facility in Oregon. No one loves a prisoner: "They get what they deserve!" But the Bible says, "Remember those in prison as if you were their fellow prisoners" (Hebrews 13:3).

Prisoners know they are guilty. However, they don't understand why family and friends can't separate what they did from who they are—a human being God created, God's Girl. Bondage occurs with or without bars. The metaphor of prison resonates with many of our own experiences. Here is the good part; the prophet Isaiah declared:

> He [God] has sent me to bind up the brokenhearted, to proclaim freedom for the captives and release from darkness for the prisoners, to proclaim the year of the Lord's favor and the day of vengeance of our God, to comfort all who mourn, and provide for those who grieve in Zion, to bestow on them a crown of beauty instead of ashes, the oil of gladness instead of mourning, and a garment of praise instead of a spirit of despair (Isaiah 61:1–3).

God holds your key to freedom. That key was cut through Jesus Christ.

Reflection: Right now, if you're ready, ask God for the key.

~ The chains of habit are too weak to be felt until they are too strong to be broken. ~

Samuel Johnson [40]

Day 39: The Great Escape

Incarcerated women often say prison was one of the best things that happened to them. They meet Jesus. He sets them free. One woman who is *not* incarcerated wrote, "I feared people. The door of my prison cell shut tight. What other people thought of me was more important than what God thought of me. I hated wearing this mask. I longed to be the woman God created me to be. I longed to be released from the prison I had locked myself in, free from the enemy's grip, but I didn't know how to get there."[41]

Yesterday we read Isaiah's words. In the book of Luke we find that same scroll was handed to Jesus. Unrolling it, Jesus found the place where it is written:

> "The Spirit of the Lord is on me, because he has sent me to proclaim freedom for the prisoners and recovery of sight for the blind, to release the oppressed, to proclaim the year of the Lord's favor." After reading it, Jesus rolled up the scroll, gave it back to the attendant and sat down. The eyes of everyone in the synagogue were fastened on him. He said, "*Today this scripture is fulfilled* in your hearing" (Luke 4:17–21, author's emphasis).

God's arms are wide open, and he accepts you just the way you are *right now* in your dark prison. I want this journey for you to be the biggest jailbreak since *The Great Escape*! You have been given the key to unlock your prison cell—break out!

Reflection: Write in your journal what freedom looks like to you today.

~ The word "hope" I take for faith; and indeed hope is
nothing else but the constancy of faith. ~

John Calvin [42]

Day 40: Adopted by God

Every day babies and children are put up for adoption and placed with new families. No doubt you know someone who was adopted, or perhaps you were. Many significant people have been adopted, including my own mother (who is significant to me). Did you know God adopted you? The apostle Paul tells us:

> For you did not receive a spirit that makes you a slave again to fear, but you received the Spirit of sonship (adoption). And by him we cry, "Abba, Father." The Spirit himself testifies with our spirit that we are God's children. Now if we are children, then we are heirs—heirs of God and co-heirs with Christ, if indeed we share in his sufferings in order that we may also share in his glory (Romans 8:15–17).

Adopted people are chosen. *Chosen people are special people.* When we accept Jesus Christ as our Savior, we receive his Spirit—the spirit of adoption—of freedom from bondage, a new life! God gives us *his* name. My name is no longer "rejected." It is "beloved daughter of the King." When I comprehend I have been adopted, specifically chosen, and am unconditionally loved, I know I am a very special person! Some people in this world may have discarded us, but God gives us a new family. If you have excluded God, remember he still loves you and is waiting for you to say the words, "Father, I need you!" The Bible says to call him Father or Abba, an intimate word that denotes the close and dear relationship between a child of God and himself. That revelation makes us want to cry "Daddy," doesn't it?

Reflection: How does being adopted into God's family change your outlook?

~ *God carries your picture in his wallet.* ~

Tony Campolo [43]

Day 41: I Am an Heir!

God, our Creator, selectively chooses us when we come to him by faith. We become part of his eternal family—never again enslaved to our old life!

> So also, when we were children, we were in slavery under the basic principles of the world. But when the time had fully come, God sent his Son, born of a woman, born under law, to redeem [*set free*] those under law, that we might receive the full rights of [*daughters*] sons. Because you are sons [*daughters*], God sent the Spirit of his Son into our hearts, the Spirit who calls out, "Abba, Father." So you are no longer a slave, but a son [*daughter*] … God has made you also an heir (Galatians 4:3–7).

What a picture! The world is cruel and unfair when we become its slave. As a believer you have been adopted into God's family. God has a new name for you: "My precious beloved daughter." You are no longer a slave to the world but an heir! Every person you study in this book is in your bloodline, which gives you the right to stand up and say, "My past, or my family's addictive or dreadful history, is not part of my future. I am in the same bloodline as Jesus Christ. I can overcome!"

Reflection: "Give thanks to your Father, who has qualified you to share in his inheritance in the kingdom of light. For he has rescued you from the dominion of darkness and brought you into the kingdom of the Son he loves, who bought our freedom with his blood and forgave us all our sins" (Colossians 1:12–14).

~ God's promise is his extended hand. When we reach out we are startled to find we have touched life and power. We have grasped the mountain-moving hand. ~

John White [44]

Day 42: Freedom and Peace

I hope you are beginning to feel like you have just been given the best surprise party in the world. Many people think because God has given them freedom and an eternal home they have to pay him back somehow because we are used to paying our own way. However, God in his grace reaches down and takes us into his family. He says, "You came through my Son who lived and paid the price, so now come and live with me." This is the theology of adoption.

"In love he predestined us to be adopted as his sons through Jesus Christ, in accordance with his pleasure and will" (Ephesians 1:4–5).

The Living Bible says, "There is all of God in a human body; so you have everything when you have Christ, and you are filled with God through your union with Christ" (Colossian 2:9–10).

Don't confuse God's love with man's love. Man's love is often dependent on performance or what you can do for someone else. God models the qualities we're looking for: love, goodness, mercy, forgiveness, and grace.

> Therefore, there is now no condemnation for those who are in Christ Jesus, because through Christ Jesus the law of the Spirit of life set me free from the law (bondage) of sin and death ... The mind of sinful man is death, but the mind controlled by the Spirit is life and peace (Romans 8:1–2, 6).

Reflection: Express your feelings to God about being adopted into his family.

~ *The real "work" of prayer is to become silent and*
listen to the voice that says good things about me. ~

Henri J.W. Nouwen [45]

Day 43: God's Girl Hannah

Freedom. Peace. Meditate on those words. They come with the privilege of being God's daughter. Do you believe that? If all we know is what we have been told our whole lives, then we wear a different name. My name is abuse. My name is abandoned. My name is prostitute. My name is ugly duckling. I have no name.

You do have a name, and it is Beloved Daughter of the King. I want you to meet a beloved sister of yours, Hannah (1 Samuel 1). A godly woman, Hannah became depressed when she had to deal with infertility and a strained relationship over a prolonged period of time.

Hannah had a godly husband, Elkanah, who loved her dearly. He was a Levite (a priest). However, Hannah lived with stress in her family. "He [Elkanah] had two wives; one was called Hannah and the other Peninnah" (verse 2). Peninnah is a hard name to pronounce; let's call her Penny!

Penny had children, but Hannah had none. Some of Hannah's stress came from living in a polygamous marriage. Polygamy was tolerated in ancient Israel. Multiple wives meant many children. In those days a woman who was barren was considered useless and divorceable.

It is likely that Hannah was Elkanah's first wife, but because she was barren, he took a second wife, Penny, to ensure his family's name would be carried on. With so much pressure to have children, you can imagine the stress put on a married woman.

Reflection: What kind of stress are you facing today?

~ *Standing in the middle of the road is dangerous. You will*
get knocked down by the traffic from both ways! ~

Anonymous

Day 44: Losing Hope

Can you imagine what it must have been like for Hannah to live with a co-wife who had no trouble bearing children? Penny kept conceiving children, while Hannah continued to suffer emotionally from her infertility. As each menstrual cycle passed, so did her hope for having a baby. Certainly she was envious and depressed. As mentioned yesterday, it was a disgrace to be barren in her culture. Children were so important that a husband was permitted to divorce a barren wife. Missionary Dorothy Pape wrote,

> Until very recently, in most parts of the world, a woman has been seen mainly as a baby-producing machine, as someone to perpetuate the family line of the father. Even Martin Luther, great Christian that he was, stated, "If a woman becomes weary, or at last dies from child-bearing, that matters not; she is there to do it." "For a woman not to become pregnant has usually been taken as a sign that she was displeasing to the gods and has been regarded as just grounds for divorce or the taking of a concubine.[46]

Thankfully, people don't look down on infertile women in today's society as they did in Hannah's day. Hannah had one great asset—Elkanah loved her and didn't divorce her. Pastor Jim Andrews wrote, "People who bear their pain and misunderstanding, their abuse and misrepresentations, in a godly manner find that God eventually rescues great gain from the jaws of enormous pain, if not now, then in eternity."[47]

Reflection: When life looks dark, we don't see our assets. Ask God to show you three of your assets. Write them down.

*~ I can't change the direction of the wind, but I can
adjust my sails to always reach my destination. ~*

Anonymous

Day 45: In Bitterness of Soul

As we examine these two women, undoubtedly Hannah played the comparison game with Penny. Think about it. Two women living in the same house, sharing the same husband! You probably could have cut the competition, pressure, rejection, and jealousy with a knife!

Penny kept adding to Hannah's stress. Verses 6–7 say, "And because the LORD had closed her womb, her rival kept provoking her in order to irritate her. This went on year after year. Whenever Hannah went up to the house of the LORD, her rival provoked her till she wept and would not eat."

Penny tormented and humiliated Hannah for years! Surely Hannah felt like a failure, very depressed. Elkanah compassionately said, "Hannah, why are you weeping? Why don't you eat? Why are you downhearted? Don't I mean more to you than ten sons?"

"In bitterness of soul Hannah wept much and prayed to the LORD. And she made a vow, saying, 'O LORD Almighty, if you will only look upon your servant's misery and remember me, and not forget your servant but give her a son, then I will give him to the LORD for all the days of his life'" (1 Samuel 1:8, 10–11). We can feel how desperate Hannah was—so desperate she bargains with God. The fact is, she turns to God and entrusts the resolution to him, looking to him to sustain her.

Reflection: What correlations to do you see between your life and Hannah's? How have you been bargaining with God?

~ *Even though I walk through the valley of the shadow of death, I will fear no evil, for you are with me; your rod and your staff, they comfort me.* ~

Psalms 23:4

Day 46: Hannah's Road to Freedom

Hannah's despair was overpowering, and even though Elkanah loved her, it appears that he was not able to console her. Hannah withdrew from life and kept silent. However, Hannah still held onto one person—God. Hopelessness has the ability to keep us silent, doesn't it?

The Bible says that in the *bitterness of soul, she wept*. Then she prays to God and negotiates for a son. Can you feel her desperation? Her resolve? Don't forget me, Lord! Give me a son! Hannah was desperate and knew God was her only source. She went to the tabernacle and cried bitterly. We feel her burden here:

> Eli observed her mouth. Hannah was praying in her heart, and her lips were moving but her voice was not heard. Eli thought she was drunk and said to her, "How long will you keep on getting drunk? Get rid of your wine."
>
> "Not so, my lord," Hannah replied, "I am a woman who is deeply troubled. I have not been drinking wine or beer; I was pouring out my soul to the LORD. Do not take your servant for a wicked woman; I have been praying here out of my great anguish and grief" (1 Samuel 12–16).

In the midst of her grief, Hannah now has to deal with a false accusation, but she finds a friend, Eli.

Reflection: When have you been falsely accused? Perhaps that is the source of your stress today. If it is, talk to God about the situation.

~ *He rides pleasantly enough who is carried by the grace of God.* ~

Thomas a Kempis [48]

Day 47: Eli's Sympathy

Hannah was depressed. Provoked by Penny's malice, she refused to retaliate. Instead she poured out her heart and soul to God, and she had an ally in Eli. He said, "Go in peace, and may the God of Israel grant you what you have asked of him" (verse 17).

Then Hannah went her way and ate, "and her face was no longer downcast" (verse 18). Hannah joined in the worship of the Lord in the morning. Her prayers were answered: "So in the course of time Hannah conceived and gave birth to a son" (verse 20).

As a result of Hannah's honest praying and faith in God, Hannah was fulfilled as a woman, capable of bearing children (she had five more). The key to understanding Hannah's dramatic turnaround is attributed to focusing on God. She turned from herself and looked up.

She also had an ally. The first step toward healing is sharing your heart, and your secret, with a trusted person. When a woman shares with me, I get extremely excited because she is taking that first baby step toward healing. Let Hannah be your pillar of hope. Her God is our God, and he hasn't changed, nor will he. His purpose has not changed either. If God loved Hannah yet allowed her to endure this pain, then he will make us not only his burden-bearers but receivers of blessings, all for his glory.

Reflection: What did Hannah know about God that you can apply to your life today?

~ *But from everlasting to everlasting the* LORD's *love is with those who fear him, and his righteousness with their children's children.* ~

Psalms 103:17

Day 48: Hannah's Prayer

Sometimes God lets us struggle until we recognize our dependence on him. In doing so, he gives our faith an opportunity to grow and mature. Hannah's heart was pointed toward God. Hannah's prayer: "There is no one holy like the LORD; there is no one besides you; there is no Rock like our God" (1 Samuel 2:2).

Hannah recognized God's holiness and the presence of God's Spirit working within her, changing a negative situation a positive one. She knows God is firm, strong and unchanging.

"Do not keep talking so proudly or let your mouth speak such arrogance, for the LORD is a God who knows, and by him deeds are weighed" (1 Samuel 2:3).

Most likely thinking of Penny's arrogance, Hannah didn't have to get even with her. She recognized that God has perfect knowledge about everything in life. He will be the judge, and that gives us confidence that he knows what he's doing.

"The LORD brings death and makes alive; he brings down to the grave and raises up. The LORD sends poverty and wealth; he humbles and he exalts. He raises the poor from the dust and lifts the needy from the ash heap; he seats them with princes and has them inherit a throne of honor" (1 Samuel 2:6–8).

Hannah learns that God is power and in control. He controls everything that goes on around us and within us, through his power and knowledge.

Reflection: How does her prayer apply to you today?

~ That which we persist in doing becomes easier—not that the nature
of the task has changed, but our ability to do it has increased. ~

Ralph Waldo Emerson [49]

Day 49: MileStone

Steps To Overcome Negative Emotions

Move Forward

Pastor and author Max Lucado poignantly expresses:

> God is for you. Turn to the sidelines, that's God cheering your run. Look
> past the finish line, that's God applauding your steps. Listen for him in
> the bleachers, shouting your name. Too tired to continue? He'll carry you.
> Too discouraged to fight? He's picking you up. God is for you.[50]

Challenge the Old Way of Thinking

Begin to put affirming thoughts into action: "Today, with God's help, I will do one
thing more than I think I can do."

- If I'm too tired to get out of bed, I will not only get up but also
  take a shower.

- If I don't have enough energy to go to work, I will get dressed then
  drive to the parking lot.

- If I just can't face the world, I will walk to the end of the street and
  back. I will reach a little further than whatever I believe my limitations to be.

- I will remember: when I take that little extra step, it seems easier
  than I thought it would, and I feel better too.

Reflect on Will Rogers's (1879–1935) wise advice: "Even if you're on the right
track, you'll get run over if you just sit there."

Day 50: Pray and Meditate

Psalm 16:1–11

Keep of me safe, O God, for in you I take refuge.

I said to the LORD, 'You are my Lord; apart from you I have no good thing.'
As for the saints who are in the land, they are the glorious ones in whom is all my delight.
The sorrows of those will increase who run after other gods.
I will not pour out their libations of blood or take up their names on my lips.
LORD, you have assigned me my portion and my cup; you have made my lot secure.
The boundary lines have fallen for me in pleasant places; surely I have a delightful inheritance.
I will praise the LORD, who counsels me; even at night my heart instructs me.
I have set the LORD always before me. Because he is at my right hand, I will not be shaken.
Therefore my heart is glad and my tongue rejoices; my body also will rest secure, because you will not abandon me to the grave, nor will you let your Holy One see decay.
You have made known to me the path of life; you will fill me with
joy in your presence, with eternal pleasures at your right hand.

Self-Soother

Angels are everywhere. Acknowledge the angels in your life and tell them thank you.

Part Five

The Creator

Encouraged by God's Word

"From the east I summon a bird of prey; from a far-off land, a man to fulfill my purpose. What I have said, that will I bring about; what I have planned, that will I do." (Isaiah 46:11)

"For I know the plans I have for you," declares the LORD, "plans to prosper you and not to harm you, plans to give you hope and a future. Then you will call upon me and come and pray to me, and I will listen to you. You will seek me and find me when you seek me with all your heart." (Jeremiah 29:11–13)

Day 51: A Story

Story adapted from Dr. Henry Cloud's book, *Changes That Heal.*[51]

Once upon a time, alien beings were bored and wanted a new god. They sent representatives to Earth and visited dozens of churches and religious institutions. The aliens returned with not one, but two new gods, and one was a *goddess!* Her name was Grace. Grace was nice and attractive. She talked about love, getting along, and forgiveness. Grace had fed the poor and visited prisoners in jail. The aliens said, "I don't know why, but Grace seems lost. Something's missing."

The other god's name was Truth. Truth was mean. Truth kept telling the people on Earth all sorts of things about them that made them feel bad. On the other hand, Truth set up campaigns against nasty enemies, such as lying, cheating, adultery, abortion, and drunkenness. This god was like a big religious street sweeper. The people that followed Grace smiled. The people that followed Truth cringed.

Grace and Truth. What do they really mean? Why are they so important? We need to know what grace and truth are because Jesus is "the Father, full of grace and truth" (John 1:14).

Reflection: In your own words, describe the attributes of both grace and truth.

> ~ *People need the direction of truth to know where to go. Then they*
> *need the empowerment of grace to help them get there.* ~
>
> Randy Alcorn [52]

Day 52: God's Grace

Grace can be difficult to not only define, but embrace. Grace is the unmerited favor of God toward people. It is not earned, meaning we don't deserve it. It is a gift. "[I]t is by grace you have been saved" (Ephesians 2:5).

I once heard a story about a man who was sitting in a restaurant when a homeless person came in and ordered a sandwich, fries, and a coke. When the waiter gave her the check and asked her to pay, she said she didn't have the money. One patron who overheard the conversation responded, "I'll pay her tab." This is grace—unconditional love and acceptance. Jesus paid your tab with his life.

As Jesus hung nailed to that cross, and today as he looks at the mess we've created in our lives, he says, "You don't have to pay. I already did." You don't need to do *anything* to be loved by God or another person. You don't need to be perfect or have to perform or please others. You cannot sin so badly that grace cannot save you. Grace ignites a determination to keep going.

Grace only comes through Jesus Christ (John 1:14, 16–17), and our faith is the channel through which we receive that miraculous, marvelous grace. Along with this gift comes the realization that God wants us to turn from godless living and sinful pleasures and to live good, God-fearing lives day after day (Titus 2:12).

Reflect on the gift of grace given to you by your Father.

~ Grace is the pardoning, purifying, and beautifying activity of God—all forever undeserved—making something winsomely useful and redemptively charming. ~

Paul S. Rees [53]

Day 53: God's Truth

If you only hear grace, then you don't hear truth. An irate father challenged his daughter, "I want an explanation, and I want the truth." She responded, "Make up your mind, Dad. You can't have both."

What is truth? Truth describes how things really are—what's real. God's truth is the law—a blueprint, or structure for people to live by. Truth is fundamental to abundant life—it offers guidance and sets limits. God and truth are inseparable. To reject truth is to reject God. Without truth the enemy has access into our life, and we begin to believe lies that keep us in bondage.

Truth without grace says, "You should do this," or, "You should be this way." I'm not accepted for the way I am. Instead I am judged.

Prior to going to prison, Elaina had complete support from her pastor's family. They helped her find a lawyer, babysat her kids when she went to court; they did all the things a loving family would do. Now that she is incarcerated they haven't answered her letters or accepted phone calls. She said, "Just like the jury, they found me guilty and have thrown me behind their bars. It really hurts me. How can I trust a pastor again?"

Truth says to Elaina, "You broke the law. Bad lady! You must accept the consequences. Take one 'Go To Jail' card." Grace plus truth says to Elaina, "You broke the law and must accept the consequences, but I still love you. We all make mistakes, and there is no one to judge you except God. I support you all the way."

Reflection: Why do you and I need a God that is full of grace plus truth?

~ *For Your loving kindness is great to the heavens and Your truth to the clouds.* ~

Psalm 57:10 (NASB)

Day 54: Grace and Truth in Jesus

Grace and truth invite the real me as I really am, warts and all, into a relationship with God and others. Grace and truth must work together. John 8: 3–11 tells the story of Jesus and the adulteress woman. The Pharisees brought a woman caught in adultery and placed her out in front of the crowd. Moses' law said to stone her to death.

Jesus stood up and said, "All right, hurl the stones at her until she dies. But only he who never sinned may throw the first!" The Jewish leaders slipped away one by one until only Jesus was left in front of the crowd with the woman. Then Jesus stood up again and said to her, "Where are your accusers? Didn't even one of them condemn you?"

"No, sir," she said. And Jesus said, "Neither do I. Go and sin no more."

Jesus shows us what it means to know grace and truth in him. He doesn't overlook her sin but offers grace in the form of forgiveness and acceptance. He basically said she didn't have to die for her sin or be separated from him. We are all sinners. Jesus accepted this woman knowing she was an adulteress. He was not shocked by what she did. He accepted her true self—a woman with a sinful nature and desires. He also gave her direction: "Go and sin no more." Let us not forget: we have not been licensed by God to punish others for their sins. Judgment is God's responsibility, not man's.

Jesus, the perfect example of God's grace and truth, sets people free. He forgives them, teaches them, and gives them the hope of God's love and salvation. He holds the same key to set us all free today.

Reflection: How does this story help you better understand grace and truth?

~ *People thirst for the real Jesus. Grace and truth are His fingerprints.* ~

Dr. Randy Alcorn [54]

Day 55: Grace and Truth Need Time

Whenever we're blue or pressed down, we no longer participate fully in life. There are so many reasons that happens, like the chronic stress of migraine headaches, the death of a loved one, the loss of a job, or a childhood trauma—all sorts of other loss, pain, and injury. God calls us out of darkness and into the light with Jesus. Jesus is the power behind the healing and transformation we are searching for.

Why does it take so long to get better? Dr. Henry Cloud says, "Time is God's way of bringing about the wholeness lost in Eden. It takes time to work the soil with his ingredients of grace and truth, and allow them to take effect."[55]

This is something God will work in us for the rest of our lives. However, if we choose to remain pressed down and isolated, God can't use time to redeem our hurts. When we come out of hiding, God uses our current relationships to provide the nurturing we desperately need.

Personally, I disagree with the statement that *time heals all wounds*. I would say that, in time, God gives us a new kind of normal. He promises to take care of us.

Reflection: When have you come up against the "mean" or hard side of truth that gives love only if you do what is right? How did that affect the way you thought about yourself?

~ *No matter how dark things seem to be, or actually are, raise your sights and see possibilities—always see them, for they're always there.* ~

Dr. Norman Vincent Peale [56]

Day 56: God's Goodness

Millions see God as distant and impersonal. Many spend a lifetime wrestling with God's authority. Those grieving the loss of a loved one or a death or a child's self-destructive behavior or a divorce may view God as a being that only wants hardship and sacrifice. We each have our own battlefronts. I had more than one. I came face to face with a God who appeared silent and unfair. I thought, *If you're so good, God, why don't you help me?* Often we question God's sovereignty and goodness.

Previously we explored our "God images." What we are talking about here is more distorted thinking about God. The Bible says over and over that God is good. "God is our light and our protector. He gives us grace and glory. No good thing will he withhold from those who walk along his paths" (Psalm 84:11, TLB).

What does that mean?

The word *goodness* often translates the Hebrew words *tov* and *tuv*, terms referring to that quality in God that causes him to bless people, deliver them, and store up future gifts for them. God's goodness is pleasant, desirable, fair, and generous.

The same goodness that brought food daily from above for the Israelites in the wilderness gives us all things richly to enjoy. This is the picture of love.

"God is love" (1 John 4:16). John is *not* saying that God is lovely or loving, but that He *is* love. He is good!

Reflection: What does this Scripture mean to you?

> ~ *I am still confident of this: I will see the*
> *goodness of the* LORD *in the land of the living.* ~
>
> King David (Psalm 27:13)

Day 57: God's Grief

As you read the Bible, you will see it is one big love letter from God. "I love you!" is repeated by God. He says, "I am love." Because he is love, he grieves.

Our culture values the ability to stand strong in times of grief. Weeping in public is often seen as a weakness. Be self-controlled! As a culture we do not value or give permission for the open expression of grief or pain.

Part of our healing process is grieving what we've lost or what we've done, which makes us feel depressed and blue. Be assured that as you grieve, the Holy Spirit within you is also grieving. God is grieving with you.

Jesus wept when his friend Lazarus died: "When Jesus saw her weeping, and the Jews who had come along with her also weeping, he [Jesus] was deeply moved in spirit and troubled" (John 11:35).

Jesus wept over the nation of Jerusalem (Jeremiah 9:1–11).

This means God grieves when we experience loss. Jesus empathizes with us and is able to help us through the grief process.

Jesus *openly* wept. We tend to stuff down our grief. Jesus loved Lazarus, and he loves you. I believe he weeps when we weep. He knows what is stuffed down inside us even when we tend to deny or avoid it.

Reflection: Express (unstuff) your grief in a prayer to Jesus right now. He knows and feels your pain.

~ Heavy hearts, like heavy clouds, are best relieved by the shedding of a little water. ~

Anonymous

Day 58: The God Who Hears Our Cries

If God hears my cries, why doesn't he bring joy back into my life? For decades I didn't think it was possible to experience joy. Maybe some happiness from time to time if I got what I wanted. Like a puppet, I allowed fear, shame, pride, and all sorts of lies to pull my strings. Once I asked Jesus to become part of my life, he cut those strings and began cleaning out the cobwebs of the past. His spirit eventually filled my spirit with joy.

Have you asked Jesus to meet your needs? He said, "Until now you have not asked for anything in my name. Ask and you will receive, and your joy will be complete" (John 16:24). The apostle James says, "You do not have, because you do not ask God" (James 4:20). You say, "I'm not worthy of asking. Look at what I've done." Do not lose sight of the fact that God has already done so much for you.

> When you were stuck in your old sin-dead life, you were incapable of responding to God. God brought you alive—right along with Christ! Think of it! All sins forgiven, the slate wiped clean, that old arrest warrant canceled and nailed to Christ's Cross (Colossians 2:13–14, Msg).

God's victory is our victory! If you are in Christ, when God sees you, your sins are wiped out—the slate is clean. God doesn't see them anymore. He sees you as pure and righteous—better than you see yourself.

Reflection: Look into God's mirror. Who and what do you see?

~ *Happiness comes from good circumstances. Joy comes from Jesus.* ~

Unknown

Day 59: God's Girl Jochebed

When our child is born, we believe life doesn't get any better than this. Regrettably, in today's world a parent's dream can shatter in a matter of minutes. Carol Kent, author of *When I Lay My Isaac Down,* knew this pain all too well when her son, a lieutenant in the navy, committed the unthinkable crime—murder.[57] Your child may not have committed murder, but you may be a mom in pain.

We meet an extraordinary woman in the Old Testament who, too, had to lay her Isaac down (Exodus 1 and 2). The Egyptian king Pharaoh saw the children of Israel as both a threat and an opportunity. Working them ruthlessly, he hoped to weaken the strong and kill off the weak. However, they grew stronger and continued to multiply. Pharaoh tried again. He mandated that the Hebrew midwives put to death every male child they delivered. They disobeyed Pharaoh and saved the babies because they feared God more than they feared the king. Surely they chose to be midwives because they valued life. Pharaoh decreed to take the baby male infants by force and drown them in the Nile.

It was during this time that a woman named Jochebed found herself pregnant with her third child, a male. She hid him for three months. Imagine the stress level trying to keep a healthy baby quiet and hidden. When she could hide him no longer, she placed the child in a water-tight basket and put it among the reeds along the bank of the Nile. The right thing to do, Jochebed must have felt tremendous pain, even depression, at the thought of never seeing her son again. However, God had a providential answer.

Reflection: Put yourself in Jochebed's place. What would your reaction, then action, have been?

~ *One with God is a majority.* ~

Billy Graham [58]

Day 60: God's Providence

Jochebed's love for her son, coupled with her faith, gave her the power to act heroically in the midst of great oppression. Pharaoh's daughter discovered the baby when she came down to the river to bathe. Jochebed's daughter, Miriam, approached the princess and suggested that her mother nurse and care for the baby. The princess bought the services of Miriam and Jochebed. Now the baby did not come under the pharaoh's decree of execution. God's providence was at work and the family reunited. After the baby was weaned, he was returned to Pharaoh's daughter, who called him Moses, meaning, "I drew him out of the water."

Commentator R. Alan Cole wrote, "Jochebed's act is just within the law. She had indeed thrown her son into the river as ordered, but in a wicker basket. It was in fact the ancient equivalent of leaving him on the steps of a hospital or orphanage today."[59]

Testing her faith, Jochebed rose to the challenge, defying Pharaoh. Jochebed had a godly heritage. It had been prophesized that the Israelites would be enslaved but that the fourth generation would be set free. Times were terrible, but evidently these parents remembered God's promise.

When times look bleak, we, too, must look to God's promises for strength. Our feelings will always be attacked, but God's Word will always stand strong.

Reflection: A wise person once said that God's will is a pillow to rest on, not a load to carry. What promise of God's will you hang onto today?

~ The Christian is bound to be an optimist,
because he has behind him the grace of God. ~

William Barclay [60]

Day 61: God's Miracles

Our God is a God of miracles. That is the hope we hang onto today. Through a series of miracles, God used Jochebed's plan of hiding her baby to begin his plan to rescue the people from Egypt. The first miracle is the fact that baby Moses lived. Hebrews 11:23 confirms why: "By faith Moses' parents hid him for three months after he was born, because they saw he was no ordinary child, and they were not afraid of the king's edict."

The second miracle is when the princess decided to take the baby in as her own son. She was Pharaoh's daughter, and there was prejudice against the Hebrew people. She could have her pick of any Egyptian boy, but God put a desire in her heart to adopt a child from another race, a race being oppressed by her own father!

Third, God so honored Jochebed's faith that he saw to it that the princess hired her to nurse and care for her own son. Moses' parents chose to trust God with the impossible, and he took their fear away. Moses was no ordinary baby. He became the Old Testament's premier leader and prophet.

The same God that intricately wove his purpose through Jochebed's life gives us the same promise. He has a better plan, a greater plan, a plan of hope: "I will be found by you and will bring you back from captivity" (Jeremiah 29:14). When we pray he will listen. And let's not forget, the children we nurture today could be tomorrow's leaders!

Reflection: What miracle do you want from God today? Ask him in prayer.

~ This is how God showed his love among us: He sent his one and only Son into the world that we might live through him. ~

The Apostle John (1 John 4:9)

Day 62: The Psalms

"O Lord my God, I pleaded with you, and you gave me my health again. You brought me back from the brink of the grave, from death itself, and here I am alive!" (Psalm 50: 2–3).

At the center of the Bible is the book of Psalms, a grand collection of songs and prayers expressing the heart and soul, the despair and the joy, of their authors. They mirror the human soul. They are not a series of religious devotionals but are filled with emotion, the same kind you and I feel today. They contain the accounts of enemies who scheme, hurt, gossip, and plot against one another. They are full of hope and faith.

For the psalmists, faith in God involves a struggle against powerful forces that often seem stronger than God. The authors often cry, "Where are you, God? Why don't you answer me, help me?" Often they feel abandoned, angry, confused, misused, betrayed—just like us. Sometimes they are elated, other times depressed, but they are always honest with themselves, therefore the psalms are of value to us.

What is common to all of them is that they cast agony on God. The psalmists cry,

"We can't bear it any longer. Take it from us and bear it for me. You God can handle suffering." Like us, the psalmists proclaimed that Jesus Christ is the only one who can help us in our suffering, for in him, God is with us. On this basis the psalms develop our trust in God.

Reflection: Like the psalmists and other biblical characters, we will learn to express ourselves to the Lord and tell Him our true feelings, fears, hopes, and dreams.

~ Sorrow looks back, worry looks around, and faith looks to the psalms. ~

Unknown

Day 63: There Is Joy in the Morning

David provincially wrote, "Weeping may go on all night, but in the morning there is joy" (Psalm 30: 5, TLB). He wrote a majority of these heartfelt psalms. Like us, David describes his depression as being a pit. But he also knew God's promise of deliverance despite his present despair.

> I will praise you, Lord, for you have saved me from my enemies. You refuse to let them triumph over me. O Lord my God, I pleaded with you, and you gave me my health again. You brought me back from the brink of the grave, from death itself, and here I am alive! Oh, sing to him you saints of his; give thanks to his holy name. His anger lasts a moment; his favor lasts for life! Weeping may go on all night, but in the morning there is joy...Hear me, Lord; oh, have pity and help me. Then he turned my sorrow into joy! He took away my clothes of mourning and clothed me with joy so that I might sing glad praises to the Lord instead of lying in silence in the grave. O Lord my God, I will keep on thanking you forever! (Psalm 30:1–12, TLB)

Our emotional and spiritual life is full of peaks and valleys, and we want immediate relief and answers. But often, as with David, the Lord calls us to wait, which is the hardest part. Look ahead to the future. There is a way out. Thank God for where he will take you!

Reflection: How has this particular psalm spoken to you? Are there any other Psalms you would consider your favorites or that have a significant meaning to you?

~ The task ahead of us is never as great as the Power behind us. ~

Anonymous

Day 64: Jairus Comes to Jesus

Because it drags on and on, we think our blue and depressed mood means we are weak and have failed. Let me assure you that God loves you just the way you, *but* he refuses to let you stay this way. If God accepts us when we are unhappy, then we can cry out like David and expect a response. For healing and spiritual growth to occur, our pain needs to be identified. God helps us do that. He comes alongside of us.

In the story of the dead girl (Mark 5:21–42), a synagogue ruler named Jairus pushes through the crowd, raises his voice above everyone else, and begins pleading with Jesus. He fell at his feet and said, "My little daughter is dying. Please come and put your hands on her so that she will be healed and live." This powerful man humbled himself because he knew Jesus was the only one who could heal his young daughter.

"Jesus went with him" (verse 24), as he will come with you.

When we look up, what do we see? The sun, thousands of stars, billowing clouds, a red-blue sky, the full moon, and possibly Saturn or Venus. If our God is big enough to create and light the celestials, then he is big enough to meet your every need.

Jesus succeeds where we fail. He brings healing when nothing else seems to work. He offers forgiveness when our hearts say it's impossible to forgive. He extends comfort and peace when the agony becomes too great to carry. He breaks through the chaos and says, "Anything is possible through me."

Reflect and ask him to come into your situation right now.

~ *These miracles showed Christ to be a conqueror of Satan, a healer of diseases.* ~

Matthew Henry

Day 65: When It Seems Over, Don't Give Up

The story continues ... Jesus went with Jairus, and a large crowd followed and pressed around him, almost crushing him.

> While Jesus was still speaking, some men came from the house of Jairus, the synagogue ruler. "Your daughter is dead," they said. "Why bother the teacher any more?" Ignoring what they said, Jesus told the synagogue ruler, *"Don't be afraid; just believe."* He did not let anyone follow him except Peter, James and John the brother of James. When they came to the home of the synagogue ruler, Jesus saw a commotion, with people crying and wailing loudly. He went in and said to them, "Why all this commotion and wailing? The child is not dead but asleep." But they laughed at him (Mark 5:35–40, author's emphasis).

Jairus pulled out his last card. Nothing left to do ... but he knew of Jesus. Jesus was perhaps his last hope. These people laughed at Jesus! *This man is a joke—she's dead!*

But this is Jesus! "He took her by the hand and said 'get up!' Immediately the girl stood up and walked around. At this they were completely astonished" (Mark 5:41–42).

Were they laughing at Jesus now?

As we learn more about Jesus, we're reminded of his miraculous healing power. When it seems like it's over, the circumstances are overwhelming, and you want to resign yourself, keep taking the problem to Jesus. As long as Jesus is in the area, there is hope. Never give up!

Reflection: How will you use this encouraging story in your present situation?

~ *A joy that is shared is a joy made double.* ~

John Ray [61]

Day 66: Ashamed and Desperate, but Determined

A central feeling in depression is shame. For decades I felt deeply ashamed of my choices and myself. I never felt good enough. Shame is an emotion associated with defeat. Often our shame is focused around our bodies, which reminds me of the story of what has been called *The Bleeding or Hemorrhaging Woman*.

The apostle Mark speaks of a mystery woman who had been slowly bleeding for twelve years (Mark 5:25–43). She had suffered a great deal and spent all her money on doctors but nothing worked. Declared "unclean," most likely she felt defective, humiliated, and desperate. At the end of her rope, she heard Jesus was coming and thought, *If I just touch him, I will be healed*, fueled by nothing but faith.

This woman risked everything. Jewish law considered her unclean and unsocial, equivalent to a leper. In her mind she probably battled, *Bad idea. I need to avoid crowds so as not to offend anyone. Maybe I shouldn't go to Jesus since there are always so many around him. Besides, I'm too ashamed of my condition.* It's easy to make excuses.

However, she presses through the fear and gathers enough courage to seek Jesus. She doesn't wait around for him to find her. As he came near, she touched the hem of his robe. "Immediately her bleeding stopped and she felt in her body that she was freed from her suffering" (5:29). Jesus asked, "Who touched me?" Reluctantly she stepped up. The faith that empowered her to stretch out her hand gave her the strength to step forward.

Reflection: Have you, in your heart, fallen at the feet of Jesus? If you never have, perhaps today is the day to come to him and touch his robe.

~ The woman, knowing what had happened to her, came and fell at
his feet and, trembling with fear, told him the whole truth. ~

The Apostle Mark (Mark 5:33)

Day 67: When It Seems Forever, Don't Give Up

We live in a microwave, fast-paced society. We want it now, which includes our healing. Time goes fast except when you are sick or hurt or lonely. However, what may seem like forever now is not forever in God's timetable. The bleeding woman didn't give up. I'm sure twelve years seemed like forever to her. Now God was ready to heal her. After so many years of suffering, she finally found peace and freedom—true joy.

No one listened before to this woman. When she reached out to Jesus, he said, "Daughter, your faith has healed you. Go in peace and be freed from your suffering" (Mark 5:34). These words represent hope! Jesus called her "daughter." This is the only time when Jesus calls a woman daughter. He gave her a name when no one else did.

Most likely she overcame any feelings of inferiority and low self-esteem. I hope she realized that she, too, was created in the image of God, equal in value and giftedness, a precious daughter of the King—God's Royal Girl! For this woman it came down to persistence, pressing through the fear and seeking Jesus, becoming completely dependent on God ... and waiting for God's timing.

What do these stories tell you about your faith and about claiming your identity? One woman disclosed, "The messages I got from my family were always negative. I never felt love or acceptance. Then I touched Jesus and realized that God loves me just the way I am!" These kinds of stories offer us encouragement. The hand that touched these women can touch you.

Reflection. As we learn more about Jesus, we're reminded of his miraculous healing power to deal with prolonged sickness like depression. Meditate on this.

~ *I alone can do it. But I can't do it alone.* ~

Anonymous

Day 68: Mile Stone

Steps To Overcome Negative Emotions

Move Forward

It is difficult to move forward most days because we are unsure of God. What if he is angry at me? Maybe he'll reject me. Why should I talk to him? He's not listening. Then we might feel guilty for withdrawing and not praying. Moving forward says you no longer reinforce this guilt. Recognize that God knows your heart and condition, and there are seasons of prayerlessness.

Moving forward says that I have the freedom to makes choices. Most importantly, I choose to know and love God and allow him to direct my life. Moving forward may look like asking others to pray for you or meditating on a psalm or merely waiting in silence before God.

These actions represent your voice to God. Moving forward means recognizing that we can control what we put into our mind, thereby determining what our attitude will be. We have a choice (even if our hormones are out of whack!).

~ True peace doesn't come from the absence of
trouble. It comes from the presence of God. ~

Unknown

Day 69: Challenge the Old Way of Thinking

You may feel God has let you down. He didn't protect you from awful circumstances or people. And you did nothing wrong! We're not usually privy to the answers as to why God allows bad stuff to happen. It is beyond our human ability to even understand the "whys" behind all the suffering in the world. The answer to these questions is God himself. Lifelong change begins with that daily adjustment.

~ I believe in the sun even when it is not shining. I believe in love even when I'm feeling it not. I believe in God even when He is silent. ~

Inscription where Jews hid from Nazis[62]

Pray and Meditate

A few moments in quiet prayer and meditation with God can rekindle the flame that guides us from within. Listen to the quiet whisper of God. Allow him to fuel your inner flame with encouragement and love.

This prayer was inspired from Psalms 42 and 43:

"Father, my heart is panting for you just as the deer pants for the water brook. I am hurting and in despair. Lord, I'm pouring out my heart and my soul to you. Help me in this misery to stop and remember the joy that I have known with you in the past. Father, I am. You know the pain I have endured. You know I feel I have failed to be all I could be and feel worthless. But, Lord, you are greater than all my failures. You can help me. Help me please, Father, today. In Jesus' name. Amen."

Self-Soother

Make a cup of your favorite tea or coffee drink and relax for one hour.

Part Six

God's First Girl

Encouraged by God's Word

"Then the Lord God caused the man to fall into a deep sleep, and took one of his ribs and closed up the place from which he had removed it, and made the rib into a woman, and brought her to the man. 'This is it!' Adam exclaimed. 'She is part of my own bone and flesh! Her name is *woman* because she was taken out of a man.' The man named his wife Eve (the life-giving one) for he said, 'She shall become the mother of all mankind.'" (The Creation Account, Genesis 2:21–23; 3:20, TLB)

Day 70: God's Girl Connie

Connie reminisces: I met Larry in Bible College. From the moment we set eyes on each other we knew we were "yoked to be." One year later we married. We both agreed it was God's desire that I be a stay-at-home mom. Larry graduated from dental school and got into a good practice in the town we both grew up in. Yes, God was good!

I became pregnant with our first child, Hannah. Two years later we had Philip. I had difficult pregnancies followed by bouts of post-partum depression. I felt overwhelmed by the responsibility of motherhood and inadequately prepared. Larry didn't appear to empathize, although I think he felt the same way but chose to hide his feelings in his work.

What I really needed from him was validation that I was a good mother. I got no encouragement. One day I was going in a million directions. When Larry came home to a messy house and a cold dinner, he asked what I had done all day, insinuating I had been sitting around watching soap operas while letting the kids run wild.

When he'd come home and the house wasn't neat, he would sarcastically point out the virtues of the Proverbs 31 woman. I would pout. Then he would say I was being too sensitive. If dinner was late, he'd state what a good servant Martha was ... and let's not forget Mary, who washed Jesus' feet! He said he was just kidding. Was he really?

Reflection: Are you walking in Connie's shoes today? How have you perceived a put down from a loved one? Take the time to draw near and talk to God about your situation. He wants to hear and help you move through the hurt.

~ *Praise be to the* LORD, *for he has heard my cry for mercy.* ~

King David (Psalm 28:6)

Day 71: Depression Is Not Terminal

Connie's story continues ... One day Larry was building a gazebo in the backyard by himself. The kids and I were sick with colds, feeling really rotten. When he came in for lunch, he said, "God said that man wasn't to be alone, and so he made him a suitable helper." Was he trying to make me feel guilty, or was I making myself feel guilty?

Dr. Valerie E. Whiffen writes:

> The relationship a woman creates with her romantic partner or spouse is a key determinant of how good she feels about herself and how emotionally well she is. A woman who feels supported and cared for by her romantic partner may go through difficult times in her life, but she is generally able to ride out such times, even grow from them. Depression occurs when a woman is alone and isolated or when she is involved in a romantic relationship that leaves her feeling uncared for and inadequate.[63]

Connie cried, "It wasn't supposed to be this way. I'm so unhappy." She elaborates ... Larry convinced me to talk to a counselor because I appeared deeply depressed. The good news was that my depression was not terminal and Larry agreed to counseling as well. I was helped because I became willing to challenge different ways to respond to problems and leaned completely on God and his Word. I learned to adapt and tolerate Larry's different sense of humor. He wasn't purposely trying to torment me.

Reflection: What is the number one issue on your mind right now? Begin talking about it to God and ask him to bring clarity to the situation.

~ Jesus does not speak about a change of activities, a change in contacts, or even a change of pace. He speaks about a change of heart. ~

Henri J.W. Nouwen[64]

Day 72: God's Girl Eve

In Genesis 2 we meet Eve, "the mother of all who have life," who came into this world perfect and at peace with God and her husband. The Bible tells us that Eve was created by God for her husband, the only other man on the planet. Just think: she never had to hear about former girlfriends or what a great cook his mother was!

When God created Eve, she was a perfect woman. She must have been a person of unparalleled beauty. She was the crown and pinnacle of God's amazing, creative work, fashioned directly by the Creator, who showed great care and attention to detail. Eve was a glorious refinement of humanity itself. A special gift to Adam, she made his existence complete.

From the beginning the Bible places both man and woman at the pinnacle of God's creation. Neither sex is exalted, and neither is depreciated.

God carefully designed Eve. "This is it!" Adam exclaimed. "She is part of my own bone and flesh! Her name is 'woman' because she was taken out of a man" (2:23, TLB). Notice that Eve was not made out of dust like Adam.

Adam felt a deep, intimate, and personal attachment to Eve—a priceless treasure, an encourager, and a partner who would love him in return. He didn't have to weigh the pros and cons; instantly he adored her and embraced her as his own.

Reflection: Has being a woman ever felt demeaning? If so, what one change can you make to bring more equality to the situation?

~ *That which is sent by God will only produce the*
perfection of His glory in your presence and future existence. ~

Madame Guyon[65]

Day 73: What Went Wrong?

Why are some people consistently lucky, while others suffer? Why did my neighbor's baby die? Why did you get promoted and not me? Why can't everybody have prosperity, joy, and security? The Bible helps to paint an answer.

Genesis 2 ends with a beautiful picture of paradise. Scripture says Adam and Eve "were not ashamed." Today so many of us live with a deeper kind of guilt called shame or self-condemnation. All God wanted was for us to live openly and honestly with him and one another, without shame.

Genesis 3 introduces a new character, a serpent "more crafty than any of the wild animals the Lord God had made." This is clearly Satan, the evil one. He was an angel who fell into sin. In the beginning God created all good angels. Lucifer, the archangel, then sinned against God by saying in his heart, "I will make myself like the Most High" (Isaiah 14:14). Lucifer wanted to be God. He rebelled and was thrown out of heaven. Lucifer's name (which means Morning Star or Light-Bringer[66]) was changed to Satan, meaning adversary; and devil, meaning slanderer or accuser. His mission was to continue disguised as an angel of light. His goal: to deceive, tempt, and destroy man. The good news is he is a created being with limitations.

Reflection: When you hear the word devil or Satan, what image do you have? (Hint: that cute little character in a red bodysuit holding a pitch fork is a fallacy.) In what ways have you rebelled against others in authority or God?

~ When we awaken to the facts of life, inner peace is
impossible unless it is received from Jesus. ~

Oswald Chambers[67]

Day 74: Paradise Lost

Scripture doesn't give us a physical description of Eve, but you probably have a vivid image of her. This was a woman who, in her original state, was flawless, unbroken, healthy, untouched by evil—perfect. She was the living picture of pure radiance and splendor, an example of the goodness of God's grace and his perfect wisdom. Do you imagine someone perfectly slender (since we place such an emphasis on being thin)?

It was paradise. Adam and Eve were the perfect man and woman, but then it was all ruined. God's plan was for humanity was to have dominion over all the created order (Genesis 1:28). Man and woman were created to have an intimate relationship with God. God had only one requirement—obey him. Women for centuries have felt the brunt for that day when Eve succumbed to temptation.

Being expelled from the Garden of Eden must have been excruciatingly painful, the loss of innocence. Our depression is like departing from a garden of paradise and waking up to a world of challenge and pain.

We, too, make wrong or hasty choices that separate us from God. We may run from him, but he doesn't leave us or give up on us. Eve's life speaks to each of us.

Reflection: Silence your heart. Hear him calling you back into his garden of peace, love, and hope.

> *~ Eve was not taken out of Adam's head to top him, neither out of his feet to be trampled on by him, but out of his side to be equal with him, under his arm to be protected by him, and near his heart to be loved by him. ~*

Matthew Henry [68]

Day 75: Eve's Temptation

Satan came to Eve disguised as a serpent. Scripture tells us what happened next:

> Now *the serpent was more crafty than any of the wild animals* the LORD God had made. He said to the woman, "Did God really say, You must not eat from any tree in the garden?" The woman said to the serpent, "We may eat fruit from the trees in the garden, but God did say, You must not eat fruit from the tree that is in the middle of the garden, and you must not touch it, or you will die." "You will not surely die," the serpent said to the woman. "For God knows that when you eat of it your eyes will be opened, and you will be like God, knowing good and evil." When the woman saw that the fruit of the tree was good for food and pleasing to the eye, and also desirable for gaining wisdom, she took some and ate it. She also gave some to her husband, who was with her, and he ate it (Genesis 3:1–6, author's emphasis).

When Satan said to Eve, "Did God really say you must not eat from any tree in the garden?" he was planting seeds of doubt in Eve's mind. (Remember, back in Genesis 2, God gave Adam the directive. Eve had not been created yet.) Satan questioned God's Word, which we assume Adam had passed on to Eve. Satan basically says, "That's a lie! You won't die! God knows that when you eat it you will become like him!"

Reflection: Every person who has lived since then has been tempted with the words, "Did God really say…?" and "God did not really say…" Faith means taking God at his Word. How have these words become part of your vocabulary?

~ *Expect the dawn of a new beginning in the dark nights of life.* ~

Lloyd John Ogilvie[69]

Day 76: What a Snake!

The story continues ... The serpent tempts Eve twice. First, he tells her she will be like God. Then he gets her to doubt God's goodness. *God's holding out on you!* Why would God "hold out" on his beloved creatures? God didn't want Adam and Eve to know evil. He wanted to protect them, just as he wants to protect you and me today.

When Satan said, "Surely you won't die," he lied! For the first time in history a lie was spoken. The perpetrator: Satan. He appeals to a virtuous desire in Eve. He basically says, God wants you to grow up and think for yourself. Use your wisdom, and God will reward you for it. She thinks, *This tree will enhance my spiritual growth.* The snake's suggestion turned out to be true in her judgment.

God asks, "Have you eaten from the tree that I commanded you not to eat from?" Adam says, "The woman you put here with me—she gave me some fruit from the tree, and I ate it." Then God says to Eve, "What is this you have done?" She says, "The serpent deceived me, and I ate" (Genesis 3:11–13).

Eve now recognizes she was deceived. Satan does the same thing to us. He tempts us by watering down God's Word or getting us to take his Word out of context. He whispers in our minds that it's okay to make our own choices, choices that appear so sensible and innocent. Instead of asking God, *Did you really say this* (and checking against God's Word), we move ahead on our own and think, *God did not really say this.*

Reflection: What has been your most recent temptation? How will you apply what you've learned so far about truth to your life this week?

~ *Short is the joy that guilty pleasure brings.* ~

Euripides[70]

Day 77: The Blame Game Begins!

After Eve sinned, she involved Adam. When we do wrong, we often try to relieve our guilt by involving someone else. That sin created a barrier not only between Adam and Eve and God, but between man (you and me) and God.

Picture Adam cowering behind a bush, lamenting, *She made me do it!* This is the beginning of the blame game. God asks Adam about eating the forbidden fruit. Adam quickly accuses Eve. He doesn't stand with her. He basically says, *Blame her, God. She's the one who got me into this mess!* Scripture says, "The man said, 'The woman you put here with me—she gave me some fruit from the tree, and I ate it.'" *It's your fault, God!*

Before the serpent entered the picture, every conversation was perfectly, completely truthful and honest. Paul Tripp, author of *War of Words*, poignantly said, "No longer do we simply reflect the image of God with our words; we also reflect the image of the serpent. No longer do we consistently speak up to God's standards; we speak down to the serpent's."[71] How often have you regretted things you have said?

Innocence and intimacy were lost after that day in the garden. Theologians call it "the Fall." As a result every baby is born with a sinful nature because we inherited the depraved nature of Adam and Eve (called *original sin*). Unfortunately, that sinful nature leads us to commit acts of *personal* sin. We will look more closely at sin on Day 86.

Reflection: Thinking back over the last two days, when were you deceived?

> ~ *It is good to be a Christian and know it, but it is*
> *better to be a Christian and show it.* ~
>
> Anonymous

Day 78: Who's Setting the Rules?

As we grow the real issue becomes who's going to set the rules—humans or God? From the beginning God gave Adam and Eve the freedom to choose. Without choice they would have been prisoners or robots. Unfortunately, temptation came into the world, and sorrow followed. Adam disobeyed. God exposed his sin. Punishment was swift. Adam and Eve were banished from paradise and the presence of God, where they had complete dominion. They decided in favor of themselves, and our world has never been the same.

Their first son was a murderer and their second son the victim. Mankind went from owning everything to owning nothing, from a life of joy to a life of toil and pain. Because of sin men would have to sweat for their daily bread, and women would suffer in childbirth and have strife with men.

I imagine Adam and Eve felt sick and ashamed. Hence lies, shame, and blame emerge. I wonder if they could hear the serpent laughing at them as he hid in the bushes. The real tragedy of their sin emerged. Not only did humanity fall from their place of dominion, but all creation fell with them (3:17–24).

Into our dominion came the serpent Lucifer: the tempter, named Satan. What had been created good was now cursed by Satan. All our broken relationships, our grief, sadness, sickness, pain—all can be traced back to that one monumental day in Eden.

But God had a plan!

Reflection: How have you changed the way you see your circumstances today?

> ~ *Lord ... Let me find thy light in my darkness, thy life in my death, thy joy in my sorrow, thy grace in my sin, thy glory in my valley.* ~

Arthur Bennett[72]

Day 79: God's Girl Rahab

We live life in a fallen world, which is disappointing and sometimes brutal. Many of us feel despair because we put our hope in the wrong people. I did. Their names were Chris, Dan, Bill, and Bob. I put my hope for a meaningful life in them, only to be deceived and rejected by each one. I became entangled with losers who kept me hopelessly enslaved to their weaknesses. I set myself up to experience depression because I felt devalued. I also realized the relationships failed because we never built true emotional intimacy. The foundation was built on the physical. And I was co-dependent. Besides, these men didn't have the answer. God did. God provides us with the light of hope that can cut through the murk. We witness the same liberation in the story of Rahab.

The action begins in the book of Joshua, chapter two, when two Israelite spies are dispatched to Jericho. However, the story isn't about the spies. Rather, it's about a woman named Rahab, a prostitute; the same woman who is listed as a member of the "Faith Hall of Fame" (Hebrews 11:31). Why was she so important?

Rahab is introduced as a harlot or prostitute, the type of woman who most likely would be written off as hopeless. In those days, although tolerated, prostitution was viewed negatively, leading men to ruin (Proverbs 23:26).

Rahab was of a low-class, a social outcast. She was used for her services but hardly included in the city's aristocratic social circles. She was a poor, landless woman. This is the picture we have of Rahab.

Reflection: Have you put your future or hope in the wrong things or people?

~ *Regardless of how it comes about, depression can hold the*
soul hostage as few other personal experiences can. ~

Dr. Jeff Olson[73]

Day 80: A Life Redeemed

Rahab's story continues … The spies went immediately to Jericho and entered Rahab's house. They were planning to spend the night there, but someone informed the king of Jericho that two Israelites who were suspected of being spies had arrived in the city that evening. The king dispatched a police squadron to Rahab's home, demanding that she surrender them.

Rahab thought quickly and hid the two spies. She covered for them and then got them safely out of the city, all at considerable risk to herself and her family. The Israelite spies were forced to depend on the courage and initiative of this one questionable woman. In return for her help, the spies swore to spare her and her family.

The story concludes, "Then the two men started back. They went down out of the hills, forded the river and came to Joshua son of Nun and told him everything that had happened to them. They said to Joshua, 'The Lord has surely given the whole land into our hands; all the people are melting in fear because of us'" (23–24).

(The rest of Rahab's story unfolds tomorrow.)

Reflection: Describe the last time you demonstrated courage and initiative in a situation? How did that feel?

> ~ *Today we need a fresh spirit of anticipation that springs out of the promises of God. We must declare war on the mood of non-expectation, and come together with childlike faith.* ~
>
> A. W. Tozer [74]

Day 81: God's Girl Moves Forward in Faith

Why would spies stop at Rahab's house? Most likely it was a good place and location to gather information, but more importantly, God directed the spies to Rahab's house because he knew her heart was open to him and she would be instrumental in the Israelite victory over Jericho.

This low-cast woman made Israel's advance into Jericho possible. She was given a choice. She could have sent the spies away and continued to live as a prostitute, or she could make herself available to God and become a woman of influence and faith at a great risk. Rahab saw something that many of the Israelites didn't—God Almighty is not an ordinary god. She used that knowledge to press through any fear or doubt.

Let's not overlook the fact that her faith was accompanied by fear. Who wouldn't have been scared? By choosing the Lord, Rahab ultimately escaped the destruction that came on those who refused to trust God. And Rahab is mentioned in Jesus' genealogy (Matthew 1:2).

She was a foreigner who joined God's plan for Israel. Transformed by God from harlot to heroine, Rahab is an inspiration for each one of us. You, too, can leave your past behind and walk forward in glorious grace, proclaiming, "God is good!" This story is a testimony to our God, the God of second chances and restoration. We have a choice to make—to move forward in faith or stay as we are.

Reflection: No matter what your past, God gives you a second chance. Which parts of the past are you ready to hand over?

~ *Faith can take us farther than any of our feelings.* ~

Anne Calodich Fone [75]

Day 82: MileStone

Steps To Overcome Negative Emotions

Move Forward

Rahab had a past, yet she was not afraid of risk. Moving forward is deciding to tackle that one obstacle that is in your way.

> I saw him again today, Lord,
> Just a glimpse, in a crowded street,
> But it was enough ...
> Enough to open the wounds again
> To allow the bitter memories of those hard words,
> broken promises, and the mistakes I made to come flooding back.
> I almost got caught, Lord.
> Caught in a wave of self pity, self recrimination, and guilt.
> And then I remembered ...
> Remembered that failure brought to you and confessed,
> Is failure forgiven, forgotten, dealt with.
> So now I can look back to that experience—
> thankful for lessons learned.
> I can look up to you—confident that you can create beauty
>
> out of the ashes of my mistakes.
> I can look forward to the future—at peace.
>
> —Marion Stroud in *Celebrate Friendship*[76]

Challenge the Old Way of Thinking

Do you have this same kind of faith that you are willing to do what God asks of you despite the risks? Renewed thinking says: "I can look up to you—confident that you can create beauty, and I can look forward to the future—at peace."

Day 83: Pray and Meditate

Lord, you are my Creator. You always know what is best for me. Thank you that you want what is best for me, and that you're able to do what is best for me. Forgive me for ever doubting you. Nothing is too hard for you.

Thank you, Father, for the privilege of being called your chosen and cherished daughter, and for allowing me the privilege of coming to you whenever I want with my prayer. your Word says, "Call upon me in the day of trouble; I will deliver you, and you will honor me" (Psalm 50:15).

Guide me as I bring each problem area to you. I trust you to give me wisdom. In Jesus' name. Amen.

Self-Soother

List three people you are thankful for and why you appreciate each one.

Part Seven

Let There Be Light!

Encouraged by God's Word

"And God said, 'Let there be light,' and there was light. God saw that the light was good, and he separated the light from the darkness." (Genesis 1:1–4)

"We look for light, but all is darkness; for brightness, but we walk in deep shadows. Like the blind we grope along the wall, feeling our way like men without eyes. At midday we stumble as if it were twilight; among the strong, we are like the dead." (Isaiah 59:9–10)

Day 84: Kris's Story

After attempting suicide, Kris disclosed, "A few months after I came home from the hospital, the cards, letters, and phone calls stopped. In my head the thought *Out of sight, out of mind* kept going over and over relentlessly. I'd wait for cards to encourage me, but they quickly stopped arriving in the mail. I'd come home after shopping to see if I had messages on my answering machine. I'd wait for the light to flash to indicate a message was waiting, but it wouldn't be flashing. I'd check my email for just a word of encouragement from anyone, but there was nothing.

"It was hard to come to the realization that people forgot about me. I know people go on with their own lives, but there is something to be said for reaching out to others, even if they don't reach back. I was in a place that was hard for others to reach. Shame filled my heart, and to try to rid it from me was difficult. In failure God always moves closer to us. People distance themselves from failure or failures."

Maybe you have walked in Kris's shoes. I would have felt hurt, disappointed, ashamed, rejected; possibly would have lost my faith in mankind. She healed, and her life was transformed into something beautiful. "God has brought me through a horrific time in my life and has given me hope to keep living. Not only to keep living, but to have more abundant life than I've ever thought possible."[77]

That is the character of God—the provider of abundance and prosperity.

Reflection: When have you felt God move closer when everyone else seemed to move further away?

> ~ *For you were once darkness, but now you are light*
> *in the Lord. Live as children of light.* ~
>
> The Apostle Paul (Ephesians 5:8)

Day 85: Where Abundance Is Found

Try to imagine being clouded and swarmed by thousands of grasshopper-like insects. In the book of Joel, a terrible plague of locusts covers the land and destroys the crops. The prophet Joel describes the devastation as a foretaste of the coming judgment of God. Let us ask ourselves, "Is God sending this plague into our lives to get our attention?" Or are we at that point where God now has our attention, and we are responding to his call to do things differently, to return to him?

God can set each one of us free from the darkness of bondage. He set Kris free. He set me free. Turn to God. Come to him with a remorseful, repentant heart, and he will make up for the lost blessings. He will make up for the wasted years—years that the locusts, worms, and snails (our sin) have devoured! The women you are meeting on these pages are testimonies to this promise.

A most comforting Scriptures is Joel 2:25–26:

> I will repay you for the years the locusts have eaten … You will have plenty to eat, until you are full, and you will praise the name of the LORD your God, who has worked wonders for you; never again will my people be shamed.

God can give us a new crop in one year that will make up for the old ones that we lost. It is never too late for a fresh beginning. This represents light!

Reflection. Describe your life right now in terms of darkness or light, or both.

~ 97-year-old Mae Laborde is just four years into her acting career and hotter than ever. ~

The Associated Press[78]

Day 86: The Darkness

Lorrie learned that her husband had fathered a child by another woman. She felt betrayed and devalued by him, and understandably became depressed. Losses, if big and bad enough, can trigger depression. Lorrie's account reminds me of the story of David and Bathsheba (2 Samuel 11:1–27). It is the Old Testament version of a soap opera: man sees beautiful married woman; man sleeps with beautiful woman; woman gets pregnant.

In our culture that's only too common, but Scripture doesn't tell us how Bathsheba felt about this. There is nothing in the text that points to Bathsheba intentionally seducing David; she was alone in her private courtyard. In that culture, death for both the man and woman was the punishment for adultery. Fear must have consumed Bathsheba. She was in quite a predicament. She knew it was wrong (a sin) to commit adultery, but to refuse a king's request could mean punishment or death. She may not have been a willing participant, but there is no doubt about David's motive.

Jesus made it clear, "I tell you the truth, everyone who sins is a slave to sin" (John 8:34). Sin can be a great deception. Retired minister and author Stanley Baldwin clarifies:

> A person ordinarily views his (or her) sins as an expression of independence, not slavery. The law says, "Thou shalt not." The person says, "I shall too." He (or she) sees this violation of the law as a matter of personal freedom to do as he (or she) pleases rather than to submit to the dictates of another.[79]

Reflection: The person who sins is not expressing freedom. She is embracing slavery. In this light, how would you have handled Bathsheba's predicament?

~ *Sin is geographical.* ~

Bertrand Russell[80]

Day 87: If Only She Didn't Get Pregnant!

The soap opera continues … David takes responsibility, but there is no sign of repentance or acknowledgment of guilt. He tries to find a way to avoid the negative consequences—both for Bathsheba and himself. He is too occupied with his problem to concern himself with moral issues. He gets desperate and does something stupid. David devises a cover-up plan, starting with a clever attempt to make Bathsheba's husband, Uriah, look like the father. One crime leads to another. David murders Uriah.

Bathsheba, we are told, mourned for Uriah; she grieved for him (11:26). He was a good soldier and a good man, and his death did not go unnoted. Then after a respectable mourning period, David marries Bathsheba. In the end, David, the man after God's own heart, breaks the sixth, seventh, ninth, and tenth commandments.

The chapter ends with a powerful understatement: "The thing David had done displeased the LORD" (11:27).

Reflection: When have you felt desperate and then done something stupid? What was the outcome? Who did it affect? What would have been a better solution?

~ *Whatever weakens your reason, impairs the tenderness of your conscience, obscures your sense of God, or takes off the relish of spiritual things, whatever increases the authority of the body over mind, that thing for you is sin.* ~

John Wesley[81]

Day 88: Every Choice Has Consequences

When God created us, he gave us free will. Unfortunately, when we make the wrong choices, no matter how right or how good they feel at the time, they have consequences. Often the consequence is separation from God—darkness.

There were consequences to David's actions. His baby dies (12:14–23), which seems cruel and unfair punishment for an innocent child. This child's death underscores an important truth; our sin affects not only ourselves, but also those around us.

I liken sin to a growing tumor. First you don't even know it is there. Then you begin to feel uncomfortable and experience a few symptoms. The tumor gets larger, and symptoms grow worse. Finally, the tumor takes over, which can lead to some very serious consequences. There's nothing you can do to stop that tumor from taking control of your life and possibly even killing you. At this point you have a choice to make. Seek a surgeon and have the tumor cut out, or let it destroy your life and be cut off from God.

We may work hard at trying to cover up our sin, but God is going to work to expose it at some point so that we can deal with it. What is certain is that David, in spite of his position and the promises God made to him, was not above the law. In fact, the story continues. Nathan the prophet is sent by the Lord to rebuke David. We are all accountable to God for our actions. Indeed, the remainder of David's reign was a spectacle of jealousy, rape, murder, and rebellion within his own family.

Reflection: What have you learned from this story that will change the way you look at situations?

~ *God delights not in punishing sin, but bringing*
sinners to Himself and giving us another chance. ~

Anonymous

Day 89: Bathsheba's Second Chance

God chose Bathsheba. He gave Bathsheba a second chance. From that point on, the Bible depicts her as a caring mother and wife. As far as we know, she lived rest of her life blamelessly. And Bathsheba is one of only four women mentioned in the Jesus' lineage (Mathew 1:6). Like Rahab, she was a foreigner who joined God's plan for Israel.

Every choice has consequences, no matter how right or how good that choice feels at the time. There were consequences to David's actions, as there are consequences to our actions.

In the Old Testament, Moses "chose to be mistreated along with the people of God rather than to enjoy the pleasures of sin for a short time" (Hebrews 11:25). The pleasure of living outside the boundaries is never more than temporary.

Think of our sin and God's mercy like a calculator. We add up all the sinful things we've done, confess (acknowledge), and turn from our sin (repentance). God hit's "clear." God forgets about it. We get to start all over again. That's amazing grace!

These words were written late in 1772 by John Newton:

"Amazing Grace"

Amazing Grace, how sweet the sound, That saved a wretch like me . . . I once was lost but now am found, Was blind, but now, I see. T'was Grace that taught . . . my heart to fear. And Grace, my fears relieved. How precious did that Grace appear . . . the hour I first believed.

Reflection: When has life seemed fun and pleasurable, only to turn to darkness? Meditate on John Newton's words.

~ Sins are forgiven but consequences carry on. ~

Chaplain Scott Delbridge[82]

Day 90: Sin and Consequences

What is sin? Sin is any lack of conformity, active or passive, to the moral law of God. This may be a matter of act, of thought, of inner disposition or state.[83] I always thought sin applied to only certain people who broke the Ten Commandments, like David. That's not what the Bible says. *We have all sinned and have come short of the glory of God* (Romans 3:23).

The apostle Paul said sin is the work of the flesh: sexual immorality, impurity, and debauchery; idolatry and witchcraft; hatred, discord, jealousy, fits of rage, selfish ambition, dissensions, factions, and envy; drunkenness, orgies, and the like (Galatians 5:19–21). What a list!

There is no such thing as a "big sin" and a "little sin." Your sin is not any bigger or any worse than my sin. That may be an eye opener for you.

Reflection: When has life seemed fun and pleasant, but that pleasure only turned out to be for a season? Pray as David did, "Create in me a pure heart, O God, and renew a steadfast spirit within me" (Psalm 51:10).

~ Some people feel guilty about their anxieties and regard them as a defect of faith, but they are afflictions, not sins. ~

C.S. Lewis [84]

Day 91: Temptation

Temptation is one weapon the enemy uses to get us to sin. David succumbed to temptation and wallowed around in his sin, leading to despair and dark thoughts. Sin may feel good, but the gratification will run its course. Then it turns to darkness. When I began bingeing and purging, I thought I found the utopian answer to weight control. Soon after, I was a captive in a dark and lonely prison with no way out.

The apostle John said, "Everyone who does evil hates the light, and will not come into the light for fear that his deeds will be exposed. But whoever lives by the truth comes into the light, so that it may be seen plainly that what he has done has been done through God" (John 3:20–21).

Light represents not only illumination but exposure. Many people don't want their lives exposed for fear of what will be revealed. They don't want to change. Now that we have started to make changes to our lives, we may encounter those who feel threatened by the light—the truth. Don't be discouraged.

God delights not in punishing sin but bringing sinners to himself and giving us another chance. He gave Bathsheba a second chance. He gave me a second, third, and fourth chance, as he did for most of the women in this book! God redeemed for good what the enemy intended for disaster. Redeemed means God *emancipated—obtained a release from captivity.*[85] He will do that for you and your loved ones too.

Reflection: Pray for yourself and those you love who are wandering in the darkness. Pray they become weary of hiding in the shadows and are attracted by shining hope.

~ Let us remember that God will never tempt us. Testing helps us grow stronger and more mature. Tempting tries to get us to do wrong. ~

Anonymous

Day 92: Spiritual Wandering

Yesterday's story teaches us that disaster is the long-reaching effect of a moment of sinful self-indulgence. We seldom pause to consider that in a moment of temptation. If we could see the results of our actions clearly, we'd say *no* more often.

The prophet Isaiah said, "We all, like sheep, have gone astray, each of us has turned to his own way" (Isaiah 53:6). This verse says that our spiritual wandering gets us in trouble. We each have followed the road of sin and turned our own way, which is away from God. Now we have begun a journey of self-examination, which means we are taking responsibility for our actions and going to God with a repentant heart.

David agonized, "My God, my God, why have you forsaken me? Why are you so far from saving me, so far from the words of my groaning? O my God, I cry out by day, but you do not answer, by night, and am not silent" (Psalm 22:1–2).

Jesus quoted that as he hung in angst, dying on the cross (Mathew 27:46).

Remember that, like us, Jesus was tempted. We can never fully understand what happened at Calvary, but what consoles me is that God is unwilling to put his children through any test that he himself has not endured. When God seems far away, he may be closest of all.

Reflect on this and thank Jesus for what he has done for you.

~ *Many a dangerous temptation comes to us in gay, fine colors, that are but skin-deep.* ~

Matthew Henry[86]

Day 93: Self-Examination

David made a choice to let go. He confessed his sin and expressed sincere repentance. The Bible says God removes and forgets our sins (Psalm 103:12; Isaiah 43:25) when we confess them and repent. "I have swept away your offenses like a cloud, your sins like the morning mist. Return to me, for I have redeemed you" (Isaiah 44:22).

God's purpose for confession and repentance isn't to beat you up with guilt and shame but to give you *freedom* by allowing you to let go. We will never be free and whole until we confess we are in bondage—that we are filthy dirty. "He [Jesus] poured water into a basin and began to wash his disciples' feet, drying them with the towel that was wrapped around him" (John 13:5).

To place our feet in Jesus' basin is to give him the filthiest areas of our lives. Once cleansed, we repent. Repentance means you acknowledge you're going down the wrong road. You say, "I've been doing life my way, and it's not working. I have to change and go in God's direction." It is a radical change of mind, leading to a complete turnaround.

Oswald Chambers wrote, "The bedrock of Christianity is repentance. If ever you cease to know the virtue of repentance, you are in darkness."[87] Once I confessed the denial and guilt over my abortion, God hit the clear button. He forgot about it. I do myself no favors by returning again and again to that guilt. That's the tool of the enemy—to get us to return to the same negative feelings that God has already cleared from our record.

Reflection: What two or three things do you want God to clear from your life?

~ *What a deterrent to sin it would be if, before the fact,*
we could be given a glimpse of its impact. ~

Charles Swindoll[88]

Day 94: Our Unconfessed Sin

God redeemed David and Bathsheba. We aren't given a picture of what Bathsheba was feeling, but she must have felt great grief and torment over her losses. The Bible says, "Then David comforted his wife Bathsheba, and he went to her and lay with her. She gave birth to a son, and they named him Solomon" (2 Samuel 12:24–25). Bathsheba soon became the favored wife and was able to obtain the succession rights for her son, King Solomon (1 Kings 1:11–31). This story has a joyful ending—a new kind of normal.

If unconfessed sin is your cause of unhappiness, let your conscience, your spirit, speak to you. Listen to the voice of God as he speaks through the Spirit. If he is putting his finger on something, get rid of it. Whatever your sin, if we confess our sins, he is faithful and just to forgive them and cleanse us from all unrighteousness (1 John 1:9).

Repentance is all that is required. No matter how far we have strayed, God is able to restore our relationship to him and rebuild our lives. It is not necessary to dwell on your past. "Everyone who trusts in him is freed from all guilt and declared righteous" (Acts 13:39, TLB). You are free! Rejoice!

Reflection: If there's a skeleton in your closet or certain sin you have not confessed, do that right now. Open the door and pull that skeleton out. Dust off the cobwebs and tell God. He already knows. He just wants to hear it from you so he can give you his supernatural touch. Then pray: Lord, I acknowledge that the things I've just confessed are the very reasons Jesus had to die on the cross—for me. Jesus, I accept your shed blood, wiping my slate clean today. Thank you, Lord! I praise you!

> ~ *Men cannot thus sin against their brethren, without offending Christ, and endangering their own souls.* ~
>
> Matthew Henry

Day 95: Light in Midst of Darkness

Darkness drains of us hope and optimism. Light fills us with energy and joy. The problem is we get comfortable hiding in the dark. It's an escape. No one need see the real me. Why do you think so many taverns don't have any windows?

We can make outside changes to ourselves like a facelift, a new hair color, a better job, polished wardrobe, or sports car. Those things won't remove the darkness. Even the wise king Solomon said, "Utterly meaningless! Everything is meaningless . . . I hated life, because the work that is done under the sun was grievous to me. All of it is meaningless, a chasing after the wind" (Ecclesiastes 2:2:17).

Only God has the power to shine. For he said, "Let light shine out of darkness," (2 Corinthians 4:6). That power is available to you because he picked you. "You are a chosen people, a royal priesthood, a holy nation, a people belonging to God, that you may declare the praises of him who called you out of darkness into his wonderful light" (1 Peter 2:9).

This verse says that you belong to God, which means you can go directly to him! He called you out of the dark for a very specific purpose to make a difference in this world—to be light! This revelation requires us to assess areas in our life that are working against us—the dark spots. We can either react to the dark spots with depression or anger. Or we can accept what we can't change and move forward, toward the light.

Reflection: Today ask God to turn on his light. Reflect on this powerful verse and image: "God is light; in him there is no darkness at all" (1 John 1:5).

~ *When a train goes through a tunnel and it gets dark, you don't throw away the ticket and jump off. You sit still and trust the engineer.* ~

Corrie Ten Boom[89]

Day 96: God's Girl Mary Magdalene

God shaped many women of the Bible and wants to do the same with you. Mary Magdalene is one such woman—a woman delivered from darkness, a woman transformed. She has been labeled a prostitute, although nothing specifically points to that. What we do know is that Jesus set Mary free from seven demons (Mark 16:9).

When Jesus found Mary, he saw a woman in trouble, in bondage, and in need of a savior. We don't know exactly what happened in Mary's life to bring on her despair, but she was in agony—at least seven kinds. No one could help her ... until Jesus. Mary Magdalene found the source of light. Demons represent darkness in our life. Sometimes they come in a package called stress, anxiety, the pressures of daily life.

Dr. Gregory Jantz, author of *Moving Beyond Depression*, said, "The pace of life can exhaust us. The patterns of life can undercut us. Unexpected dilemmas, such as a loss of a job, the illness or death of a loved one, a financial crisis, the necessity of a move, or personal health problems, can erode our emotional equilibrium. Difficulties like these attack our sense of security and can rob us of happiness."[90]

Many of us accept this as part of life, but that is a lie. No one could help Mary ... until Jesus. Jesus relates to women. We are equal reflectors of God's image.

Reflection: First, define the foremost pressures in your day-to-day life. Then ask Jesus to help you prioritize and bring light to these pressures.

~ What's the world's greatest lie? It's this: that at a certain point in our lives, we lose control of what's happening to us, and our lives become controlled by fate. ~

Paula Coelho[91]

Day 97: God's Agenda

Tick. Tock. Tick. Tock. I want it to stop!

So often we get overwhelmed with the world's time clock, and what we need to do is reset our clocks to God's time. This usually means slowing down and listening for God's agenda. Life's stress (especially in the peri-menopausal years) is often the biggest factor in depression because there is a lot going on.[92]

Or perhaps you are caring for an ill parent or grieving a parent's death. You may have your own health concerns. You may feel the pressure to retire but are not prepared financially. But amidst it all, God has a plan. You and I can't figure it out, and in reality, I'm glad his plan doesn't depend on me or you, because then ... yikes!

We are daughters of light, therefore we need to do whatever it takes to remove stress (darkness) from our lives, so eventually we may become light givers. Take Jesus' hand and remember his promise: "I am the light of the world. Whoever follows me will never walk in darkness, but will have the light of life" (John 8:12).

This is a message of hope and love from an awesome God who has a distinct purpose for your life. It's a promise of healing and restoration and wholeness with an opportunity attached to experience everything amazing God has to offer.

Reflection: What is one way you will use today's lesson and Scripture to change, or light, your life this week?

~ We need life's stress. Character cannot be developed into its strongest and most beautiful forms without it. ~

Walter B. Knight[93]

Day 98: The Cracked Vase

Jasmine attended a seminar on self-esteem and returned with an attitude I'd never seen in her before. She re-created the speaker's demonstration for me. There were two vases placed side by side on a table. The speaker held up the first vase. "This is beautifully shaped, flawless, a fine vessel." Inside the vase was a candle, which she lit. She then said, "You can't see anything, can you? But let me assure you it is a perfect vase that can hold anything you put inside of it, including this lit candle."

Then Jasmine held up a second vase that looked similar to the first. But this one had some very large cracks in it and countless hairline fractures. She said, "Who wants this broken and cracked vase?" No one responded. She proceeded to light the candle placed in this vase. "What do you see?" The group responded, "Light!" She posed, "Where is it coming from?" One woman said, "From inside." "How is that possible?"

The group concluded that the light was coming through the cracks. Jasmine pointed to each crack and clarified what each one represented. "This one is sexual abuse. This one is a failed marriage. This one is rejection. This one is an abortion. This one is loneliness." We are the vase. Our vase is composed of cracks, dings, and chips. It is within each crack, each ding, and each chip that God meets us. The almighty potter himself creates each one of us and then fills us with himself—light.

Reflection: Contrary to how you may feel, you are a beautiful and cracked vessel. Read and meditate on 2 Corinthians 4:6–12.

~ People are like stained-glass windows. They sparkle and shine when the sun is out, but when the darkness sets in their true beauty is revealed only if there is light from within. ~

Elisabeth Kübler-Ross[94]

Day 99: Your Divine Purpose

Peeking into the lives of the characters in this book is like looking into a mirror. We each have that inward tendency or preference for the things that are not good for us. Things that are not part of God's plan. When this tendency is expressed outwardly, it creates strong, negative behavior patterns. The more we carry out the negative, the less we can resist. We can live in slavery for a long time and not even know it. It's when we want to change that we learn we are not really free and happy at all.

When I realized I was drowning in quicksand, I wanted to take my life back. Little did I know God had done that for me. "Even though we were spiritually dead and doomed by our sins, he gave us back our lives again" (Ephesians 2:5 TLB).

God made us alive with his Son, Jesus, and forgave *all* our sins, which means he wiped out your bad record. He has a magnificent plan for your life that can be said in a single phrase, "to make holy," which means "to separate." Romans 5:10 says we are enemies of God before we accept Jesus. But the moment someone trusts Jesus Christ as her personal Savior, she's adopted into the Lord's family and set apart as God's child for a sacred purpose. To be holy is to be set apart, above the norm, and to be extraordinary.

Reflection: What has gotten in the way of your fellowship with God, and are you willing to remove those obstacles no matter what? Pray about the answer to this question.

> ~ *The old word for holy in the German language, heilig, also means healthy.*
> *And so heilbronn means holy-well, or healthy-well. You could not get any*
> *better definition of what holy really is than healthy—completely healthy.* ~

Thomas Carlyle[95]

Day 100: Ground Zero

We were created to have companionship with God and bring him glory and honor. Because of our stubborn self-will, we chose to go our own dependent way and fellowship was broken. Today many of us are not experiencing God's wonderful plan because we are separated from God by our sin. We are at Ground Zero.

That term has become synonymous with the World Trade Center and the September 11, 2001, disaster. Life as many knew it was destroyed, and they had to start all over—at ground zero. Today may be your personal turning point. Perhaps you are unsure of your relationship with God and need to deal with this choice now. When we receive Jesus, we experience a new beginning. We are born again and get to start all over again—at ground zero. The first step is receiving Jesus Christ as your personal Savior.

God loves you and has a wonderful plan for your life (John 3:16). Jesus said, "I have come that they may have life, and have it to the full" (John 10:10). You must have a personal relationship with Jesus to discover God's perfect plan. The *only way* to bridge this gap is to profess our belief that Jesus' died on the cross and rose three days later. In other words, we must be saved. We acknowledge we are all sinners. We ask God's forgiveness. We recognize Jesus as personal Savior and commit our life to him. If you are not ready today, you can come back when you feel the Holy Spirit prompting you.

Pray: "Dear Lord Jesus, I do believe you are the son of God and that you died on the cross to pay for my sin. Forgive my sin and make me part of your family. I now turn from going my own way. Thank you for the gift of eternal life and for your Holy Spirit, who has now come to live in me. I ask this in your name. Amen."

Day 101: MileStone

Steps To Overcome Negative Emotions

Move Forward

Before we were Christians, we lived in darkness. Everything about us, including our hearts, was dark—black. Then we received Jesus Christ as our Lord, and he covered us with his shed blood. The moment we trust Jesus, wonderful things happen.

> *All* of your sins (past, present, future) are forgiven. In this way God took away Satan's power to accuse you of sin (Colossians 2:13–14).

> You become God's child—God's Girl (John 1:12; Romans 8:15)—and receive eternal life (John 5:24).

> God rescues you out of the darkness and gloom of Satan's kingdom and brings you into the kingdom of his Son, Jesus (Colossians 1:13).

> You become a new person inside. You are not the same (2 Corinthians 5:17); Jesus dwells within you (Colossians 1:27; Revelation 3:20).

> God takes the sinless Christ and pours into him our sins. Then, Jesus pours God's goodness into us! (2 Corinthians 5:21)

> "Because it is written, You shall be Holy, for I am holy" (1 Peter 1:16).

Scripture describes the stable and secure identity we have in Jesus Christ. It is our privilege to be his children and experience his love, forgiveness, and power through the Holy Spirit (Read Acts 2).

> *~ A season of suffering is a small price to pay for a clear view of God. ~*

Max Lucado [96]

Day 102: Challenge the Old Way of Thinking

When we receive Jesus Christ as our Lord, he covers us with his shed blood and darkness turns to light. Our hearts go from darkness to gold, so to speak. Many of the chains that bind us break. We experience a new birth, a renewal, a transforming resuscitation, called regeneration. Dr. Robert McGee says that regeneration is not a self-improvement program, nor is it a cleanup campaign for our sinful natures. He says that regeneration is nothing less than the impartation of new life.[97]

What chains do you want to break? What do you have strong emotions about?

Where do you feel stuck or bound? What things are you doing that you wish you would stop? Compulsive behaviors? Crying all day?

Pray and Meditate

Meditate on this passage: Titus 3:3–7. Then in your own words tell God what your regeneration means to you.

At one time we, too, were foolish, disobedient, deceived, and enslaved by all kinds of passions and pleasures. We lived in malice and envy, being hated and hating one another. But when the kindness and love of God our Savior appeared, he saved us, not because of righteous things we had done, but because of his mercy. He saved us through the washing of rebirth and renewal by the Holy Spirit, whom he poured out on us generously through Jesus Christ our Savior, so that, having been justified by his grace, we might become heirs having the hope of eternal life.

Self-Soother

Call someone special to you that you have not spoken with for quite a while.

Part Eight

Become What You Are—God's Girl

Encouraged by God's Word

"The apostle Paul said, "Get rid of the old yeast that you may be a new batch without yeast—as you really are." (1 Corinthians 5:7)

In the Old Testament any grain offering made to the Lord could not have yeast because it was a fungus or mold, and therefore a symbol for sin. In other words, because Christ has delivered us from the slavery of sin, we should have nothing to do with the old yeast—sins of the past. With God's help we become who we really are.

Day 103: God's Girl Karlie

Karlie recalls, "Have you ever had a day when it takes incredible fortitude to even get out of bed? I had this kind of day, times one hundred. I figured out I must be depressed. When my marriage of eight years began rapidly falling apart, I felt beaten up and emotionally drained.

"Then our two children picked up on the conflict and began to act out and then refused to go to school for days. And then there was talk of lay-offs at work. I could handle one, maybe two conflicts, but not all this. Everything was falling apart.

"As I dragged myself through each day, I felt as though I were wading through never-ending quicksand. I felt overcome by hopelessness and despair, and often found myself wide awake in the middle of the night, worrying about my children and our future. I also started to binge eat in the middle of the night. I became less and less reliable, causing my family and employer great concern.

"With the help of a Christian counselor, antidepressant medication, and a committed sister in Christ, I started climbing out of the pit of quicksand. Each was a strand of the lifeline God threw to me."

Reflection: Do you see yourself reflected in Karlie's story—the worry, fear, tiredness, and feelings of inadequacy? Perhaps you should consider following up with a counselor, or a physician, and a friend in Christ.

~ *When walking through the valley of shadows, remember; a shadow is cast by light.* ~

H.K. Barclay[98]

Day 104: Miserable Men of the Bible

Men are not immune from the blues either. Some great men in the Bible felt despair. Job, a righteous man, cried, "My heart is broken. Depression haunts my days" (Job 30:16, TLB).

The great leader Moses asked to die: "If this is how you are going to treat me, put me to death right now" (Numbers 11:15).

King Saul was miserable. He believed David caused his inner mayhem. *If it weren't for David, I'd be a happy king!* Misery fortified with self-pity.

Jeremiah is another man who struggled in darkness, "My heart is broken within me; all my bones tremble" (Jeremiah 23:9). A true champion, he pressed on. He couldn't see light, just as we may not be able to see light, but he was still faithful to his Lord.

Elijah wanted to die too. "I have had enough, LORD," he said. "Take my life; I am no better than my ancestors" (1 Kings 19:4). They didn't hold back their feelings. Some even blamed God.

In Moses' case we see an outstanding personality shaped by God. God did not change who or what Moses was. Instead he took his characteristics and molded them until they suited his purposes. God touched these men because they sought him.

God is trying to take what he created in you and use it for his intended purposes. The Spirit of God working in us can bring what is withered, even dead, back to life.

Reflection: Instead of telling God what he should change about you, ask him how you should use what he has already given you. This will be your starting point.

~ *Inwardly we are being renewed day by day.* ~

The Apostle Paul (2 Corinthians 4:16)

Day 105: The Barriers

Stand in front of a mirror. What do you see? When I looked in my mirror, I saw failure, liar, faults, broken promises, and a closet full of secrets called guilt and shame.

Someone once said that we are as sick as our secrets. Layers and layers of fear or shame or hopelessness often keep us from disclosing our innermost feelings or secrets, creating a barrier to becoming who God intend us to be.

We'd rather keep the mask on than to lose face. Sometimes an appearance of godliness and performance, or no appearance at all (isolation), becomes more important than matters of the heart.

David must have felt a similar sting when he said, "But how can I ever know what sins are lurking in my heart? Cleanse me from these hidden faults. And keep me from deliberate wrongs; help me to stop doing them" (Psalm 19:12–13, TLB).

David was imploring God to show him and then cleanse him of his dark chambers and secret faults.

We, too, have hidden away similar feelings either out of ignorance or simply not wanting to deal with them. But today is a new day. Look into the mirror and see your faith—your Savior. See what God sees—his beloved, unblemished, beautiful daughter!

Reflection: Ask God to help you identify those feelings today.

~ Nothing makes us so lonely as our secrets. ~

Paul Tournier[99]

Day 106: Put Your Past Behind You Today

When I was twelve I began to shoplift and take things that didn't belong to me. I didn't need the stuff. The act of not getting caught was a game, a high. I held secret after secret for decades, imbedding destructive roots deep within my soul like a cancer. I'd read a self-help book or try to distract myself by doing something "good and normal," but symptoms returned. I ended up discouraged, depressed, and convinced that God must not love me because my prayers went unanswered. The enemy rejoiced!

Jesus said, "There is nothing concealed that will not be disclosed, or hidden that will not be made known. What you have said in the dark will be heard in the daylight, and what you have whispered in the ear in the inner rooms will be proclaimed from the roofs" (Luke 12:2–3).

We all have that *stuff* that needs to be exposed, and only God can show us what it is and how. No matter what hides beneath the layers, God is always there. Right now God sees you just as he created you. Proclaim who you are:

"They [*you*] are like the angels. They [*you*] are God's children" (Luke 20:36).

"You also, like living stones, are being built into a spiritual house to be a holy priesthood" (1 Peter 2:5).

"… you will be my treasured possession" (Exodus 19:5).

Whatever is important to you is important to God!

Reflection: How does it make you feel to know you are God's child? Share any secrets you have with God in prayer right now.

~ We have to go for what we think we're fully capable of, not limit ourselves by what we've been in the past. ~

Vivek Paul

Day 107: Cleaning Out the Attic

When was the last time you looked at the state of your attic? If you flooded your dark attic with light, you might see a real mess. As I began my journey, I asked Jesus to clean out my attic. He began by penetrating the darkness and not only exposed, but cleansed and healed the dark areas. God wants to expose us to truth and light to free us from bondage so in the end we may serve and bring him glory. Jesus said, "Everyone who does evil hates the light, and will not come into the light for fear that his deeds will be exposed. But whoever lives by the truth comes into the light, so that it may be seen plainly that what he has done has been done through God" (John 3:20–21).

It is comforting to know that God's power to save and heal is not limited to how good we are or how attractive we might look or how spiritual we are. God understands we all have times of ups and downs; we're in the kitchen surrounded by family one minute, only to be found hiding in the dark, musty attic by ourselves one minute later.

Jesus came to convict of us of our sin (the darkness), but more importantly to offer us a way out through the light—himself. God's plan was never one of depression, failure, poverty, abuse, sickness, or pain. There is no valley of depression so dark that God can't touch it and bring light out of it. He's been doing so for millennia, and he can do it for you today. Jesus said, "You are the light of the world. A city on a hill cannot be hidden" (Matthew 5:14).

Reflection: Right now catch the vision of what you could be apart from the negative circumstances or people in your life. Ask God right now in prayer to flood your soul with his presence and light.

~ *What is the past, what is it all for? A mental sandwich?* ~

Ashbery, John[100]

Day 108: Made in the Image of God

The cartoon character "Popeye the Sailor" man was famous for always settling and moaning, "I yam what I yam." We too often grumble, "That's just the way I am, and I will never change." Throw out this complacent thought. One of the greatest obstacles to living life as God's Girl is looking for what's wrong with us—our body, our clothes, our relationships, our children, even our friends, and then dwelling on it. "I yam what I yam!" Don't worship your problem!

Grab a hold of this fact: "God made you in his image" (Genesis 1:27).

That is profound! It means that God used a template of himself to make you like him in many ways. Romans 8:29 also tells us, "For those God foreknew he also predestined to be conformed to the likeness of his Son." That's not the message our culture promotes, is it?

Growing up, most of society's messages told us that our physical appearance was most important because the body is a measure of female attractiveness and social success. Women are also expected today to attain the superwoman persona. Add to that any family variables, such as high achievement and perfectionism, and you can see why we don't see ourselves as God sees us.

Reflection: Describe yourself—first your physical appearance and then how other people see you. Do you think this description lines up with God's image of you?

> ~ *I am not what I might be, I am not what I ought to be, I am not what I wish to be, I am not what I hope to be. But I thank God I am not what I once was, and I can say with the great apostle, "By the grace of God I am what I am.* ~

John Newton[101]

Day 109: The Power to Shape Our World

Human beings are the only creatures made in God's image. In fact, we are the only creatures that can laugh and cry! We have the power to shape our world according to God's purpose. It means we have the ability to reflect his character in love, patience, forgiveness, kindness, and faithfulness. It also means we have the ability to connect; and we have imagination, passion, intellect, and creativity.

However, we can't reflect God's attributes of being all knowing, all powerful, and being everywhere (though we try and fail miserably). Even as Christians we often ask God why he made that person better or prettier than how we perceive ourselves. We've heard the saying a hundred times: "God doesn't make mistakes." Believe it! Think of the image of God as a mirror. In God's mirror all of his children have a designer label that reads, "Gorgeous!"

Genesis 1:31 tells us that God saw that all he had created was very good. He is pleased with how he made you! You are a one-of-a-kind woman, extraordinaire. No one else has ever been created to be and do what God has in mind for you. Today he wants to use everything about you—your personality, your background, and yes, even your pain. The Bible says God laid out a plan for each of us long before we made an appearance on this earth. You have a destiny!

Reflection: Now that you are aware of God's gift to you, how can you use it wisely?

~ It is only possible to live happily ever after on a day-to-day basis. ~
Margaret Bonnano[102]

Day 110: Looking in God's Mirror

I'd look at a beautiful or talented woman and think, *God, why'd you make her so beautiful? I must be leftovers.* Or, *How come she has so many gifts, and I can't do anything?* I was that kid in gym class who usually got picked last to be on a sports team. I hated that I had no physical talent—more rejection. *God made a loser!* No, he didn't. Those were lies from the enemy. It's hard to see ourselves the way God's see us, isn't it?

Philip Yancey wrote, "God created us so that when he looked upon us, he would see reflected something of himself."[103]

How do you think it makes God feel when we look in that mirror and say, "I'm ugly." "I'm a loser." "No one loves me." "I have nothing." Because we bear God's image, criticizing ourselves is criticizing God himself. We are saying, "God, I don't like your work." We were created with the capacity to reflect the very character of God. Adam and Eve sinned and could no longer reflect God's glory, but God did not leave us in this predicament. By grace we have been given the Holy Spirit so we may become more and more Christlike in order to reflect that image.

Reflect on these words from the book of Hebrews: "Keep your lives free from the love of money and *be content with what you have*, because God has said, 'Never will I leave you; never will I forsake you'" (Hebrew 13:5, *author's emphasis*). Now answer: "What have I done in my life to make me feel second-best to someone else?"

~ Satan is an identity-theft master. ~

Anonymous

Day 111: A Portrait of God's Girl

Pastor and author Charles Swindoll said, "The most important asset I possess, apart from my relationship with Christ, is my character. The problem is that as human beings high moral character is not our 'default setting,' sin is."[104]

When we begin our relationship with Jesus, the Holy Spirit begins to reset those defaults. Every woman who believes in Jesus Christ is God's Girl, which means God desires to do powerful things in her life. An all-wise, all-powerful, and all-loving God intentionally and purposely created you.

A. W. Tozer instructed, "True faith requires that we believe everything that God has said about himself, but also that we believe everything he has said about us!"[105]

In order to fulfill God's specific plan for us, we must first see ourselves the way he sees us. Then we begin to grow and prosper in each area of our lives. The Bible provides many powerful examples: Jonah was captive in the belly of a fish, surrounded my gunk and gastric juices. Then the fish expels Jonah, and he is used to reveal God's goodness and mercy to a wicked, rebellious people.

Daniel was in the lion's den, no doubt face to face with a lip-licking lion, when God miraculously delivered him. And who could forget poor Joseph? Left in a pit by his brothers with no way out—no hope. Joseph takes a God-detour and ends up royalty—a governor in Egypt. These are the stories of the Bible. One near-death, hopeless experience after another. This is our hope!

Reflection: Write down five positive virtues or characteristics about yourself.

~ He that does not love the image of God in his
people, has no saving knowledge of God. ~

Matthew Henry

Day 112: God's Girl Is Royalty

Max Lucado writes:

> There are many reasons God saves you: to bring glory to himself, to appease his justice, to demonstrate his sovereignty. But one of the sweetest reasons God saved you is because he is fond of you. He likes having you around. He thinks you are the best thing to come down the pike in quite awhile…[106]

Why wouldn't God think that? You're his daughter! Where you are today is a reflection of how you see yourself. More than likely you have a negative self-image of yourself since most women do. Through this journey we will discover, cultivate, and express those virtues and characteristics that are innate to being God's Girl. The Bible says, "For *we are God's workmanship, created in Christ Jesus* to do good works, which God prepared in advance for us to do" (Ephesians 2:10, author's emphasis).

No matter what our current situation, we can change our self-image by speaking and meditating on God's Word and spending time with God. God's Girl learns firsthand that God loves her just the way she is but out of that love refuses to leave herself this way. That's what the God's Girl journey is about—transformation. She knows she is created in the image of God. She sees herself with a crown on her head, even though she is not perfect. A co-heir of Jesus Christ, she sees herself as a real princess!

Reflection: Describe how your vision of yourself differs from how God sees you?

~ Remember always that you have not only the right to be an individual; you have an obligation to be one. ~

Eleanor Roosevelt

Day 113: God's Girl Is a Champion

"See I am doing a new thing! Can you not perceive it?" The Bible says that (Isaiah 43:19). Notice it doesn't say that God is *going* to do a new thing maybe next week, next month, or next year. God says, I'm doing something new in your life right now! God wants to do something new in your life *today*.

As you let go of the past, take hold of all the wonderful plans and changes he has in mind for you. You will envision yourself as a champion. God's Girl presses through circumstances and negative feelings, "for everyone born of God overcomes the world. This is the victory that has overcome the world, even our faith" (1 John 5:4).

With God as her trainer she becomes a CHAMP: Courageous, Humble, Awesome, Mindful, and Persistent.

Reflection: Which of the CHAMP qualities and characteristics describe you? Why?

~ If you'll persevere ... God will open doors for you. ~

Joel Osteen[107]

Day 114: God's Girl Is Victorious

Each week before I enter the gates of the correctional facility where I volunteer, I pray reverently. I have created a beautiful image. As I near the facility I picture a dozen warrior angels waiting for me at the prison entrance. Each is covered in bright, shiny majestic armor. As I drive through the main gate, they surround me and I sense God's protection. This representation is so emotive that it always brings tears to my eyes. I know God and his army will protect me based on my faith and trust in him.

You have the power of faith within you to overcome whatever comes against you. The Bible says that faith comes by hearing the Word of God (Romans 10:17). God's Girl hears the Word of God and stores it in her heart. God's Word is only truth, and God's Girl fights for this kind of truth in her life. The Bible says God loves truth and hates deceit: "The LORD detests lying lips, but he delights in men [women] who are truthful" (Proverbs 12:22).

Her faith in God grows stronger each day. She knows her enemies and recognizes that a victorious life won't just come, but she must fight for it. When the enemy attacks her feelings, by faith she battles him through the power of Jesus Christ—the truth.

Reflect on David's heartfelt words as your own: "O Lord, the king [David] rejoices in your strength. How great is his joy in the victories you give!" (Psalms 21:1)

~ *Victory at all costs, victory in spite of all terror, victory however long and hard the road may be; for without victory, there is no survival.* ~

Winston Churchill

Day 115: God's Girl Loves

Holocaust survivor Corrie Ten Boom wrote:

> I discovered that it is not on our forgiveness any more than on our goodness that the world's healing hinges, but on God's. When He tells us to love our enemies, He gives, along with the command, the love itself.[108]

Nothing can stop God from loving you. He gives God's Girl the Holy Spirit to lead her through the gradual process of having the character of Christ formed in her (Galatians 4:19). This means first developing a love for God through an intimate relationship with him. Then she has the ability to receive and give love to others.

The phrase "I love You, God" means different things to different people. It's easier to define what love is not rather than what love is. Some use "I love you" to express their feelings about the Lord. Others make up their own ideas of God's desires for them. Jesus taught that only those who obey God's commands truly love him.

God's Girl not only loves God and her family, but also others, whether they deserve love. She loves herself and loves life!

Reflection: How much do you love yourself? God? Your family? If not very much, talk to God about what love means in your life right now.

~ *Always forgive your enemies—nothing annoys them so much.* ~

Oscar Wilde[109]

Day 116: God's Girl Is a Friend

Why do we see the glass as completely empty rather than as half full? Discouragement and self-pity become comfortable, and we fear that discarding them will leave us vulnerable. Seeing the glass as empty is a sign that our thinking and attitude are holding us back. Unfortunately, negative thinking (like sin) is seductive. We actually find pleasure in feeling sorry for ourselves. Sometimes we even imagine staying in that isolated place forever. It's then that we need the warmth of loving friends.

Dr. Larry Crabb, author of *Connecting*, wrote, "We were designed to connect with others; connecting is life … tears without an audience, without someone to hear and care, leave the wounds unhealed. When someone listens to our groaning and stays there, we feel something change inside us. Despair seems less necessary; hope begins to stir where before there was only pain."[110]

I know it sounds like too much work to let people in and cultivate friendships. It's a lot like physical therapy: just five more reps and you're done. We may try to ignore those reaching toward us, but with the Holy Spirit's guidance, soon we feel stronger and welcome their presence.

Jesus also said, "Love each other as I have loved you. Greater love has no one than this that he lay down his life for his friends" (John 15:12–13).

Jesus is saying we should be connected to others. Once we embrace friendship, then we become that much-needed shepherd or mentor friend to other women, and we begin blossoming like never before!

Reflection: How have you become isolated from friends and family?

~ *To like your sex, you have to like yourself.* ~

Heidi Brennan[111]

Day 117: God's Girl Honors

So many of us are wounded; a parent abused you, your husband left for another woman, your son is a drug addict, your teacher told you you'd never amount to anything, you didn't get the promotion you worked so hard for, or your best friend moved. You have reasons to be hurt and angry, but you also have a choice to make. "Do I keep these feelings torched, let my feelings turn from hurt to hate and keep going deeper into this pit, or release them to God and seek my purpose for existence?"

Why do I exist? Vey few people can answer that. Our purpose for existence is to glorify God. Another word would be to honor or value God. As Christians it is not a choice but a biblical mandate to honor God. We honor God because he merits our devoted obedience.

With obedience to God in mind, we work to release feelings of unfaithfulness and wrong. We work to honor our marriage, our parents, and other people (and some who are very unlovable). We ask the Holy Spirit to guide us where we need strength and help.

God's Girl also honors what God has given her. She honors the people and relationships God has put in her life. It is out of her ability to honor God that God's Girl is then able to honor others and more importantly, herself. And she honors her body by taking proper care of it.

Reflection: List three ways you can honor yourself. How can you implement those ideas this upcoming week?

~ There are three classes of men; lovers of wisdom, lovers of honor, and lovers of gain. ~

Plato[112]

Day 118: God's Girl is Light!

As new creations God makes us beautiful and enables us to reflect his image. *His image is love and light.* That is why we are here, to love and be loved by God … and love others. Everything God has done, He did with us in mind—from creation to redemption. Redemption means we have been bought out of sin and slavery (bondage). We were bought with Jesus Christ's blood, not gold or silver—His blood. When we comprehend that sacrifice, and how much God loves us, we change and begin to give of ourselves.

Jesus said, "I have set you an example that you should do as I have done for you" (John 13:15).

We are called by Jesus to be light—to speak and act as His representative. What begins to matter most is the heart behind what we do. God's Girl does not live for *self* anymore. She is a portrait of a woman used by God—a woman of light. She reflects the fruit of the Spirit: joy, peace, love, patience, kindness, goodness, and faithfulness.

More than likely you are feeling that you are not living up to the potential God has given you. That is only temporary. You will be beset by what God has in store for those who diligently seek him. God has huge plans for your life if you let him in!

Reflect on his Word and how this applies to your life today: "I can do *all things* through him [Jesus] who strengthens me" (Philippians 4:13, author's emphasis). Notice what Paul is not saying: *I can do nothing, so I'll wait around for God to step in and take over.* Paul is saying: *I can do it, but not without depending on Jesus' strength.* We can't do what we're called to do without partnering with Jesus.

> ~ *When we keep claiming the light, we will find*
> *ourselves becoming more and more radiant.* ~
>
> Henri J.W. Nouwen[113]

Day 119: God's Girl Lives a Balanced Life

Most of us fooled around on a teeter-totter when we were a kid. What happened if one of the "teeters" suddenly got off? The balance was broken. The other "totter" crashed to the ground or flew off, sometimes with dire repercussions. The same thing happens in our spiritual and emotional life. If we teeter too much to the side of sin or negative thinking, we lose perspective, and God is left out of the picture.

Living a balanced life brings peace, joy, and health to every area of our life. That may sound scary and unrealistic right now, but with the Holy Spirit's help, you can do anything because He serves as our counselor, instructor, and source of spiritual power. Who exactly is the Holy Spirit? The Holy Spirit is the third person of the Trinity. The Holy Spirit is considered to act in concert with and share an essential nature with God the Father and God the Son (Jesus.) His primary purpose is to glorify Jesus and bring attention to him. The Holy Spirit directs and teaches us, and guides us into the truth of the Scriptures (John 16:13). It is through the Holy Spirit's power that the love of Jesus flows through us to others. That power produces spiritual fruit.

Don't put off doing the things you know God has instructed you to do. When you do your part, stepping out in faith, the Holy Spirit will do his part. Watch, God will pour out his blessings and favor, and you will experience the balanced life he has for you.

Reflection: What does a balanced life look like to you? What areas today are you procrastinating? Envision how your life will be more harmonious once those areas are put back into balance.

~ *Never compete. Never. Watching the other guy is what kills all forms of energy.* ~

Diana Vreeland[114]

Day 120: MileStone

Steps To Overcome Negative Emotions

Move Forward

It takes courage and honesty to move forward. This may be one of the greatest challenges of your life today, but the Lord will provide everything you need to persevere.

Moving forward means you begin to see yourself the way God sees you. He sees you as rising above and triumphing over. He sees you as a precious stone in his crown. He sees you above, and not beneath. He sees you growing and excelling, and living a life of joy and success!

Challenge the Old Way of Thinking

Becoming what we were created to be may seem scary at first. This takes humility, trust in God, and energy. How we begin:

We rely on the Holy Spirit, not our self.
Examine what we expect of ourselves.
Make a list of things we are good at.
List what we are thankful for.

Remember, in God's eyes, there are no surprises. We humans, with our limited viewpoint, are often stunned by what he allows. But God always has a plan and a provision.

Day 121: Pray and Meditate

God, I want to let go of my grief, the worry, all of my problems, and focus on the fact that you are doing something good in me right now. I believe your plans for me are good. Help me to acknowledge your presence and to experience the life of victory that you designed just for me. God, I am your child and that means I am destined to live a life of victory. Help me be the unique individual you designed.

Help me use my special gifts, not hide them. When the world gets to be too much for me to bear, remind me to take comfort in your Word. Help me to begin to store up Scripture verses in my head and my heart to help me overcome the trials I will face in this world. In Jesus' name. Amen.

Self-Soother

Buy yourself one item under seven dollars that will make you feel pretty.

Part Nine

God's Girl Confronts Truth

Encouraged by God's Word

"Today, God answers our prayers just as He did thousands of years ago: "Because he loves me," says the LORD, "I will rescue him; I will protect him, for he acknowledges my name. He will call upon me, and I will answer him; I will be with him in trouble, I will deliver him and honor him." (Psalm 91:14–15)

Day 122: Love Is Blind

After one date with Bill, I (Kimberly), was sure he was "Mr. Right." Superficially charming and handsome, he swept me off my feet. We fell in love quickly, and we decided to get married. I should have known there was something wrong with the dream when he asked to borrow money from me to buy my own engagement ring!

Swiftly the relationship began to deteriorate. He was bar-hopping and picking up women, taking pleasure in throwing his indiscretions in my face. I also discovered he had been using my gasoline credit card and forging my signature, but I was willing to forgive. I believed it was somehow my fault, and I needed to change.

Bill was a narcissist (one who has excessive love or admiration of oneself characterized by self-preoccupation and lack of empathy[115]). He'd accuse me of lying, and no matter what I said, it never made any difference. I wasn't allowed to defend myself. A few times he got so angry that he put his fist through the wall. He really didn't want to be married. I should have been relieved, because he hurt me deeply with his infidelity and rejection. But I fought to keep the relationship alive, as painful as that was. *At least I have a man ... It could be a whole lot worse—look at so and so ...*

It was less painful to blame myself for this ill-treatment than consider the possibility that Bill didn't really love me. Love is certainly blind, and I had several blind spots—things about this relationship I didn't want to see. This was a pattern with me. I would never have considered the man I needed in my life would be Jesus.

Reflection: Take some time to consider your blind spots.

> ~ *For many of us, life is like walking through a very*
> *dark house with no lights for illumination.* ~

Dr. Robert S. McGee[116]

Day 123: The Truth Hurts

At first I told myself that I had nothing to complain about. There are women in far worse situations. I couldn't see just how weak I was—unable to tolerate the normal problems of living. My self-esteem hit rock bottom when I realized he probably never cared about me and was only using me. *This is my fault for being so stupid! Why do I always pick these kinds of men?* I didn't blame him for the betrayal. I blamed myself. When I lost the relationship, I lost my identity because my self-esteem was dependant on Bill's approval.

I found acceptance and refuge at my favorite bar, because all my inhibitions and low self-esteem vanished! Other drunks complimented me. I felt at home. I couldn't sleep, became depressed, and considered getting sleeping pills from a doctor I knew, but decided against it. So, I just swam in my own murk. I had a sales territory, and I worked it so that I actually didn't have to do very much. God wasn't welcomed in my life either. I wallowed around in self-pity. Instead of looking up, I was looking down.

Reflection: Would you say bad relationships are a revolving door for you? What one step can you take to stop that door from revolving around again?

~ *Am I a prisoner of people's expectations, or liberated by Divine promises?* ~

Henri J.W. Nouwen

Day 124: God's Girl Faces Despair

Would you be surprised to learn I got fired from my job? Probably not. I entered into a cycle of grief—the emotion of loss, anguish, sorrow, regret, and longing for a time in my life that was gone. I thought I had lost everything—no man, no job—no security. Because I put everything I had into this relationship with Bill, I had few friends left to turn to. What else is left for me? I obsessed about how I could have done things differently. I concluded I was a failure.

I considered moving to California. I stayed with a friend in Los Angeles and decided this is the place for me: movie stars, hunky men with money, sun, and beaches! Bill and I continued to talk on the phone every couple of weeks. Then he announced he was coming to L.A. Amazingly, I didn't get excited. I realized I didn't have the same feelings anymore.

When he got to L.A. I chose not to answer his phone calls! God gave me eyes to see my worth, and the strength and courage to close the door to this abusive relationship. For the first time in my life I chose to set boundaries. No Bill!

As a child of God I could not be defeated. I faced my grief. I said farewell to this chapter of my life and started over in California, but it was *not* the last time I would meet Mr. "Maybe" Right. The future looked brighter because I realized my past, and my sin, was covered by Jesus' blood—it was finished!

Reflection: Are you wallowing around in self-pity as a result of a broken relationship? What one step can you take to start digging out?

~ *I rest my faith in Him alone Who died for my transgressions to atone.* ~

Unknown

Day 125: The Wizard of Oz

It's been said that depression is like the movie *The Wizard of Oz* when the color goes out and everything turns gray. We don't know how to turn the color back on. Helen Keller is quoted as saying, "A happy life consists not in the absence, but in the mastery of hardships."[117]

As strange as it may seem, facing despair is one of the best things we can do. The thought can be frightening. What does it take to turn the color back on? A better question is, what does it take to find hope? It takes a dose of courage.

Remember the cowardly lion from *The Wizard of Oz*? The lion sings, "What makes a king out of a slave? Courage." The lion eventually got courage from the Wizard, Hollywood's version of the omnipotent one. We get our courage from God, our omnipotent, all-powerful source to begin facing the darkness.

Jesus too felt despair in the Garden of Gethsemane (Matthew 26:36–38). Jesus shared his anguish with close friends, those whom he trusted. It is natural for us to carry our despair alone, but when we share our burden with another person and God, we shatter the darkness by enlightening our situation, and the healing begins.

Reflection: Think of a trusting person you may be willing to share your burden with. What one step can you take today to move a little bit closer to her (or him)?

~ *True* courage *is facing danger when you are afraid.* ~

L. Frank Baum, American writer, "The Wizard of Oz"

Day 126: God's Girl Faces Pain

We've all been there: You go into a store for a justifiable purchase and suddenly the clearance rack dares you to stop. If you're like me you buy things you don't need just because they're on sale. *Look what I saved!* Why do we do it? It makes us feel good. Shopping gives us an emotional jolt like eating chocolate. It may be a coping mechanism, like drinking alcohol or popping pills, deadening our pain.

Healing cannot take place unless we acknowledge the hurts. It does no good to keep deadening the pain. I know. I tried for twenty years! We need to start the process of resolving disappointment and loss so that God can draw close and unravel and restore what we have raveled and braided together.

Developing the courage to face despair is also an exercise in faith development, and that takes time. God is working, and you must do your part by being patient as you move toward wholeness. Dr. Gregory Jantz wrote:

> Remember that evening and morning do not come all at once. There is a transition time from one stage to the next. As you consider your depression, realize that while a significant event may have happened suddenly, your state of depression evolved over time. Just as the sunlight of joy dimmed gradually, it will take time for the increasingly bright rays of hope, joy, and peace to permeate the gloom. Keep working. Keep trying. Morning will come.[118]

Reflection: What do you believe God intends for your life?

~ *Remember your word to your servant, for you have given me hope. My comfort in my suffering is this: Your promise preserves my life.* ~

Psalm 119:49–50

Day 127: God's Girl Faces Doubt about God

I've lost so much, therefore, God doesn't care. Perhaps you fee the same. Your faith in God has slowly been dying or you feel betrayed by God. You may feel that he doesn't care about you any longer, so the desire to read your Bible or go to church has diminished. You undoubtedly feel hurt, even angry. It's easy to blacken God's character because he never answers back. It's easy to turn away from God and abandon any hope for relief and redemption. This may provoke despair because of the guilt associated with being mad at God. Maybe you don't believe you are even worthy of his love.

It's okay to question God. David questioned God quite a bit in the Psalms. Jeremiah poured out his doubts to God. Jacob spent a dark night wrestling on a riverbank with God's angel. Job painted God as a villain. Many mothers of the Bible who lost children have struggled with God's goodness. Even God's own Son cried, "My God, my God, why have you forsaken me?" (Matthew 27:46)

Psychologist Jeff Olson wrote:

> Struggling with God is no light matter. It exhausts all the energy we can muster. But it's in our exhaustion that we are more apt to be humble and quiet before Him. It's as if our soul runs out of breath and we have no more energy left to speak. This is when God shows Himself to us in ways that are life changing.[119]

Reflection: Have you been wrestling with God? How has God shown his divine hand to you in the middle of the unrest?

~ *Pain is temporary. Quitting lasts forever.* ~

Lance Armstrong

Day 128: Why Doesn't God Prevent Suffering?

We have all asked the puzzling question, "Why would a good and loving God allow his children to suffer?" Author and pastor Chip Ingram wrote:

> The price tag for a loving relationship among people is freedom. Human freedom means we have the willful opportunity to say yes and to love God, but we also have the willful opportunity to freely love or reject him, knowing that our freedom would result in pain. But he allowed it, knowing that the only remedy for that pain would be Jesus—he would come and die to pay the price that restores that relationship.[120]

Imagine a bear in a trap and a hunter who compassionately wants to free the bear. He tries to win the bear's confidence, but can't, so he shoots it with a tranquilizer gun. The bear now thinks the hunter is trying to kill him. It doesn't realize he is doing this out of kindness. In order to get the bear out of the trap, the hunter has to push it further into the trap to release the tension on the spring. If the bear were awake, he would be even more convinced the hunter was his enemy, intentionally causing the suffering and pain. However, the bear would be wrong.

I believe God does the same to us. We can't comprehend why he does it any more than the bear can understand the motivations of the hunter. We do not always understand the path through which God leads us, but we may be certain it is always born of love.

Reflection: Write down some specific things you know about God. How has he been faithful to you?

~ *Pain nourishes courage. You can't be brave if you've*
only had wonderful things happen to you. ~

Unknown

Day 129: God's Girl Abigail

This is a story of one of the Bible's most mismatched couples, the *Beauty and the Beast*. Scripture says, "A certain man in Maon, who had property there at Carmel, was very wealthy. His name was Nabal (which means "fool," which is probably a nickname to reflect his character, rather than his actual name) and his wife's name was Abigail. She was an intelligent and beautiful woman, but her husband, a Calebite, was "surly and mean in his dealings" (1 Samuel 25: 2–3). Arranged marriages were the custom of the day, so most likely Abigail wed Nabal for his wealth. He was evil. She was good.

In this story, Nabal and his servants would begin celebrating following the task of shearing this enormous flock. Storyteller Jennie Afam Dimkoff wrote, "You could hear Nabal shouting, "Get out of my sight, you lazy so and so!" Profanities followed. "Where's my wife? Where's my wine?" Abigail agonized when she heard his voice. Composing herself, she walked over and joined her husband.

"Wide awake later that night after meeting Nabal's demand for food, wine, and sexual pleasure, sadness overwhelmed her for a moment about her circumstances. To stay with a man that was cruel and foolish, she practiced forgiveness daily, trusting God for strength, wisdom, and ingenuity to face each new day. She was a woman of faith. She knew God had a plan for her life."[121]

Reflection: God brings peace into broken relationships. Abigail experienced this. So can we. Talk to God about your specific needs today.

> ~ *There are many things we are capable of, that we could be or do.*
> *The possibilities are so great that we never are more than one-fourth filled.* ~
>
> Katherine Anne Porter[122]

Day 130: A Woman of Integrity

Abigail's story continues … Meanwhile, David was running from King Saul, and his men moved into the wilderness just a few miles away. David (through his servants) asked Nabal to provide some necessary sustenance, but Nabal refused. David was livid because Nabal should have been in debt to him for protecting his herd. David swore that by morning not one male belonging to Nabal's household would remain alive.

A humble peacemaker, Abigail sprang into action and loaded a hoard of food on donkeys, but did not tell Nabal. "When Abigail saw David, she quickly got off her donkey and bowed down before David, "My lord, let the blame be on me alone. Please let your servant speak to you; hear what your servant has to say. May my lord pay no attention to that wicked man Nabal. He is just like his name—Fool, and folly goes with him. But as for me, your servant, I did not see the men my master sent" (1 Samuel 25: 21–25).

David's anger may have been dissuaded by the smell of food, but Abigail's skillful speech won him over. Such diplomatic wisdom! She accepts full blame and dissociates herself from the fool. David realizes this woman was sent by God to stop him, and he was overwhelmed with gratitude.

How tempting it must have been for Abigail to allow David to dispose of Nabal! But Abigail faces reality. She knows she's married to a worthless, wicked man. Instead of a pity party she jumps into action at great personal risk, and puts on her persuasion hat.

Reflection: What would you have done in Abigail's shoes?

~ If any of you lacks wisdom, he should ask God, who gives generously to all without finding fault, and it will be given to him. ~

The Apostle James (James 1:5)

Day 131: Back at the Ranch

Abigail's story continues ... When Abigail returned home, Nabal was in the house holding a banquet like a king. He was inebriated. She told him nothing until daybreak. Then it reads like a movie—when "his wife told him all these things (that she had been on a mission that saved his life) his heart failed him and he became like a stone. About ten days later, the LORD struck Nabal and he died" (1 Samuel 25: 37–38).

Like a happy fairy tale ending, David sees Nabal's death as justice and seeks Abigail's hand in marriage. She becomes his queen. What a story! From the wife of a fool to the queen of Israel! Abigail's life was grim, but she fixed her eyes on God. This is an example of increasing inner strength. There was no question in David's mind that Abigail brought him God's Word. The ability to hear God speaking and to listen to advice, even when it comes from unexpected sources, is a sign we're walking with God.

How easy it would have been for Abigail to believe she wasn't worthy—that she deserved this kind of husband, or wallow in self-pity and bad-mouth Nabal. The cycle of abuse would most likely have continued, had God not intervened. It is the incredible grace of God that puts our past behind us and hands us a future filled with promise and possibility. Like Abigail, we may find when we've walked through the pain, God gives us a better life than we expected.

Reflection: What have you learned from Abigail's story that you can use to increase your inner strength today?

~ A stumbling block to the pessimist is a stepping stone to the optimist. ~

Eleanor Roosevelt

Day 132: God's Girl Faces Reality

Unfortunately, as long as we live on this side of heaven we will confront un-desirable circumstances and people like Nabal that charge up our emotional responses. We probably had a different dream for our future, or wished we had somebody else's' life. When dreams don't come true, often the "poor me" pity party begins. *I'm a lousy mother. My husband deserves better. Nobody loves me. Oh misery! I'm a failure.*

When Mr. Right number three, Bob, "just left" out of the blue after two years of bliss (my perception was bliss), I expected that he would come to his senses and regret the decision. Even though he had left me for another woman, I was sure he'd realize I was "Mrs. Future Right," come back, and beg for forgiveness. This was denial clothed in hope. At the very least he'd give me an explanation of why she was the better choice, and I'd have closure. In retrospect, it was probably good he didn't tell me why because that would have lead to a far worse pity-party of self-condemnation.

The truth was he couldn't provide closure because of his personality type. I didn't exist to him anymore. That reality was like a sharp knife to my heart. That was his pattern—someone who hurt women. Looking back, he did the same thing when I came on the scene. It's devastating to face reality. *Poor me. Loser me.* Pity party!

Reflection: Rick Warren wrote, "Focusing on ourselves will never reveal our life's purpose."[123] Honesty is painful. Which relationships have caused you to have a pity-party? What one step can you implement today to overcome that?

> *~ In the end, denial, bargaining, binges, and anger are mere*
> *attempts to deflect what will eventually happen to us all. Pain will*
> *have its day because loss is undeniably, devastatingly real. ~*

Jerry Sittser[124]

Day 133: Cancel Your Pity-Party

I had come to depend on this man (actually *all* men) to fill me up. I had to learn to fill myself up with the Holy Spirit. I found that when we don't rely on other people in our lives to do and be "it" for us, we will find happiness if we let Jesus do and be "it." And remember, no one can take your dignity from you unless you hand it to them on a plate.

Moving forward says that we cancel that pity-party. Where do we begin?

Focus on God's Word: Life, people and situations change, but God's Word always remains the same. It is the voice of truth that will enable you to overcome worry and fear—two weapons of pity-parties.

Know your Father's character: When we focus on our problems, we tend to lose sight of God's character, centering solely on the circumstances. Life loses its joy. Disappointment overwhelms us. We become frustrated and irritable.

Praise God for what he is doing in your life: Provided you are not depressively ill, praise can transform your daily experience into one of joy. I praise God not for the tragedy, but that I know him to be faithful *in* the tragedy, and that every trial in my life might have been allowed to do a deeper work in my spirit, to bring freedom.

I praise God for bringing great good out of something not so good or evil. In praise we discover we are uplifted, purified, and strengthened. However, praise is not a psychological technique. We praise God because he is worthy of honor, not for the benefits we receive.

Reflection: Praise God for your current situation. List five positive thoughts.

~ *Christian renewal begins when we focus on God's power and not our problems.* ~

John Maxwell[125]

Day 134: Focus On the Needs of Others

Years ago I read a cartoon picturing a smiling woman jabbering on and on to a glum-faced woman. The smiling woman finally said, "Well enough about me! Now let's talk about you. What do you think about me?" When we focus on ourselves we miss those that need us the most, our family and close friends. Take a trip to a local homeless shelter or prison. We soon realize that others have far more problems than we do.

Self-pity is the natural human response to troubled times, and rehashing the details of our situation only makes it worst. We actually grieve the Holy Spirit when we do not encourage ourselves or others (Ephesians 4:30). Self-pity is the work of the devil. On the other hand, *praise* focuses our attention on God instead. Every trial comes through his permissive will, which means he has complete control. Whatever his reasons, he is faithful to see us through, and we are told to give thanks in "all" circumstances. "Give thanks to the LORD, for he is good; his love endures forever" (Psalm 106:1).

Thankfulness is the awareness that if it were not for God's touch, you'd be planning another pity-party, hurt and bitter and broken. As we learn to confront the truth and avoid myths and fantasies, we will be less inclined toward disappointment and disillusionments. We've been learning to paint on a new face, the face of reality. Now we will begin to put on the virtues of God's Girl, the next phase of our journey.

Reflection: How ready are you for the next phase of the journey? What obstacles do you need to be aware of as you continue moving forward?

~ *You must keep yourself fit to let the life of the Son of God be manifested, and you cannot keep yourself fit if you give way to self-pity.* ~

Oswald Chambers[126]

Day 135: MileStone

Steps To Overcome Negative Emotions

Move Forward

We may have learned to be miserable, but we can choose to unlearn it. Humans are adaptive creatures. Just as we learn negative coping mechanisms, we can unlearn them. We can't control what happens to us, but we can determine how we will take in and react to what happens. We can moan about the things we don't like, using them as excuses for self-pity, or we can accept what we can't change and change what we can.

One: Refuse to be secretive about your anxieties and pain any more. Write your feelings in a letter to God. Include everything that you have felt associated with your loss and pain: anger and unforgiveness; broken dreams; loneliness; doubts about God.

Two: Now think of a special person you are willing to share this letter with. Plan to discuss the letter with this person, and consider this person a potential accountability partner for future exercises. This can be a friend, minister, mentor, relative, parent, adult child, or spouse. What is important is the person is able to provide comfort, reassurance, and support, especially during stressful times. Women who have at least one person to confide in are at much lower risk for depression than women who lack a confidante.[127]

Challenge the Old Way of Thinking

Set up a time to read your letter to that special person. Openly own your feelings, even if it seems out of character for you. Remember God forgives your secrets.

Day 136: Pray and Meditate
Psalm 42

As the deer pants for streams of water, so my soul pants for you, O God. My soul thirsts for God, for the living God. When can I go and meet with God? My tears have been my food day and night, while men say to me all day long,

"Where is your God?" These things I remember as I pour out my soul: how I used to go with the multitude, leading the procession to the house of God, with shouts of joy and thanksgiving among the festive throng. Why are you downcast, O my soul? Why so disturbed within me? *Put your hope in God, for I will yet praise him, my Savior and my God.* My soul is downcast within me; therefore I will remember you from the land of the Jordan, the heights of Hermon—from Mount Mizar. Deep calls to deep in the roar of your waterfalls; all your waves and breakers have swept over me. By day the LORD directs his love, at night his song is with me—a prayer to the God of my life. I say to God my Rock, "Why have you forgotten me? Why must I go about mourning, oppressed by the enemy?"

My bones suffer mortal agony as my foes taunt me, saying to me all day long, "Where is your God?" Why are you downcast, O my soul? Why so disturbed within me?

Put your hope in God, for I will yet praise him, my Savior and my God.

Self-Soother

Open the curtains in each room and let the sunshine flood the room. If it's raining, open the window and smell the rain.

Part Ten

The Royal Girl

Encouraged by God's Word

"Now if we are children, then we are heirs–heirs of God and co-heirs with Christ, if indeed we share in his sufferings in order that we may also share in his glory." (Romans 8:17)

Day 137: The Fairytale

When I was a little girl I loved creating plays and playing the star. I had two younger brothers. I gave them the part of a tree or a gate, something insignificant. They'd threaten to quit, but Mom and Dad would convince me to give them better parts. *Okay, they can be a frog or a dog*, something that at least breathed.

No matter what the theme of the play I always played the same part—the beautiful princess over a huge kingdom. She was a cross between Snow White and Cinderella. At night she'd fall asleep to the tune of "Someday My Prince Will Come." One day, the little princess turned into a woman, but she didn't live happily ever after. Her kingdom walls came crumbling down. Most of us have heard the story of the *Beauty and the Beast*. My real life fairytale the *Princess and the Monster*.

Most of my life I wanted to be a princess. Maybe not a beauty contestant, but the kind that was beautiful and admired by a kingdom! I was addicted to approval from man, not God. No matter how hard I tried, and what I did to change myself, I never got the recognition I desired. I wore myself out trying to meet other people's expectations, trying to attain the princess image. I admitted defeat in the form of always feeling down.

I eventually met my prince—Jesus Christ—and I became God's Royal Girl: Princess Kimberly! I had a new kingdom and title. Little did I know when I was a kid, playing the part of the princess, I was playing myself!

Reflection: It has been said that in man's quest for a perfect and benevolent world, we create fantasies in order to survive, and illusions are developed where we don't have to confront overpowering fears. What is your fantasy or illusion?

~ *Jesus has the power to transform—not fairy godmothers!* ~

Kimberly Davidson

Day 138: I Really Am a Princess!

Did you know you have royal blood soaring through your veins? It's true! The Bible says that we are co-heirs with Christ. "The Lord who created you, O Israel, says: Don't be afraid, for *I have ransomed you; I have called you by name; you are mine*" (Isaiah 43:1, TLB, author's emphasis).

You are an heir—a princess! That means you are a noble woman—God's Royal Girl! You may not feel like a princess, but you are. Let me give you an illustration. If I offered you a hundred dollar bill, you would most likely take it, right? What if I stomped on it, crumpled it, and crushed it into the ground, would you still want it? Most likely, because the one hundred dollars still held its value.

Often in our own lives we are dropped, crumpled, ground into the dirt by the choices we make, or circumstances and people that come our way. We feel worthless and dirty. No matter what happens to us, we never lose our value in God's eyes. Dirty or crumpled, we are still priceless to him.

Consider how valuable you are to God, given the price he's paid for you through his Son. Grasp how precious, important, desirable and deeply loved you must be for God to let Jesus, his beloved Son, die to rescue you for himself. The Bible tells us over and over that in God's eyes we have value that can never be equaled.

Reflection: What sort of dreams or fairytale images do you still have? How well have those dreams served you?

> ~ *The best and most beautiful things in the world cannot be seen*
> *or even touched. They must be felt within the heart.* ~

Helen Keller[128]

Day 139: Royalty and Self-Esteem

Young Colleen was found standing in front of her bedroom window during a lightning storm. Her dad asked what she was doing, to which she replied, "I think God is trying to take my picture."

Why don't most of us feel this important? Instead do we say, "Why is he looking at me?" When we're wandering around our wilderness we have feelings of inadequacy. As we withdraw from others, we tend to become preoccupied solely with ourselves. The blues become our way of life, our identity. Having a low sense of self-worth and little self-love makes it increasingly difficult to bear our circumstances.

Having positive self-worth, or personal significance, is characterized by a sense of self-respect and satisfaction. Unlike pride, having positive self-worth is not based on our success or prestige or appearance. One of the most powerful weapons in Satan's arsenal is low self-esteem or self-worth, which is a gut-level feeling of inferiority, inadequacy, and low self-worth. This shackles women (and men) in spite of positive and rewarding experiences, and in spite of their faith.

Reflection: Do you have low, medium, or high self-esteem? Why? What one thing can you do immediately to increase it if it's low to medium?

~ *Everyone needs to be valued. Everyone has the potential to give something back.* ~

Princess Diana[129]

Day 140: "Get Self-Esteem!"

Once a teacher told me to "get" self-esteem. *Why? Do I need more confidence? Do I have to do something that will bring me success?* She said it meant valuing myself. It means first knowing who you are, and then liking who you are. It is my feeling of significance. Self-esteem is a confidence and satisfaction in oneself.[130] It is your overall evaluation of your own worth and how you value your own attributes—that deep-down feeling you have about yourself.

Dr. Robert McGee says whether labeled *self-esteem* or *self-worth*, our feeling of significance is crucial to our emotional, spiritual, and social stability, and is the driving element within the human spirit. We must understand that our hunger for self-worth is God-given and can only be satisfied by God. Our value is not dependent on our ability to earn the acceptance of people; rather, acceptance is the receiving of God's love. God created us, and only he knows how to fulfill all our needs.[131]

How high or low your self-esteem is depends on how you compare what you'd like to be with how you actually see yourself. It is often the result of what significant others (our parents, teachers, friends, peers) have said about us. We place great weight on what others think about us. The first step toward higher self-esteem is to realize that your self-image shouldn't come from what other people think of you.

Reflection: On a scale of one to ten (one is the lowest; ten is the highest), where does your self-esteem fall? Reflect on why you assigned it that particular number.

> ~ *Self-esteem is about how we value ourselves, and is based on the sum total of our attitudes and beliefs.* ~
>
> Dr. Rick Kausman[132]

Day 141: Being Your Real Self

"You're fat! Go on a diet!" Someone once told me that. Since our society does not value "fat" people, I assumed I was a loser. I lost fifteen pounds and took great pride in the compliments I received. We usually speak, act, and react as the person we *think* we are. We tend to get what we expect. If we believe we're insignificant, ugly, unqualified, unworthy of love, then we tend to act this way. Often that is what we are told by a parent, or teacher, or boss. We are made to think we are valueless.

Some of us are filled with self-contempt because of what we do to ourselves. We may allow others to control or put us down. We're "grateful for small favors" and settle for disrespect, neglect, and indifference. There are no boundaries.

Today, middle-aged women are feeling pressured to be not only thin, but youthful and sexually vibrant, which is often unattainable. As long as we get our self-image from external sources, we will never be the woman God created us to be, God's Royal Girl. Instead, we will be at the mercy of others.

Unquestionably, healthy self-esteem is one of the key factors in our joy. As we develop a more intimate relationship with God, he can help us identify the obstacles that prevent us from seeing ourselves as his royal daughter. As his Word begins to penetrate our soul, we will discover our God-given gifts, beauty, talents, and unique design.

Reflection: Describe what does your "real" self looks like today?

~ *Before you try to keep up with the Joneses, be sure*
they're not trying to keep up with you. ~

Erma Bombeck[133]

Day 142: Three Views of Me

There are three different views of every individual: the view that God has of us, the opinions that others hold concerning us, and the perception we have of ourselves.

One: *God's vantage point.* The Lord does not observe people merely outwardly, as most humans do; rather, "The LORD looks on the heart" (1 Samuel 16:7). The Lord "knows the hearts of the children of men" (1 Kings 8:39). If some of the world's "beautiful people" were turned inside out, and revealed as God sees them, they would be quite unattractive.

Two: *Our peer's vantage point.* Many people hold an opinion of us that is greatly exaggerated or wrong. Look at those in the public eye. Often they are idealized and idolized. There are those who are authentic and real who are maligned unjustly. Jesus certainly did not deserve the hateful reproaches that were heaped upon him. The apostle Paul suffered unmerited character assassination.

Three: *Our vantage point.* It is important that we have a healthy view of ourselves. That is, how you evaluate yourself in terms of important characteristics like what you are good at, what you are not so good at, and the kinds of situations you prefer or avoid. We are healthy when we can look in the mirror and not focus on changing our outside features, but turn from the mirror and focus on asking God to help us change our inside features, particularly our heart.

Reflection: How do others perceive you? How would you like to see yourself? In what ways do the two descriptions differ?

~ May today there be peace within. May you trust God that
you are exactly where you are meant to be. ~

Mother Teresa[134]

Day 143: I Am What I Am

Like many of us, the apostle Paul felt he was not worthy to be called royalty: "But whatever I am now it is all because God poured out such kindness and grace upon me and not without results: for I have worked harder than all the other apostles, yet actually I wasn't doing it, but God working in me, to bless me" (1 Corinthians 15: 9–10, TLB).

When I look at my transformation, I say "ditto." What matters today is not what you were, or what you did, or who you wanted to be, but who *you are now*. I gave my life to Jesus mid-life, when I was thirty-four years old. But I didn't become his disciple until I was forty-five. I have regretted wasting so much time. Paul is telling me that it is not the time of your entry into the kingdom that matters, but the fact that you are now in the kingdom. It's foolish to mourn what could have been.

Scripture says: "By the grace of God I am what I am" (1 Corinthians 15:10). What am I? Forgiven. Reconciled to God by the blood of his Son Jesus Christ. A child of God. A joint heir of Jesus. This is who I am today! If someone reminds you that you were that "bad" or untrustworthy or unreliable person, do what Paul did. Say: "You're right! I was that. (Paul was a bad dude before his transformation!), but I've been transformed."

As royalty we must live in a manner consistent with that position. When Prince Charles visits America, I doubt he stays at Motel 6, rents a car from "Rent-A-Wreck" or eats at McDonald's. He doesn't live as a commoner, nor should we.

Reflection: Do you believe you now a member of the kingdom? What was the turning point in your transformation?

~ *Smile, it enhances your face value.* ~

Dolly Parton

Day 144: Jacob's Girls

Manipulated by their father, the women in this story did not have a voice concerning their life and relationships. Meet Rachel and Leah (Genesis 29).

Jacob, son of Rebekah and Isaac, was sent to live with Rebekah's brother Laban. Jealousy, deception, favoritism, betrayal, selfishness, anger—these were the family legacies Jacob took with him to his new home. He meets Rachel and her sister Leah. Rachel was the younger, very beautiful sister. It was love at first sight for Jacob and he asks to marry Rachel. Apparently, Leah did not have the same appeal. We all know a Rachel, don't we?

Laban says yes and Jacob agreed to work for Laban for seven years, for very special wages, his attractive daughter Rachel. It appears no other suitors were asking for Leah's hand in marriage. Laban wanted his oldest daughter married and devises a scheme. (He is one of the most subtle villains in the Bible.)

In that culture, daughters literally belonged to their fathers and could be paid out as wages for labor. "Jacob served seven years to get Rachel, but they seemed like only a few days to him because of his love for her" (29:20).

What a romantic thought—that your man would work seven years for your hand in marriage.

Reflection: Do you believe there are still gallant men out there? Why or why not?

~ I always looked for a man to rescue me and bring me happiness. I bought into that myth, of course, and looked for my own Prince Charming. ~

Linda Evans[135]

Day 145: The Trick!

Rachel's story continues...On the wedding night, Laban slipped Leah into Jacob's bed because it was customary for the older daughter to be married first. Jacob, who had tricked his blind father, was now the deceived one. What a surprise to be married to and wake up with a different woman!

Jacob was betrayed by Laban into working seven more, hard, years in order to marry Rachel. Now Jacob had two wives, one imposed on him through fraud. (Later, it was forbidden to marry or have relations with your wife's sister: see Leviticus 18:18).

You may wonder how that could happen. It was customary for the bride to wear a heavy veil and not speak on the wedding day. The room was dark.

Jacob's proposition to work seven years for the hand of Rachel in marriage was more acceptable to Laban. He could marry off the less attractive Leah to him first and so gain more free labor after the seven years expired. Laban had dared to play this unscrupulous trick because he was certain that Jacob would never be content without the one whom he set his heart.

Reflection: What do you think the two girls thought of what just happened? I wonder how the family kept Rachel quiet that night. Scripture doesn't tell us. Have you been in a similar situation? How did you feel?

~ *Our hearts will never be at rest away from the One*
who made them, and it's still true today. ~

Saint Augustine[136]

Day 146: Leah's Blessing

In this story, Jacob favored Rachel above Leah. Most of us can relate to Leah. She must have been deeply hurt—her self-esteem wounded. All she wanted was his love, and although not his first choice, he did accept her as his wife. Don't we all have a story of that special guy breaking our heart over that popular or pretty girl, someone that made us feel worthless? Leah had to have been not only hurt, but angry. Did she practice forgiveness everyday? We don't get a glimpse into her deepest thoughts and emotions.

The Bible says that when God realized Leah was unloved he opened her womb. It was a sign that God knew her misery and that her husband would love her (she hoped) because she could now bear children. God saw inside her heart. God shows us great compassion and love when we feel unloved. His power is that of life giver. However, even the birth of four sons did little to comfort her. She longed for the affection of her husband.

Capable of enduring love, Leah thought she'd have to live the rest of her life in Rachel's shadow, but God had different plans. He blessed her with many sons and one daughter. Now Rachel was the one seething with envy and competitiveness.

God sees our miseries no matter how big or small they may seem. He knows every detail of our circumstances, our heart, our feelings and all the hurts. As in Leah's life, God is willing to step in and begin something new and beautiful in us.

Reflection: When was the last time you were seething with envy and competitiveness? What were the results?

~ *Envy is a waste of time.* ~

Author Unknown

Day 147: Rachel's Envy

Rachel's story continues…Rachel longed to be part of God's plan but wouldn't trust God to make it happen. Scripture says, "When Rachel saw that she was not bearing Jacob any children, she became jealous of her sister. So she said to Jacob, "Give me children, or I'll die!" Like Hannah, her soul felt bitterness. Jacob became angry, "Am I in the place of God, who has kept you from having children?" (Genesis 30:1–2).

Rachel's next move was to adopt a tactic used by women before. She gave her servant girl, Bilhah, to Jacob, an attempt at surrogate motherhood, understanding that any child born would be hers. Bilhah became pregnant with a son. Rachel named him Dan, meaning "Justice," for she said, "God has given me justice, and heard my plea and given me a son." Bilhah became pregnant again. Rachel named him Naphtali, meaning "Wrestling," for she said, "I am in a fierce contest with my sister and I am winning!"

Whenever we compare ourselves with anyone whose circumstances seem better than ours, we face the temptation to envy her or him. We may not even want the better circumstance; we just resent their having it. Was it better to have love but have no children? Was it better to have love but no children? Or be unloved with a brood of children? Rachel did not have maturity of faith to accept that unpleasant circumstances were part of God's providential plan. It is not an easy lesson to learn when others around us are apparently having no difficulties.

Reflection: Talk to God in prayer about any situation where you may be feeling jealous or envious of another person.

~ *If malice or envy were tangible and had a shape, it would be the shape of a boomerang.* ~

Charley Reese[137]

Day 148: Retaliation

The sister's story continues...When Leah realized that she wasn't getting pregnant anymore, she gave her servant girl Zilpah to Jacob, and she, too, presented him with a son named him Gad, meaning "My luck has turned!" Then Zilpah produced a second son, and Leah named him Asher, meaning "Happy," for she said, "What joy is mine! The other women will think me blessed indeed!" Don't we often focus on what others think about us (especially other women), instead of what God is thinking?

Leah thought she'd have to live the rest of her life in Rachel's shadow, but God had different plans. Leah conceived again and bore Jacob a sixth son, and some time later gave birth to a daughter named Dinah. In the end, God exalted Leah by giving her a kingly tribe and she is honored as one of the mothers of Israel (Ruth 4:11).

What happened to Rachel? Scripture says that God remembered Rachel's plight, and answered her prayers by giving her a son. "God has removed the dark slur against my name," she said. She named him Joseph, meaning "May I also have another!" for she said, "May Jehovah give me another son" (34:22–24).

This story reveals that God, not Laban, had the last word. However, there was another storm ahead for Leah and Jacob...there are always consequences.

Reflection: How has God given you the last word in certain situations? How well have you been listening?

~ *Establish your foundation not on fluctuating emotions but on the authority of God.* ~

Dr. James Dobson[138]

Day 149: God's Girl Dinah

Perhaps if you didn't relate to Leah, you may relate to the sad story of Leah and Jacob's only daughter Dinah (Genesis 34:1–7). It has been suggested that Dinah was indulged by her parents, ignored, and considered vain. She wanted to see the daughters of the land, perhaps see what was fashionable among them.

Dinah went to be seen where she met Shechem, son of Hamor the Canaanite. Scripture says he "took and violated her." No one is certain if she was raped or merely made a bad consensual choice. Shechem decides to marry her, not out of love or pity, but because she was from a wealthy family. He unknowingly brings disaster to his people.

By today's moral standards, this story would not make headlines, but I believe feelings of guilt and shame plague us despite changing times. Research shows that teenagers who have sexual relations with a number of partners are less likely to have stable, committed relationships in their thirties.[139] The Center for Data Analysis states that sexually active teenagers are more likely to be depressed and to attempt suicide.[140] Reckless choices may be accepted, but ultimately they leave us scarred, damaging our present and future relationships.

Maybe this hit a nerve with you. Or maybe you see your daughter in this story. God knows the torment. You can take any sexual baggage (the pain and the shame) to him right now. "In my anguish I cried to the LORD, and he answered by setting me free" (Psalm 118:5).

Reflection: When have you ventured out to where you should not have? What were the consequences?

~ *All growth that is not toward God is growing to decay.* ~

George MacDonald[141]

Day 150: The Plot

Dinah's story continues…Now Dinah was damaged goods and her family was insulted. Jacob failed to provide any type of leadership so Dinah's two older bothers, Simeon and Levi, took matters into their own hands. The rape was seen, not from the point of view of Dinah, but as a wrong against her father, who lost his right to make a suitable match for his daughter and so forfeited the bridal gift that should be paid to him. The marriage was to mark the permanent alliance between two peoples. It was all part of a plot on the part of Dinah's brothers, whose burning anger sought revenge.

Unknown to Jacob, his sons came up with a wicked suggestion: if the Canaanites would accept circumcision, they would accept the marriage. Hamor agreed because he wanted to share in Jacob's wealth. Three days later, while all of them were still in pain from circumcision, Simeon and Levi took their swords and attacked the unsuspecting city, killing every male. They took Dinah and left (Genesis 34:25–26).

One assault on a girl provoked a revenge that wiped out many innocent people and ruined every family in that city. The brothers profited, and Dinah slipped back into oblivion—a forgotten victim. What happened to Dinah's heart and soul? Did her pain surface as depression? Dinah's life shows us that sometimes simple, foolish decisions impact us in a negative way and can have serious consequences.

Reflection: How do you see yourself? As a Rachel? Leah? Dinah? Other?

~ *Living in Los Angeles during the Rodney King riots was*
frightening. One assault on an African-American man led to
riots that ruined a number of cities and destroyed many families. ~

Kimberly Davidson

Day 151: Royalty and Purpose

If you've gotten this far, I trust you are beginning to change your destiny away from discontentment toward a life of hope, peace, and joy, realizing that when you give your circumstances to God, in his time, he works adversity together for good (Romans 8:28).

Remember, you have the power to move from where you are now to where you want to be. That's called purpose. Purpose gives you a reason to get up in the morning. Purpose is your unique calling. The Bible tells us our purpose is to glorify God. That's why we exist! *How* we do that is dependant on how God has created and gifted us.

When I started seminary I remember reading my first theology syllabus. It looked like a foreign language. The enemy whispered, *Who do you think you are to go to seminary? You don't have the brains to succeed. Give it up. Go back to working behind the scenes.* I became overwhelmed with insecurity and doubt. I felt a voice louder than the enemy's come through, "My child, just ask me, and I will see you through."

God reminded me of the circumstances that got me to seminary. I knew he wanted me there. More importantly, his Spirit would lead and guide me through each class.

We often build up events in our minds and panic. God does not ask us to go where he has not provided the means to help. This was the first time in school that I ever received consecutive A's. *I am worthy of attending graduate school!* The waves of insecurity, fear, and doubt dissipated. God certainly gets the glory!

Reflection: How has God used your fear and insecurity for his glory?

~ Many persons have a wrong idea of what constitutes true happiness. It is not attained through self-gratification but through fidelity to a worthy purpose. ~

Helen Keller[142]

Day 152: Our Character

As God's daughter, his ultimate goal is developing our character. Romans 8:29 states that from the very beginning God decided those who came to him (you and me) should become *like his Son*. This is our destiny, to be created in Jesus' image. God can change us to resemble his character, like his son Jesus, which is called Christ-likeness. We can never be exactly like Jesus, because we have innate sin nature, but we can make a choice to develop a relationship with God and let him mold our character, and we do become more like Jesus, more Christlike, every day. I often tell women that *beauty is a Christlike character* which often means giving up some of the comforts of life.

As a culture we've become addicted to comfort and ease. However, God is more concerned about what we *are*—our character. When we leave this earth and meet God in heaven, we won't arrive with our earthy processions or our careers or our sculpted body—we take our character. It is the Holy Spirit's job to produce Christlikeness in each one of us, but we must have the desire to do our part.

Reflection: Are you ready to give up some comforts of life? Why or why not?

~ Lord God, I have no idea where I am going. I do not see the road ahead of me. I cannot know for certain where it will end ... But I believe that the desire to please you does in fact please you. And I hope I have that desire in all that I am doing ... Therefore will I trust you always though I may seem to be lost and in the shadow of death. I will not fear, for you are ever with me, and you will never leave me to face my perils alone. ~

Thomas Merton[143]

Day 153: MileStone

Steps To Overcome Negative Emotions

Move Forward

Max Lucado wrote, "God sees us with the eyes of a Father. He sees our defects, errors, and blemishes. But he also sees our value. What did Jesus know that enabled him to do what he did? He knew the value of people. He knew that each human being is a treasure. And because he did, people were not a source of stress but joy."[144]

Moving forward is seeing yourself, and others, through the eyes of your Father.

Challenge the Old Way of Thinking

You are God's treasure, and he tells you that in his love letters to you in the Bible. Remind yourself of the importance of "rejoicing" by searching the Bible (both Old and New Testaments) for God's instructions in this area. Also consider what other great things God has done for you.

Look up and write out Scriptures that confirm this. Meditate on them daily; memorize them, and tape your favorite verses on your mirror. Try a Scripture search using a concordance. Start with:

John 1:12; John 15:15; 1 Corinthians 6:19–20; Colossians 2:10; Romans 8:1–2, 35–39; Philippians 1:6; 1 John 5:18; John 15:16; 2 Corinthians 6:1; and Ephesians 2:10.

Day 154: Pray and Meditate

Lord Jesus, I am your child, and I refuse to allow depression to settle over me. Because I am your daughter, I don't have to be weighed down with anxiety or fear (or *fill in the blank*). Your Spirit lives in me, and I want to leave a legacy for you. Please give me wisdom to make godly choices in a world that usually tells me the opposite. Lord, give me hope and a contagious joy that comes with living for you and furthering your kingdom. I want to be remembered as a woman with character, and want to leave a permanent mark of your love on the people who cross my path. In Jesus' name. Amen.

> ~ *I was regretting the past, and fearing the future. Suddenly, my Lord was speaking: 'My name is not 'I was.' When you live in the future with its problems and fears it is hard, I am not there, for my name is not 'I will be.' When you live in this moment it is not hard, I am here, for my name is 'I am.'* ~

Unknown

Self-Soother

Sometime today you're sure to find a few minutes that will be wasted. Take those few minutes and do something you consider to be creative.

Day 155: Would the Real Miss Universe Please Stand Up

As women we are usually never satisfied with the package God gave us. Our culture is quick to point out what is wrong with us, inch by inch. Extreme makeovers are all the rage. I am reminded of a woman who received God's extreme makeover.

This woman never had plastic surgery or a Botox® treatment. She never wore make-up. She wore the same clothing day after day. This woman carried sick, dying, and abandoned people off the streets. She was far more beautiful than any Miss America finalist. Her name was Mother Teresa. She died a few days after Princess Diana of England. Diana's death got all the attention because the media painted Diana as the ideal, not Mother Teresa.

Diana was beautiful, young, rich, powerful, and idolized, yet she was not a happy person. Throughout history, some of the most beautiful women have lead tragic lives. Behind those beauty marks were scars and dark tears.

Mother Teresa wouldn't qualify as a beauty contestant in the United States. What made her so different was an inner beauty that radiated. Even Mother Teresa bemoaned darkness and loneliness. Rev. James Martin, author of *My Life with the Saints*, a book that dealt with reports of Teresa's doubts, wrote, "I've never read a saint's life where the saint has such an intense spiritual darkness."[145] Mother Teresa was human, just like us. But unlike many of us, she turned her battle wounds into beauty marks. In God's eyes, and the eyes of those she helped and rescued, she was the "Miss Universe" of all times.

Reflection: Who do you know that reflects Mother Teresa's kind of beauty? What battle wounds or scars are you ready to turn into beauty marks?

~ *Being a princess isn't all it's cracked up to be.* ~

Princess Diana[146]

Day 156: Intimately Acquainted

I got married at the mature age of thirty-seven. My husband was forty-seven. We decided not to have children because of the season of life we were in. In many ways it bothered me. Then I was diagnosed with lupus which attacked the joints in my hands and arms. I was truly blessed as God's healing touch fought the lupus through modern medicine.

Later, I found out from my mom it can be dangerous for a woman with lupus to have a baby. She said, "God may have saved you a lot of physical problems. We never know, do we?" I had never looked at my circumstance from this vantage point.

I believe Psalm 139 is one of the most personal passages in all of Scripture and it spoke to me about this situation. This psalm reveals an intimacy between David and God. David says, "O Lord, you have searched me and you know me" (verse 1).

Sometimes we feel that no one understands us. This verse says God knows everything about you; he understands you. It also means that you can't hide anything from him either. God examines us and knows *everything* about us.

David continues, "You know when I sit down and when I rise up; You perceive my thoughts from afar. You scrutinize my path and my lying down, and you are intimately acquainted with all my ways" (1–4, NAS).

David firmly believes he matters to God. You matter to God.

Reflection: Do you feel that you truly matter to God? Why or why not?

~ Sometimes the Lord offers no explanation or interpretation of His response to our requests and cries, except by inference, 'This is My will for you.' ~

Dr. James Dobson[147]

Day 157: Fearfully and Wonderfully Made

Through all of his trials and temptations, David always finds a way to put God first. In Psalm 139 David says that God goes ahead of us and scrutinizes our path. God in his perfect way goes before us with his magnifying glass, looking for every single stone that would hurt us and then kicks them out of the way. He leaves some in our paths for the specific purpose of drawing us close to him through those trials.

David sees himself as God sees him. "I am fearfully and wonderfully made; your works are wonderful. My frame was not hidden from you, when I was made in the secret place. When I was woven together in the depths of the earth, your eyes saw my unformed body" (13–16).

In this passage David is emphasizing God's sovereignty over the creative process. There is awesomeness in the way I am made. To fear the Lord means we hold him in reverence, with respect and in awe. Because we are stamped in God's image, we too are to hold ourselves up in reverence with great respect.

Wonderfully made means you are magnificently created, distinctive, set apart, one of a kind. Do you feel fearfully and wonderfully made? You should, because this is spiritual truth.

Reflection: Say out loud: "I am fearfully and wonderfully made! God made me and God doesn't make mistakes."

~ God does not make junk! ~

Unknown

Day 158: Mirrors Reflecting Glory

Would you ever have considered yourself capable of being a mirror that brightly reflects the glory of the Lord? Impossible! As the Spirit of the Lord works within us, we become more like him. Possible!

In order to accomplish his goals, God created us unique and equipped our spirit with unique gifts, abilities, and personality. That portrait can be found in Galatians 5:22–23. Paul tells us that when the Holy Spirit controls our lives he will produce fruit in us: love, joy, peace, patience, kindness, goodness, faithfulness, gentleness, and self-control. These virtuous qualities portray our Father who is perfect love. To reflect the fruit of the Spirit is to be *like* Jesus Christ.

This is where all of our negative circumstances and the pain come in. There is no such thing as instant fruit. God develops our character by allowing (not causing) these negative circumstances, which is how he builds us into godly women.

The weight loss, the cosmetics, the drinking, the search for plastic perfection were not what I was addicted to. I was addicted to approval and attention. Addiction was a bulls-eye on my back that said something is wrong. Basing my self-worth on what I believed others thought about me caused me to become addicted to their approval.

God had a plan all along. It was more than about me and what others thought about me. He wanted me to focus on what he could do *through me, in me, and with me,* for other people. It was about them! That is my purpose. That is what brings God glory.

Reflection: How do you want God to use your life today to touch someone else?

~ *It's not about you.* ~

Rick Warren (The first sentence in *The Purpose Driven Life*)[148]

Day 159: Who Are You?

What do you want to be when you grow up?" As we developed into adults we focused on what we wanted to *do* as a vocation or a role, not *who* we wanted to be. Today people ask us, "What do you do?" But let me ask you, "*Who* are you?"

If you answered "Tommy's mom" or "a nurse" or "Bob's wife" you need to redefine yourself. Your identity is not your vocation or relationships. We're usually taught that our personal identity depends on the roles we play and our relationships. So, if we experience a devastating loss, we may feel like our self has been amputated.

Loss can lead to a confusion of identity. *I've always seen myself as Bob's wife. If Bob leaves me or dies, who am I now? If I'm one of the most competent employees at work and I get laid off, or if my teenager starts drinking, what does that say about "me?"*

Role is a function or position, whereas identity is who you are, your personal characteristics, the unique work of God. Sometimes God needs to break us into pieces because it's the only way he can rebuild us into the woman he created us to be. Then we are able to fulfill his purpose for our lives. That becomes our identity. If you think of yourself differently than God thinks of you, who is mistaken, you or God?

Once I got my head out of the toilet (literally) I found my purpose and my identity as I developed my relationship with Jesus. I have been chosen and appointed to bear fruit (John 15:16). It's not about the troubles; it's about the victory through Jesus.

Reflection: What difficult or unexplainable thing in your life is God using for his purpose today?

> ~ *I had kind of a classic identity crisis which was a shock to me, because I thought that all of my self-image was tied up in being a songwriter.* ~
>
> Rosanne Cash

Day 160: Royalty and True Identity

Eating disorders are a dilemma of our culture. Experts debate whether depression causes the disorder, or the nutritional imbalance causes depression. For years, eating disorders were considered the province of teenage girls and young women. Today, they are diagnosed in girls as young as five and in women well into their senior years.[149]

Like all these young girls and women, instead of finding my identity and self-worth in Jesus, I looked for it in my appearance. Rather than focusing on Jesus, it was all about the outside stuff: beauty, performance, status—the wrong pursuit of happiness.

Everyday we make choices: Follow the crowd to fit in, *or* follow Jesus. Be a people pleaser, *or* a God pleaser. Giving up the things we know and are comfortable to us is called sacrifice. I heard someone say that in America, when it comes to sacrifice, we only know how to spell the word. God can help us move forward in this direction.

The Bible says that once we have accepted Jesus Christ as our Savior, he is born into our mortal flesh, and we become his daughter. The Son of God is born *into me* by the direct act of God. Think about that! Jesus said, "I have given them the glory that you gave me, that they may be one as we are one: I in them and you in me" (John 17:22–23).

When we can accept ourselves just as we are, the way God created us, we can accept those situations and relationships in our lives that we can't change. We can make sacrificial relationship choices without fear of rejection. This is what it means to have a healthy self-esteem. It is crucial to loving ourselves and loving others.

Reflection: How much do you use this formula?

Appearance + Performance + Other's opinions + Status = My Self-worth

~ Hold on to what you have, so that no one will take your crown. ~

Revelation 3:11

Day 161: God's Girl Mary of Nazareth

How did you answer yesterday's question? The formula I strive to attain is:

God's Word about me + Obedience to God = My character and self-worth

Mary, the mother of Jesus, is often ignored except at Christmas time when she is dusted off and put in the nativity scene. Mary can teach us much (Luke 1:26–37). It's easy to read stories about Mary and reflect on her perfection. Many of us think, *Of course Mary was holy and sinless and perfect, she was the mother of Jesus! She's out of my league.* Maybe not ... Mary was young, poor, and female, all the characteristics to the people of her day that made her unusable by God for any major task.

But God chose Mary for one of the most important acts of obedience ever demanded of anyone. Before she was Mary, the mother of Jesus, she was just Mary, an ordinary girl like you and me. God was acting, moving, and revealing his love and purpose in Mary long before anyone knew what was happening. He was at work in the womb of this chosen woman, just as he is at work in you.

Your self-worth comes from what God says about you. His Word says, "Yet to all who received him, to those who believed in his name, he gave the right to become children of God" (John 1:12). However, we must claim that position. The beauty of walking with Jesus is that it is never too late to claim our position as his child. Someone once said, "If we will accept our position we can change our condition."

Reflection: Right now in prayer, claim your position to change your condition!

> ~ *God cannot give us a happiness and peace apart from Himself,*
> *because it is not there. There is no such thing.* ~
>
> C. S. Lewis[150]

Day 162: Part of His Divine Plan

I used to think, *Why would God want to use me? I have nothing to offer.*

We meet a little servant girl in 2 Kings 5 who compassionately said to her mistress, "I wish my master (Naaman) would go to see the prophet in Samaria. He would heal him of his leprosy!" (Leprosy was one of the most feared diseases.) We don't know much about this little girl except that her brief words brought healing and faith in God to this powerful Aramean captain. God placed her there for a purpose, and she was faithful.

For years I considered myself "recovered" from an addiction. Recovery meant a journey of willpower and inner self-control that would last a lifetime. It was a woman that stood up in front of her addicted peers and said, "I'm Kimberly, a bulimic and an alcoholic." One day I felt God tell me to take my blinders off and open my eyes.

He broke through, *I'm the one who healed and saved you.* I realized it wasn't any inner strength or will power, but it was Jesus who set me free. Truth prevailed! Freedom is not the same as being in recovery. Freedom is the woman who stand ups and says, "I'm Kimberly, a new creation in Jesus. I am no longer a bulimic and alcoholic."

That is where my significance came from—Jesus. From that moment on, I recovered God's plan for my life, and he's been using me every since. That's recovery!

Reflection: God can use you if you allow him. How has your position changed?

~ Teach me, O God, so to use all the circumstances of my life today that they may bring forth in me the fruits of holiness rather than the fruits of sin. Let me use disappointment as material for patience. Let me use success as material for thankfulness. Let me use pains as material for endurance. ~

John Baillie[151]

Day 163: His Divine Plan Includes You!

Dr. John Trent wrote, "Those who are able to honestly and courageously deal with the past as a learning and shaping tool will take the road that leads to authentic living. That's a way of life that enables us to honestly accept ourselves for who we are—warts, weaknesses, and all."[152]

As we continue moving forward we have questions. The more we learn, the more questions we have. There is no one-size-fits all answer, just as there is no one-size-fits all God. What we do know is he is the person who created you to be a specific kind of woman with a specific purpose. You are "fearfully and wonderfully made."

You are a vital part of God's divine plan! Nothing is wrong with the way God designed you. The issue is discovering and developing who you are, not becoming who you are not.

You may not even realize it right now, but God has given you dreams and desires. As you continue to develop your relationship with him, and put Jesus at the center of your healing, he will reveal himself to you in ways you never thought possible. Those dreams and desires will come to pass.

Yes, God wanted each one of us precisely the way we are—warts and all!

Reflection: There is simply no way to comprehend the full implication of God's love! Do you feel that love? Why or why not?

~ Eternal Father, it is amazing love, that You have sent Your Son to suffer in my stead, that You have added the Spirit to teach, comfort, guide, that You have allowed the ministry of angels to wall me round. ~

A Puritan Prayer[153]

Day 164: Royalty and Perfection

Thankfully this journey we're on isn't about perfection or accomplishment, even though it may seem like it. Many of us have become slaves to perfection. I've heard it said that perfectionism is slow suicide and anxious slavery.

Consciously or unconsciously we all have experienced this feeling that we must meet certain arbitrary standards to attain self-worth. I never considered myself a perfectionist until I heard a psychologist say that a perfectionist couldn't tolerate mistakes in others or herself. That was me!

In other instances we may find ourselves searching for the perfect person, the handsome prince, or the perfect housekeeper or teacher. I have bad news for you: they don't exist! Let me introduce you to Alice, a perfectionist, people-pleaser and performer.

Even though Alice did not have the time in her schedule, she volunteered to bake a cake for the church's annual bake sale, which she forgot. Rummaging through the cabinets, she found an old angel food cake mix and whipped it together. But when Alice took the cake from the oven, the center had dropped flat. She panicked, "I knew I shouldn't have volunteered! There's no time to bake another cake."

This cake was so important to Alice, because she wanted so much to fit in, and she didn't want anyone to think she was not perfect. She looked around the house for something to build up the center of the cake. *Ah-ha! A roll of toilet paper!* Alice plunked it in the cake, and covered it with icing. Not only did the cake look beautiful, it looked perfect, just like Alice!

Reflection: What do you have in common with Alice?

~ *Progress, Not Perfection* ~

Alcoholics Anonymous slogan

Day 165: Alice's Story Continues ...

Alice gave her daughter specific instructions to be at the bake sale the minute it opened so she could buy the cake. When she arrived she found that the cake had all ready been sold. She called her Mom and gave her the news. Alice was horrified. *Everyone would know. What would they think? I'll be ostracized, talked about, and ridiculed. I'll have to move or kill myself!* All night Alice lay awake in bed thinking about people pointing their fingers at her and talking about her behind her back.

The next day she had been invited by one of the women to a luncheon bridal shower. Alice tried not to think about the cake and focused on having a good time. To Alice's horror her cake was presented for dessert. Alice felt the blood drain from her body when she saw the cake. She thought, *I can't tell the hostess, because what would she think of me. But I should tell her, that's the Christian thing to do.* Before she could make a decision, someone said to the hostess, "What a beautiful cake!" The hostess said, "Thank you, I baked it myself" (making herself look good). Alice smiled and thought, *There is a God.*

Alice was determined not to make a mistake. It paralyzed her. We have so much God-given potential we have never recognized because we want to avoid the risk of failure. As a Christian, we have the power to lay aside deceptive thinking and be renewed in our minds by the truth of God's Word (Romans 12:2; Ephesians 4:21–25).

Reflection: How are you a perfectionist? A people-pleaser? A performer?

~ Try as hard as we may for perfection, the net result of our labors is an amazing variety of imperfectness. We are surprised at our own versatility in being able to fail in so many different ways. ~

Samuel McChord Crothers

Day 166: I Am Not Perfect!

How did you answer yesterday's reflection question? Perfectionism is a problem with spiritual roots. It is striving to be something in the flesh that we can only be in heaven—without flaw or blemish. It isn't that we should give up our desires to do the best job we can do; it is that we should acknowledge that even our best, even our award winning moments are marred by errors. We are not perfect. We are sinners in constant need of the grace of God (Romans 3:23).

If you are a first born (like myself) that can easily account for your perfectionism and why you are constantly trying to please the world by achieving standards that always seem out of reach. Dr. Kevin Leman said, "Life's challenges don't force you to be a perfectionist. You are forcing yourself by continually raising the bar a bit higher, setting goals that are too ambitious, setting yourself up for failure and frustration and another ride on the pleaser merry-go-round."[154]

We keep trying to get life right. We give it to Jesus, then we take it back. Like the little red engine, "I think I can ... I think I can."

Maybe you don't struggle with perfectionism. What about the other two p's: pleaser or performer. (Thought so!) God doesn't require us to be perfect. Part of life is accepting the fact that we are not and will never be perfect Christian women. If we were perfect, God wouldn't have had to send Jesus, the perfect sacrifice for us. We can learn to accept what we can't change and change what we can with God's guidance and grace.

Reflect on this: if we could just see what God sees then we would not driven to perfection.

~ *You're going to make mistakes in life. It's what you do after the mistakes that counts.* ~

Brandi Chastain

Day 167: Grace, Works, and Me

God is not surprised by our inabilities, imperfections, or faults. He created us! That is grace. Grace is God's acceptance of me. If God accepts me, shouldn't I accept me? Grace is one of the hardest lessons for us to learn about God. We show our ignorance of God's grace by working hard to be good enough, the perfect performer. We think if we're perfect enough then God and others will give us their stamp of approval. *I'll be accepted and loved!* It doesn't work that way.

> Because of his kindness, you have been saved through trusting Christ. And even trusting is not of yourselves; it too is a gift from God. Salvation is not a reward for the good we have done, so none of us can take any credit for it. It is God himself who has made us what we are and given us new lives from Christ Jesus; and long ages ago he planned that we should spend these lives in helping others (Ephesians 2:8–10, TLB).

God did not change me to love me. God loved me and wanted to change me into God's Girl. God is not after a perfect performance. He is after relationship.

Learning to be happy with yourself is an important key to enjoying life. Our job is to get up every day and do our best using the gifts and opportunities God has provided. It's a spirit of excellence. We do the best we can, and expect God to do the rest! When we fail, we know it is part of his plan to build us into a stronger God's Girl.

Reflection: Starting today, appreciate your life where you are right now!

~ Have patience with all things, but chiefly have patience with yourself. Do not lose courage in considering your own imperfections but instantly set about remedying them, every day begin the task anew. ~

St. Francis de Sales [157]

Day 168: MileStone

Steps To Overcome Negative Emotions

Move Forward

Most likely, prior to reading this book, who you thought you were, did not line up with who God said you were. Many of the women we've talked about looked in the mirror and saw "inferior" and "worthless," but when Jesus looked into their mirror, he saw "daughter," "princess," and "superior."

Define Who You Are. Begin to say what you like, what you want, what you will do, and what you think. This is your identity. Make a pact with yourself to offer an opinion, make a choice, and express a need. We uncover a new freedom in knowing who we are while not having to convince everyone else who we are.

Define Who You Are Not. Often we try to do things we are not gifted for. Or we strive to be a certain person God did not create us to be. This imbalance causes a tremendous amount of stress on ourselves (competition, jealousy, hatred), and we're not in God's will, which means we don't have his blessing! So we're miserable.

Challenge the Old Way of Thinking

Begin to write down and talk about your good points; your strengths, and how you are growing in Christ. What do you like? Don't like? Balance your self-criticism with self-encouragement. You will goof up. Go easier on yourself and laugh about it! Say or write out: "I am special. I have no need to be perfect or prove my value. God created me this way and I am happy with me!" Stand up for yourself!

Day 169: Pray and Meditate

God knows everything about us, and he still accepts and loves us. God is with us through everything, protecting, loving, and guiding us, which gives us a deep sense of meaning and purpose. Read this psalm slowly, mediating on each verse.

Oh, thank God—he's so good! His love never runs out. All of you set free by God, tell the world! Tell how he freed you from oppression, then rounded you up from all over the place, from the four winds, from the seven seas. Some of you wandered for years in the desert, looking but not finding a good place to live, half-starved and parched with thirst, staggering and stumbling, on the brink of exhaustion. Then, in your desperate condition, you called out to God. He got you out in the nick of time.

He put your feet on a wonderful road that took you straight to a good place to live. So thank God for his marvelous love, for his miracle mercy to the children he loves. He poured great draughts of water down parched throats; the starved and hungry got plenty to eat. . . . Some of you were sick because you'd lived a bad life, your bodies feeling the effects of your sin, you couldn't stand the sight of food, so miserable you thought you'd be better off dead. Then you called out to God in your desperate condition; he got you out in the nick of time.

He spoke the word that healed you, that pulled you back from the brink of death. So thank God for his marvelous love, for his miracle mercy to the children he loves; offer thanksgiving sacrifices, tell the world what he's done—sing it out! (Psalm 107: 1–9; 17–22, Msg)

Self-Soother

This is self-worth day. Do something nice for yourself that is inexpensive. For example, buy some flowers, get a manicure or pedicure, etc.

Day 170: That Word *Beauty*

Can you imagine looking in the mirror and saying, "Thank you Lord for making me so gorgeous"? No way! It seems we all think we can improve on God's design. I did. When I looked in the mirror, all my disagreeable features were magnified.

Models taught me that physical beauty was the road to being accepted, successful, and being loved. I believed false promises such as, *If I'm beautiful, I will be happy and successful. I'll be desirable to men. I'll be secure, important, significant, and confident.*

In our culture beauty has its advantages. "Good-looking" people will confirm that their looks serve their ambitions well. Isn't that why cosmetic surgery is so popular today? We say inner beauty is more valuable, but do we really believe it?

I believed in God, but I worshiped different gods and idols. Inevitably they made me feel worthless and humiliated because I couldn't measure up to their standards. My self-esteem became related to my body and self-image. Because I couldn't attain that supermodel perfection, I never felt good about myself. I exercised obsessively, binged and purged food (bulimia), all to stay thin. It was never enough. I kept pouring money into all the industries that promised to make me beautiful and restore youth—cosmetics, fashion, nutrition, plastic surgery, and weight-loss. All the outside dressing up did nothing to clean up the inside mess.

Reflection: Compare your outside dressing to your inside dressing. If you feel creative, draw a picture that depicts both.

~ *Break down every idol; cast out every foe. Now wash*
me and I shall be whiter than snow. ~

James Nicholson[155]

Day 171: Gobble-Gobble

In my early forties I was convinced *everyone* was younger than me. The crow's feet and wrinkles only accented this realization. Every day that I had looked in the mirror I saw turkey-neck. Time for action! I found a reputable cosmetic dermatologist that promised a new youthful, confident me. I opted for a mini-liposuction treatment for the neck. It was a simple non-invasive procedure where a small amount of fat is sucked out through a needle. The doctor said my neck would tighten up naturally within six months.

Six months later I was horrified. Gobble-gobble. The skin didn't tighten up. I bought turtlenecks in every color. Millions of people watch television shows that portray makeover segments as the answer. Plastic surgeons dramatically alter people's faces and bodies for their magical moment. But what happens after the television cameras go away?

Don't get me wrong! Beauty is an important part of our identity. There is nothing wrong in desiring to be the best we can be. The Bible talks about the beauty of many women. I'm not saying ditch the makeup or jewelry because that would make me a hypocrite. But God warns us not to love the world and anything in the world (1 John 2:15–17). Those things are merely cheap substitutes.

God's thoughts are not our thoughts, nor even close! We're thinking, *Preserve the face and body.* He's thinking, *I love her so much. I want to save her soul.*

Reflection: Write a prayer asking for God's comfort in this difficult area called self-improvement, or any other painful area that God brings to your mind.

> ~ *Each morning I awaken to the face of an older man and*
> *I pray for his wisdom for the coming day.* ~
>
> Justin Matott[156]

Day 172: The Right Beauty Prescription

Who hasn't at one time thought, *There has to be something more than my stuff, or dieting, or clothes and shoes.* Even Jesus said, "Life is more than food, and the body, more than clothes" (Luke 12:23). My relationship with God was the beauty prescription I needed. One day I heard a very simple sermon about the Potter and the clay (Jeremiah 18:1–6). In this parable by Jeremiah, God is the potter. He tells Jeremiah that Israel (man) is the clay. In other words, you and I are the marred clay on the Potter's wheel.

My question to the Potter was, *What is your purpose in putting me on your wheel? Is your answer to bring out my inner beauty?* Why do I say this? The Bible says that God doesn't make decisions the way we do. People judge by outward appearance, but God looks at a person's heart (1 Samuel 16:7). Molding and shaping implies designing. As a potter molds and shapes each clay pot, God in his divine creative act designed us.

God changes our hearts and minds, and that changes how we feel about ourselves. The Holy Spirit began reversing how I saw myself in the mirror, and God's Word became my catalyst to overcoming my obsessions. I learned that beauty doesn't carry the promise of happiness but that beauty is who we are in him. When God measures us, he puts the tape measure around our heart, not our waistline. When we choose Jesus, we can look into the mirror and say, "Thank you, Lord, for making me, if not gorgeous, just right!

Reflection: How do you want God to mold you? In your mind, what should he lop off and what should he refine?

~ *Years I spent in vanity and pride; Caring not my Lord was crucified.* ~

William R. Newell[157]

Day 173: A Counter Cultural Definition of Beauty

This culture is caught in a quest for youthfulness. We look to cosmetic surgery, vitamin and health food remedies to renovate our bodies. But do we get the intended results? Dr. Randy Alcorn, author of *Heaven*, wrote, "If we saw Adam and Eve as they were in Eden, they would likely take our breath away. If they could see us the way we are now, they would likely be filled with shock and pity."[158] I guess the answer is no.

Many women who feel depressed seek a physician for pills only, instead of exploring the possible causes and God's Word. Why not, if you think this life on earth is all there is? The Bible promises us eternal youthfulness and joy. It's not ours now, but it will be. That is our hope.

Any effort to improve our physical beauty won't have much relevance for the world beyond. The book of Revelation describes a future scene in which Jesus embraces and restores all those who have suffered and died, with a perfect body! He wipes away their tears and heals their brokenness. Then he welcomes them into the bliss, splendor and peace of his eternal kingdom (Revelation 21).

Our real life as God's Royal Girl is to be spent with him in eternity. Paul said that everyone who competes in the games goes into strict training to get a crown that will not last; but we do it to get a crown that will last forever (1 Corinthians 9:25). We need to ask ourselves daily, "How am I investing my time today for eternity?"

Reflection: Close your eyes and see yourself wearing your eternal crown of glory.

> ~ *If everyone knew the truth do you think we'd keep*
> *devouring positive-thinking books by the millions?* ~
>
> Unknown

Day 174: The Inside Says It All

Someone once said, "Be more concerned with your character than your reputation, because your character is what you really are, while your reputation is merely what others think you are."[159]

Our journey is about allowing God to develop our inside, our character—the Fruit of the Spirit. The remedy is quite simple. The apostle James said we need to look intently *into the mirror of God's Word* to see ourselves as we really are, and see where change needs to take place (James 1:22–25). We don't want to be beautiful to gain the approval of man; we want to be beautiful so that we can fulfill our purpose while we are still here on earth. We want people to be attracted to us because then they are attracted to Jesus.

As you begin to change your self-image and see yourself living the life God has planned for you, you will experience his fulfillment, peace, and power.

Reflect over these two verses:

Genesis 1:27: "So God created man in his own image, in the image of God he created him; male and female he created them."

Genesis 1:31: "God saw all that he had made, and it was very good."

How does your self-image line up with who God says you are?

~ *Character cannot be developed in ease and quiet. Only through experience of trial and suffering can the soul be strengthened, ambition inspired, and success achieved.* ~

Helen Keller[160]

Day 175: God's Girl Queen Vashti

Drama, power, romance, intrigue—this is the stuff great novels are made. The story begins in the book of Esther with Queen Vashti refusing to obey an order from her husband, King Xerxes, to parade before the king's all-male party. The Bible says, "Let a search be made for beautiful young virgins for the king...Then let the girl who pleases the king be queen instead of Vashti" (Esther 2:4).

Any modest woman can understand why she preferred not to appear before the king and his party. They were inebriated! One source interpreted "display her beauty" to mean "appear naked" or "dance."[161] Refusing the king's wish was dangerous for it made Xerxes look as if he had no control over his own wife, let alone his country.

Then the king huddles with counsel: "Queen Vashti has done wrong...For the queen's conduct will become known to all the women, and so they will despise their husbands...There will be no end of disrespect and discord" (1:16–18). The king had no option but to depose her.

I have sympathy for Vashti. Subsequently she was banished and the search began for a new queen.

Reflection: When have you felt banished or blamed for something you had no control over? Is that part of your angst today?

> ~ *It is one of the encouraging things in life that, again and again, that which looks impossible can be done, when it has got to be done.* ~
>
> William Barclay[162]

Day 176: The Queen Deposed

Vashti, queen of Persia, was the most powerful woman in the Middle East, yet she made a decision that had dire repercussions. The Bible doesn't tell us exactly why Queen Vashti refused the king. Possibly because it was against Persian custom for a woman to parade herself in front of men. Some suggest that Vashti was pregnant she did not want to be seen in public in that state. Basically, Vashti had no rights in relation to her husband, and therefore reasons were irrelevant. Scripture says that Vashti is never again to enter the presence of King Xerxes.

The omission of the title "Queen" from this point on is noteworthy. If she will not come when summoned, then she'll never be seen by the king again. Vashti's refusal to obey her husband has helped to secure her stature as a folk hero of the modern feminist movement as well as a villain because of her disrespect for her husband.

Interestingly, "Later when the anger of King Xerxes had subsided, he remembered Vashti and what she had done and what he had decreed about her" (2:1). This suggests that the king's mood changed. It implies some uneasiness over the incident, but the king was trapped by his own legislation *decreed against her.*

When a queen is deposed, such as Queen Vashti, what happens to her? We're not told but it seems likely she might have remained in the area because of her son.

Reflection: When have you been so angry at someone that you did something that you later regretted? Is anger or regret an emotion you are battling today? If so, speak to God about the situation.

~ *It's not the dress that makes the woman, but the woman who makes the dress.* ~

Coco Chanel[163]

Day 177: God's Girl Esther

The story continues ... A search begins for a new queen. The king gathered all the beautiful young women and Esther was chosen. "Immediately he provided her with her beauty treatments and special food. He assigned to her seven maids selected from the king's palace and moved her and her maids into the best place in the harem" (an Old Testament version of *Extreme Makeover*, Esther 2:9).

Esther was an orphan who lived with the Jewish exiles in Persia. Her cousin Mordecai adopted her. He was a government official and covert leader of the Jewish community. "The king was attracted to Esther more than to any of the other women, and she won his favor and approval more than any of the other virgins. So he set a royal crown on her head and made her queen instead of Vashti" (2:17).

Something else is going on behind the scenes. Haman, a high official, is plotting to destroy the Jews (3:1–6). Mordecai pleads with Esther to help. She has to decide whether she will play the part God offers. After Esther's coronation, she discreetly won king Xerxes' confidence by informing him of this assassination plot.

God is developing Esther's character as she waits obediently. She appears to be a bold woman, with a teachable spirit. She knows God has put her in this place for a reason. Like Esther, God will show you his plan for your life. He has no intention of hiding his desires from you.

Reflection: Who do you relate to more: Vashti (rejected) or Esther (uncertain or fearful)? Or both (treated as an object)? Begin to pray about God's plan for you.

~ If you don't like the way the world is, you change it.
You have an obligation to change it. ~

Marian Wright Edelman[164]

Day 178: God Moves Powerfully

Interestingly, the book of Esther makes no mention of God, yet we see him move powerfully through her to save the entire Jewish race. The writer of Esther affirms that God was indeed with them, and in control. Esther was just one woman. What could she really do? To speak up was to risk her life. It would be much safer to stay quiet, unnoticed. But she had the perfect opportunity and her own unique qualifications.

Esther had access to the person with ultimate power. All this created a great responsibility and a weighty moral pressure.

"For if you remain silent at this time, relief and deliverance for the Jews will arise from another place, but you and your father's family will perish. And who knows but that you have come to royal position for such a time as this?" (Esther 4:14)

Walking through the fear, Esther moves out of her comfort zone and faces danger. Then God gives her a heart to gain an audience with the king. This meant possible failure and fear. She knew her limitations and need to go to God. She prepared spiritually by praying and fasting for three days. Esther was willing to die for her people. What courage! Her call (or mission) was more important than herself.

Reflection: Begin working toward greater spiritual balance. Ask God what you must do to get back into fellowship with him? His Word says, "He who began a good work in you will carry it on to completion until the day of Christ Jesus" (Philippians 1:6).

> ~ *Every trial endured and weathered in the right spirit makes*
> *a soul nobler and stronger than it was before.* ~
>
> James Buckham[165]

Day 179: Royal Timing

Esther prepared the banquet asking that both Haman and the king attend. The king, wanting to grant her request, asked her to state it. Instead, she asked them to attend a different banquet the following day (5:8). Esther approached the king, which could have cost her life if he refused her, but fortunately the king received Esther's application. You have to wonder, why two banquets? Perhaps the situation with Haman was not yet adequately developed for her to expose him.

Esther asked for her petition, saying "... grant me my life–this is my petition. And spare my people. For I and my people have been sold for destruction and slaughter and annihilation" (7:3–4).

When the King discovered that Haman was the guilty party he ordered Haman hung on the gallows, the same gallows that Haman intended to use to kill Mordecai. This was Esther's strategy. She knew Haman's weaknesses and waited until he was in a position to hang himself. The Lord gave her perfect timing.

Esther's royal position was not an accident. She was in this of influence for a very specific reason. Your position in life is not an accident either. Hopefully the story of Esther has changed your thinking about God and his plan for your life.

Reflection: Describe a time when the Lord gave you perfect timing. What do you think God might have for you to do right now?

> ~ *How lovely to think that no one need wait a moment, we can start now,*
> *start slowly changing the world! How lovely that everyone great and small*
> *can make their contribution toward introducing justice straight away ... And*
> *you can always, always give something, even if it is only kindness!* ~

Anne Frank[166]

Day 180: Submission to God's Plan

In Esther's day God preserved his people in spite of opposition and danger. God's power worked first through Vashti; she lost her throne in order that Esther could rise up and save her people. In the end justice prevailed for Vashti when she reigned as "queen mother" over her son, Artaxerxes.

Esther submitted to and followed God's plan, which took wisdom and courage. She is a woman that was persuasive, politically savvy, influential, obedient, and she respected authority. She was patient for the right timing.

Esther and Mordecai were providentially placed at the heart of the Persian empire with power to act politically on behalf of their people. Esther, like Jesus, put herself in the place of death for her people. This book reveals another threat to destroy the Jewish people, and thus, the messianic line. Earthly powers were working to destroy and kill, *but* God, far more powerful, was at work to save and preserve. God continues to preserve his people in spite of opposition and danger.

Reflect and pray: "God, I was made in your image and that means, like Queen Esther, I am a conqueror and can do all things! Thank you for your confidence in me. Help me to stay focused on your loving plan for my life. In Jesus' name. Amen."

> ~ *Life was meant to be lived, and curiosity must be kept alive. One must never, for whatever reason, turn his (her) back on life.* ~

Eleanor Roosevelt[167]

Day 181: The Royal Girl's Purpose

Esther, an orphan in a foreign land, displayed courage in the midst of crisis. You may feel that God can't use you because you are not perfect, or brave, a queen Esther type. This is a lie. God uses cracked pots (not crack pots) to do his work. As Christians, we are containers that God wants to fill with his goodness and light (Day 98). God's unseen hand often guides, directs and preserves his people by working out circumstances, sometimes in the most unexpected ways.

In Esther's case, her obedience and willingness to transcend the fear of failure saved her Jewish people from possible annihilation. Esther knew the responsibility for guidance is always Gods, but the responsibility for obedience is always ours. Her circumstances were more than meant to be. They were brought about by a sovereign God who had a plan for Esther's life, and for the lives of his people.

Though God's name appears nowhere in Esther, his divine intervention is evident everywhere. We serve the same God. He even said, "I the LORD do not change" (Malachi 3:6). There are times when most of us have questioned events in our lives and wondered where God was. The story of Esther tells us that God is always present and involved in our individual lives. Esther's position was not an accident. Your position is not an accident.

Reflection: Do you recognize that God wants *you* to make a difference in "such a time as this"? How have you been delivered like the Jews in Esther's story? Celebrate your deliverance!

~ *This could be the day I see my miracle.* ~

Joel Osteen[168]

Day 182: A Risk for the Sake of Others

Queen Esther gives us confidence to take a risk for the sake of others. For me it meant giving up a career and a comfortable salary. It was hard, but it was the right thing and at the right time. It was easy to feel sadly inadequate in the face of such a challenge.

Like Esther, I needed to be reminded of my opportunities, my qualifications, and responsibilities. There is no force too strong, no position too sure, to prevent God's will from prevailing. God is always planting new seeds in our heart. He wants us to discover our gifts and begin to use those gifts habitually and creatively.

You, too, are called to carry that goodness and light into a dark world, sharing it with people everywhere you go. The key is to believe, and allow, God's seed to take root and grow into a beautiful floral arrangement. Don't be afraid of your flaws and cracks; acknowledge them and allow God to use you anyway. Don't worry about what you're not. Give God what you are and let him do the rest.

You can touch somebody. You can encourage and exhort those around you. You can use your gifts and talents to serve God and learn to enjoy every day of your life.

Reflection: What does God want to show you about your life? Make of list of six things you think you need to do to enhance yourself. They may be physical, spiritual, medical, or relational things.

> ~ *I shall pass through life but once. Let me show*
> *kindness now, as I shall not pass this way again.* ~

William Penn

Day 183: Royalty Meets the Potter

As you walk through difficult circumstances the Potter comes into your life (see Day 172). That circumstance is the wheel of God, and the purpose is to bring you against the pressure of the His hand. If you do not resist, if your will does not spoil the work by murmuring, grumbling, or complaining, or feeling resentful and bitter, and you accept the working of the Potter, then the pressure is relieved, and the pot (the vessel) takes shape.

If there is resistance, if the human will, like some imperfection in the clay, chooses something other than what the Potter has in mind, then the Potter can do nothing else but smash it down to a lump and start over. Beginning with the same lump, he will make it over into an earthen vessel, which suits his heart. The great lesson Jeremiah learned at the potter's house was that of the sovereign control of God.

The reason it took me so long to meet the Potter was because I was too busy being a people pleaser and idolizing the wrong things. Herbert Bayard Swope said, "I cannot give you the formula for success, but I can give you the formula for failure—try to please everybody."[169] I tried to be like other women. It never worked out because I tried to change myself into someone I wasn't created to be. I didn't let the Potter work me on his wheel and mold me into what he created me to be. I had to make a choice: be a God pleaser or a people pleaser.

Reflection: When have you ever admired someone so much that you tried to be like that person? What were the results?

~ *Self-esteem is rooted in unconditional acceptance of*
yourself as an innately worthy being, regardless of mistakes. ~

Matthew McKay and Patrick Fanning[170]

Day 184: People or God Pleaser?

Most women understand what it means to be a people pleaser. It's easy to fall into that trap which is why we must let God work us over like clay. The apostle Paul explains:

> But this precious treasure—this light and power that now shines within us—is held in a perishable container, that is, in our weak bodies. Everyone can see that the glorious power within must be from God and is not our own. We are pressed on every side by troubles, but not crushed and broken. We are perplexed because we don't know why things happen as they do, but we don't give up and quit. We are hunted down, but God never abandons us. We get knocked down, but we get up again and keep going. These bodies of ours are constantly facing death just as Jesus did; so it is clear to all that it is only the living Christ within who keeps us safe (2 Corinthians 4:7–10, TLB).

Paul's message does not put the focus on the perishable container; our outsides, but on its priceless contents; God's power dwelling within us.

Reflection: This is a powerful passage. Read it again. What do you think God's message to you is?

~ *O God, may we simplify our lives that we be not so concerned with unimportant things that we miss the real thing.* ~

Theodore Parker Ferris[171]

Day 185: No Way, Jose!

Yesterday's message reminds us that we may think we're at the end of our rope, but we are never at the end of hope.

When I told you that you were created in God's image, that everyone can see God's glorious power within you, that you are God's Royal Girl, you may have said, "No way, Jose!" But Jesus says, "Yes way" and "I am the way" (John 14:6).

Let us not forget that "these bodies" can never be completely satisfied with earthly pleasures. Because we are created in God's image we will always have that spiritual thirst that only the eternal God can satisfy.

The Potter showed me that my purpose was to glorify him. Another word is *revere*, which means to respect and stand in awe of God because of who he is. In this life, it's not what we know or who we know or how good we are at such and such, but *knowing God personally*. Purpose in life starts with knowing our Father. It is impossible to fulfill our God-given role unless we revere God and give him first place. Then he'll open our eyes to incredible blessings.

I thank God for remolding me, showing me I am a true princess, royalty, a treasure in a clay jar. He has given me everything I need to be that ray of light that our broken world so desperately needs. He will do the same for you.

Reflection: How well do you feel you know your heavenly Father? If not so well, what obstacles stand in the way of knowing him better?

> ~ *The world was made round so that we would*
> *never be able to see too far down the road.* ~
>
> Isak Dinesen[172]

Day 186: MileStone

Steps To Overcome Negative Emotions

Move Forward

Congratulations! You've made it past the halfway point to another MileStone!

Ethel Barrymore said, "You grow up the first day you have the first real laugh—at yourself."[173] A sense of humor helps the Royal Girl move forward.

Having a good laugh actually strengthens relationship bonds making for a stronger emotional heart. Laughter, like water, flushes toxins out of our body. When we laugh we have the ability to diffuse the pain by physically increasing the body's production of endorphins, the body's natural painkillers. *Laughter is not only good for our health, but for coping and survival.* It can break the ice, lower blood pressure, reduce your risk of developing heart disease, and improve your mood. [174]

Challenge the Old Way of Thinking

Using humor as therapy affects us in many ways. Humor has the power to reduce tension and create a relaxed atmosphere. It puts an individual in a frame of mind conducive to constructive interchange with others. Humor can lead to insight into the cause of conflict and emotional disturbances, and it allows us to be silly so we can find respite from our serious selves and responsibilities.

Begin by spending time with people who laugh and see the humor in situations. All in all, laughter and humor can reduce our emotional pain. And besides, as a comedian once said, "It is bad to suppress laughter; it goes back down and spreads to your hips."

Day 187: Pray and Meditate

Today we're going to have a little fun and meditate over the truth of the following story.

By the time the Lord made woman, he was into his sixth day of working overtime. An angel appeared and said, "Why are you spending so much time on this one?"

The Lord answered, "Have you seen her specs? She has to be completely washable, but not plastic, have over two hundred movable parts, all replaceable and able to run on diet coke and leftovers, have a lap that can hold four children at one time, have a kiss that can cure anything from a scraped knee to a broken heart, and be able to do everything with only two hands."

The angel was astounded. "Only two hands! No way! That's too much work for one day. Wait until tomorrow to finish."

I won't," the Lord protested. "I am so close to finishing this creation. It's so close to my heart. She already heals herself when she is sick and can work eighteen hour days."

The angel moved closer and touched the woman. "You have made her so soft, Lord!"

"She is soft," the Lord agreed, "I have also made her tough. You have no idea what she can endure or accomplish."

"Will she be able to think?" asked the angel.

The Lord replied, "Yes, and she will be able to reason and negotiate."

The angel then noticed something, and reaching out, touched the woman's cheek. "Oops, it looks like you have a leak in this model. I told you that you were trying to put too much into this one."

"That's not a leak," the Lord corrected. "That's a tear!"

"What's the tear for?" the angel asked.

The Lord said, "The tear is her way of expressing her joy, sorrow, pain, disappointment, love, loneliness, grief and pride."

The angel was impressed. "You are a genius, Lord. You thought of everything! Woman is truly amazing."

Yes she is, and you are this creation! Women have strengths that amaze men. They bear hardships and they carry burdens, but they have the ability to hold happiness, love, and joy. They fight for what they believe in. They don't take no for an answer when they believe there is a better solution. They go without so their family can have. They go to the doctor with a frightened friend. They love unconditionally. They cry when their children excel and cheer when their friends get awards. They are happy when they hear about a birth or a wedding. Their hearts break when a friend hurts. They grieve at the loss of a family member, yet they are strong when they think there is no strength (source unknown).

What are men good for? Lifting heavy objects and sometimes killing a spider!

Self-Soother

Watch a funny movie with someone today.

Part Eleven

The Champion Girl

Encouraged by God's Word

The Champion Girl presses through negative circumstances and pessimistic feelings:

> "For everyone born of God overcomes the world. This is the victory that has overcome the world, even our faith." (1 John 5:4)

> With God as her trainer she becomes a CHAMP:

> Courageous—Humble—Awesome—Mindful—Persistent.

Day 188: The Stress of Moving

When I was a kid we moved a lot. Every kid fears that first day of school. *Will they like me? Will anyone sit next to me?* First we moved from the USA to England. I immediately met with rejection and opposition because I was "different." I struggled in school and began what seemed like a never-ending parade of tutors in and out of my life.

High school was rather uneventful. I wasn't really good at anything. I never went to a prom. I couldn't wait to get out of high school and go to college because then life would be different! My parent's thought they were sending me off to get a BS degree. However, my intention was to get my MRS. degree.

I was encouraged to join a sorority. Again, gripped by fear, I wondered if they would accept me. Dr. James Dobson courageously called sororities a "flesh market."[175] Each sister discusses each girl's attributes and defects. They have the power to break dreams and tear apart hearts. Once "in," I too became part of the rampant negative behavior and cruelty. My newfound sorority became my identity. I belonged!

By my junior year my grades were getting worse and worse, and there was still no future Mr. Right. Most of my friends found their Mr. Right, so in my mind I failed again. Then I got that dreaded notice that I was on probation. *What will I do if I flunk out of school? What will happen to my life now? Loser!* Fear penetrated my very being.

Reflection: Can you feel the despair and fear? What similar feelings do you have today? Give them to God as you identify them.

> ~ *Optimism is the faith that leads to achievement. Nothing can be done without hope and confidence.* ~
>
> Helen Keller[176]

Day 189: More Moving, More Stress

By the grace of God I ended up graduating. I moved back home and began the next phase of my life. The first job I landed was the coveted role as a pharmaceutical sales rep. I thought I was pretty "hot" even though my clients intimidated me. Little did I know I had just set myself up for failure because I didn't really digest that sales meant doors slamming in my face over and over again—more fear and defeat.

I eventually got fired because I didn't have what it took to succeed. I moved to California. Sales job number two didn't go much better. *I'm a loser.* My insecurity was encased by panic and fear. However, I continued to take sales jobs because that was what (I thought) I knew. I was like a square peg trying desperately to fit into the round hole.

After each defeat I would retreat further into bulimic behavior and depression. God must have been watching over me, because I eventually got a sales job that fit my personality and temperament. Within a few months, I met my future husband, who introduced me to Jesus Christ. I ended up staying with this employer for nine years.

Do you think that was a coincidence? Jesus gave me the courage to overcome my fear and insecurities, eventually moving me toward pursuing a healthy career—one that used my gifts and talents as God purposed.

Reflection: When you look at your past, do you tend to focus on the victories or the failures? Identify one recent victory.

> ~ *In those times I can't seem to find God, I rest in the assurance He knows how to find me.* ~
>
> Neva Coyle[77]

Day 190: The Champion Overcomes Fear

Fear and insecurity are two of Satan's most powerful tools because they steal away what God wants to give us. Fear distorts God's purpose for our life. In the Bible, frequently God is quoted as saying, "fear not." Since we can't run away or hide from our fear, we must confront it and stand on God's promises of protection.

One of the most powerful verses in the Bible is Isaiah 52:12: "But you will not leave in haste or go in flight; for the LORD will go before you, the God of Israel will be your rear guard." Isaiah is saying that God has you completely covered. If that is the case, and we know his Word is truth, then what is there to fear?

In today's world we have so many reasons to fear. Jesus' words regarding worry:

> Therefore I tell you, do not worry about your life, what you will eat; or about your body, what you will wear. Life is more than food, and the body more than clothes. Consider the ravens: They do not sow or reap, they have no storeroom or barn; yet God feeds them. And how much more valuable you are than birds! Who of you by worrying can add a single hour to his life? (Luke 12:22–25)

Reflection: Get a hold of a concordance and look up the words fear and worry, or any other emotion that is holding you captive. Then look up "fear not" or other verses that behold God's promises. Allow God to speak to you through specific verses, and then memorize those verses. Tape them on your mirror.

~ *So much has been given to me; I have no time to ponder over what has been denied.* ~

Helen Keller[178]

Day 191: Jesus on Fear and Worry

What is the opposite of fear? According to the Bible, it is love! "There is no fear in love. But perfect love drives out fear, because fear has to do with punishment. The one who fears is not made perfect in love" (1 John 4:18).

Love will do what fear cannot. Many of us today are battling financial fear. Let's continue with Jesus' teaching from yesterday: "Do not set your heart on what you will eat or drink; do not worry about it. For the pagan world runs after all such things, and your Father knows that you need them. But *seek his kingdom, and these things will be given to you* as well" (Luke 12:29–31, author's emphasis).

Jesus avoids giving practical advice and doesn't comment specifically on personal disputes about finances. He sees money as a spiritual force. Jesus explains that money operates much like idolatry, dominating a person's life, ultimately diverting attention away from God. Jesus challenges Christians to break free from money's power, even if it means giving it all away. Our wealth is in knowing we have eternal life.

Reflection: When it comes to finances, what are your current worries? If not financial, name your primary fear and talk to God about it.

~ *Let our advance worrying become advance thinking and planning.* ~

Winston Churchill

Day 192: Instructions for Finding Lasting Joy

Jesus strongly warns against putting faith in money to secure the future. To emphasize his point, he points to King Solomon, the richest man in the Old Testament. Jesus wants us to see that Solomon's wealth vanished. Even in his prime, he was no more impressive than a common wildflower.

His message: better to trust in the God who lavishes care on the whole earth than to spend your life worrying about money and possessions. The key to using money wisely is to see how much we can use it for God's purposes.

Paul says, "Don't worry about anything; instead, pray about everything; tell God your needs, and don't forget to thank him for his answers" (Philippians 4:6, TLB).

He gives us clear instructions for finding lasting joy, financial or otherwise: do not to worry, but pray about everything and thank God for everything.

"If you do this, you will experience God's peace, which is far more wonderful than the human mind can understand. His peace will keep your thoughts and your hearts quiet and at rest as you trust in Christ Jesus" (Philippians 4:7, TLB). This kind of peace is so powerful. Does thankfulness characterize you?

Reflection: God is calling you to come to him and release your fears. Earnestly ask him to bring to mind an unresolved issue that needs healing. Thank him for this opportunity. Ask for strength and wisdom to begin peeling away the fear and worry.

~ *Anxiety is what happens when the worry machine is*
working without anything to work on. ~

John Cowan

Day 193: The Champion Overcomes Negativism

Lewis L. Dunnington said, "What life means to us is determined not so much by what happens to us as by our reaction to what happens."[179]

Most of us have been hurt—many tragically. Leila Rae Sommerfeld recounts her tragic rape:

> Boulders of unremitting agony weighed me down, crushing any positive thoughts I might have had. I felt like a time bomb of rage, tears, and fear, ready to explode at the slightest provocation. Many days I sat on the hillside, with my head buried in my lap, crying for hours. With feelings of hopeless abandonment, I slept too much and cried relentlessly.[180]

There are legitimate circumstances that call for us to react in anger or despair. Many of us mull around in this caustic acid. Instead of healing, we often move from hurting to hating. Then we become a victim. The more we focus on wounds of the past, the more we are victimized by them. The negative overwhelms us, and then we get stuck in the toxic muck. We think we're worthless. The future will be bad. There's no way out!

If we believe we have some control, we are less likely to feel depressed. The Champion Girl presses through powerlessness. She asks God to give her the strength and courage to take the reins of control.

Reflection: Is this a description of you? If it is, talk to God about your situation. Ask him for wisdom and help in taking back some of the control you have lost.

~ *Man is the only creature that refuses to be what he is.* ~

Albert Camus[181]

Day 194: That Victim Mentality

Counselors agree that people who believe they are powerless cope by avoiding or ignoring problems. *If nothing I do makes a difference, then why should I bother?* If we do nothing, nothing changes. Our feelings of powerlessness are confirmed. I lived with a victim mentality for decades. The apostle Paul says I did these things ignorantly in unbelief because I was wearing blinders before I was a Christian (2 Corinthians 4:3–4). Today Jesus Christ is my Savior, and any guilt is the work of the devil.

Satan cannot rob us of our salvation, but he can rob us of our joy with guilt. *You're a failure, you miserable Christian! Look what you did!* These thoughts are a ticket to our own road of self-destruction. Norman Vincent Peale said, "We tend to get what we expect."[182] We must stop looking in the rearview mirror. Remember what happened to Lot's wife when she looked back—she turned into a pillar of salt! (Genesis 19:26)

If we call ourselves victims, we'll soon be inviting more people and situations to victimize us. However, when we take God's hand, we take our focus off our past, and off the guilt, shame, worthlessness, and helplessness, and start envisioning a better future. Wounds heal, and God uses our holy scars. We become champions—survivors.

Don't lose sight that what's happened is just one event in a whole lifetime of events. Choose to move forward. *I will not let this situation define who I am!*

Reflection: In prayer take God's hand and ask him to help you stop focusing on the bad circumstances, and begin to focus on what he has in mind for you.

~ We have no right to ask, when sorrow comes, "Why did this happen to me?" unless we ask the same question for every joy that comes our way. ~

Philip S. Bernstein[183]

Day 195: Thankfulness and Gratitude

We can be bent toward an all-or-nothing attitude. If all is not well, so the reasoning goes, then nothing is well. This mindset is certainly in play when we allow our lives to be defined by the presence of problems. Such thinking does not have to be!

Let's prepare our hearts and minds for an all-is-well day:

Appreciate the simple things that go right. Even in the midst of unwanted circumstances, there is something good. The grocery store offers food few other countries can enjoy. You have heat and water in your home. Your dog eats meat.

Examine life outside your own personal confines. You know people who have had positive experiences. Listen to their stories. Be happy for them, not envious of them.

Remember acts of kindness. In the recent past, surely someone has acted nicely toward you. Reflect on those events, no matter how small.

Acknowledge your capacity to improve. As you consider the events that have produced frustration, focus on your resolve to move forward as a stronger, more compassionate person, using them as an opportunity to grow.

Be attentive to elements of beauty. Appreciate the wonder of the seasons. Soak in the radiance of a child's smile. Be aware of color and music and pleasant aromas.

Reflection: What do you enjoy doing? Begin to dig inside of yourself and recognize your talents. These become your goals. And thank God!

> ~ *I will tell of the loving kindnesses of God. I will praise him for all he*
> *has done; I will rejoice in his great goodness ... his mercy and love.* ~

Isaiah (Isaiah 63:7, TLB)

Day 196: The Champion Overcomes Anger

I had a bratty younger brother who found humor in sneaking up behind me on a mission to pull down my pants. One day as I napped blissfully he attacked. I kicked him off, and he literally flew off the bed, face first onto the hardwood floor. All I heard was "M-o-m!" His front tooth was chipped in half.

"You deserved it, you little brat!"

He darted out, opening a floodgate of tears. Dad came in declaring, "You're grounded. You're older and should know better."

I don't know whom I was angrier at, my brother or my father.

Jesus tells a parable (Luke 15:28–30) about the lost son who was in a similar predicament. The story is about two brothers. The younger boy broke his father's heart by taking his inheritance and running off. He squanders everything and lives a wild life and then decides to return home, hoping his dad will give him a job on the farm and a place to live. He finds his father kept his place setting at the table and the porch light on every night. The older brother became angry and refused to go in. So his father went out and pleaded with him. He says "All these years I've been slaving for you and never disobeyed you. But when this son of yours who has squandered your property with prostitutes comes home, you kill the fattened calf for him!"

It appears both sons spent time in the pigpen. One in the pen of rebellion, the other in the pen of self-pity. The older brother said the same thing I said: *It's not fair!*

Reflection: What parallels does your life have to this story? What isn't fair?

~ *He who angers you, controls you!* ~

Anonymous

Day 197: Unforgivable Pain

What if you got a note like this from your mother: "I wish you had never been born. You were one of the biggest mistakes I've ever made."

Author and speaker Sheri Rose Shepherd did. She tells about the time she became pregnant with her first baby. Wanting to put aside her estranged relationship with her mother, Sheri Rose wrote her mom a letter expressing her joy, and then received a package. *Great! Mom sent a gift for the baby!* In the box she was surprised to find all of her baby things, along with her birth certificate and that heartbreaking note.[184] She opened the box with joy in her heart, only to have that joy turn to grief.

You may have a parent like this. This is an example of unforgivable pain because someone we love and trust has betrayed us. We may not be able to avoid bad circumstances, but God gives us the ability to choose how we will react.

Since we cannot eliminate emotions such as anger, worry, and sadness, Dr. Binford Gilbert, author of *The Pastoral Care of Depression*, suggests that we learn to schedule them into our life. Once we accept our negative emotions, we can make conscious and informed decisions about how much time we want to spend with them.[185]

Reflection: Before moving forward, consider Dr. Gilbert's suggestion. At this point what might scheduling your feelings into your schedule look like?

> ~ *You can choose, like some, to put away your hurts before they become hates. You can choose to go to the party.* ~
>
> Max Lucado [186]

Day 198: Our Appointment with Anger

Many of our emotions are like unwanted company or extended family that doesn't fit in our mold. We're stuck with them. We can fight them until they eat a hole in our stomach, deny and stuff them away, or acknowledge they exist and learn to manage them. This may sound silly, but this works: Dr. Gilbert suggests worrying as effectively as possible; it will eliminate the burden of carrying this emotion with you twenty-four hours a day.

Unforgiveness is another emotion that most people who have been hurt face. Like worry it will make us sick, physically and spiritually, especially if we play the same tape of pain over and over again. Settling debts is not only unhealthy but a miserable occupation. You may believe you deserve the apology, but your debtor may never agree.

Each person usually passes through four stages from anger to forgiveness: *hurt, hate, heal,* and then *hug.* Welcome to the next challenge. Get out your mountain boots!

Reflection: Acknowledge any anger or hurt or other negative emotion holding you captive. Decide on the length of time you want to spend each day talking to God about the situation, and then schedule a follow up appointment, as you would with a counselor. Maybe you need fifteen minutes, or maybe an hour. You decide.

> ~ *He who is devoid of the power to forgive is devoid of the power to love.*
> *There is some good in the worst of us and some evil in the best of us.*
> *When we discover this, we are less prone to hate our enemies.* ~
>
> Martin Luther King Jr.[187]

Day 199: Four Stages from Anger to Forgiveness

When we are initially wounded we hurt. This is normal and not a choice. When we hurt, our defense mechanism is anger. We hang onto anger as a means of protection. But since the Bible tells us that God delegates justice in our society (Romans 13:1–5) and "takes vengeance on his foes" (Nahum 1:2), it our responsibility to give the situation to God. He alone is judge (read Romans 12:17–20).

When we're full of bitterness, we must ask, are we giving it all to God? Part of it? None? We come to a fork in the road and make a choice. We can turn it completely over to God and keep giving the situation to him every day (during our appointment) until our heart and attitude are changed. Or we can move from hurt to the next stage, hate. Sometimes that anger hurts very deeply, and we can't help but hate. Hurt wasn't a choice. *Hate is a choice.*

Reflection: What rejection, attack, or threat might be driving your anger? How has this anger affected those close to you?

Assignment: Write an anger letter (not to be mailed) to the person(s) involved. The purpose is to let out any pent-up emotion surrounding this incident. Amazingly, God often opens up a new area of emotion, and we find we're expressing emotions we did not know we had. Take as much time as you need. Write about your life and emotional state before the incident, and then after.

*~ There are two things a person should never be
angry at, what they can help, and what they cannot. ~*

Plato[188]

Day 200: The Champion *Learns* to Forgive

The ability to forgive is essential for victory—for getting out of the pit. Anger and bitterness are like a caustic substance that eats through our heart, hindering our growth. We can follow God's rules for managing our life, but if we bypass the forgiveness step, we remain in bondage. The enemy loves that because then we are not doing what God created us to do. Ask yourself, *Do I want to be bitter or better?*

If we stay bitter, we die spiritually and emotionally. No one will want to be around us and vice-verse. There is a negative price tag tied around our neck. We can continue to be bitter or even hate, or we can choose a journey to forgiveness and let God work it out with our offender. Forgiveness is not natural and not easy. It does require the supernatural intervention of God. The apostle Paul said, "Do not take revenge, my friends, but leave room for God's wrath, for it is written: 'It is mine to avenge; I will repay,' says the Lord" (Romans 12:19).

What will unforgiveness cost us? Besides medical, relational, and emotional problems, unforgiveness separates us from God! Jesus warns us: "For if you forgive men when they sin against you, your Lord will also forgive you. But if you do not forgive men their sins, your Father will not forgive your sins" (Matthew 6:14–15). Now we see that forgiveness is a command. What has unforgiveness cost you?

Reflection: Identify three reasons you struggle to forgive.

> ~ *Holding on to anger, resentment and hurt only gives you tense muscles, a headache and a sore jaw from clenching your teeth. Forgiveness gives you back the laughter and the lightness in your life.* ~

> Joan Lunden[189]

Day 201: Seventy Times Seven

Many wise people have said, "It is easier to forgive an enemy than to forgive a friend." Would you agree? Jesus gives us more instruction on forgiveness in the parable of the unmerciful servant (Matthew 18:21–35).

Peter asks Jesus (thinking he's got the answer), "Sir, how often should I forgive a brother who sins against me? Seven times?"

"No!" Jesus replies, "seventy times seven." Then Jesus launches into the parable about a servant who owed his master a large debt that he could never hope to repay.

A newly forgiven servant comes upon a fellow servant who owes him money. He demands payment, and the fellow servant also asks for more time. The newly forgiven servant refuses and has his debtor thrown into prison until he can pay in full. Learning this, the master becomes angry. He has the servant turned over to the jailer to be tortured until he can repay all he owes. Jesus reprimands, "This is how my Lord will treat each of you unless you forgive your brother from your heart."

Paul said, "Forgive anyone who does you wrong, just as Christ has forgiven you" (Colossians 3:13). What did it cost Christ to forgive us? It cost him his life. The first kind of forgiveness is the forgiveness the Lord purchased for us with his own life. We receive it simply by believing that he died for us. Like the servant, our debt was cancelled (2 Corinthians 5:21). What an awesome gift!

Reflection: What unbiblical attitudes and actions have you discovered in yourself as a result of pondering this material?

~ *We cannot afford to harbor bitterness in our soul. The price we must pay is too great!*~

Luis Palau[190]

Day 202: Acknowledge the Hurt

God cannot relate to us when our hearts are full of destructive emotions, because then we are like the unmerciful servant. Unforgiveness must be resolved before we can go on; therefore we begin with confession. I am fond of Dr. Neil Anderson's description, "Confession is simply being truthful with God and living in continuous agreement with Him. The opposite of confession is not silence, but rationalization and self-justification, attempting to excuse or deny your behavior."[191]

Genuine confession shows realization of sin—an awareness of God's holiness and a willingness to turn from that sin. God already knows what we did. We simply agree with God that our behavior is wrong.

If we don't confess, we sentence ourselves to a life imprisoned by pain. We hang onto the past, weigh ourselves down with that heavy chip on our shoulder, and become incarcerated in grief, which isn't a very healthy solution. Anybody harboring an unforgiving spirit is cheating herself out of fellowship with God . . . and joys of life . . . and the beauty of a Christlike character.

Confession means we acknowledge the hurt to God in prayer. We ask him to help us repair the situation and our heart, and to instill in us the capacity to forgive. We often find that either God changes our heart, or he changes the other person's. Depending on the circumstances, we may need to go to the person who harmed us and ask forgiveness (ask God for wisdom about this). We choose to forgive them for what they have done. We release them, let them off our hook, and put them on God's hook.

Reflection: Think about how much time you spend thinking about how you have been hurt compared to how you might have hurt or offended God.

~ *It's worth losing the battle to win the war.* ~

Sherri Rose Shepherd[192]

Day 203: Then We Heal

Confession begins the healing process. We will always remember the painful situation or loss, but we *choose* not to play that tape repeatedly. We *choose* to take our eyes off the offender and focus on God. Then we move into the third stage, healing.

Healing is a choice and the best stage to be in. Are you instantly healed when you forgive? Probably not. It is the process of releasing and forgiving time and again. It may take years, depending on how deep the wound. That freedom moves us into the fourth stage: *we hug.* We come back into relationship with God and others.

We can either choose to forgive (heal and hug) or not to forgive (hurt and hate). Whatever choice we make, we will be changed. Is the forgiveness journey easy? No! It's hard work. You have to ask yourself, *How bad do I want it?* God is righteous and sovereign. If you have been deeply hurt, nothing can happen that is beyond his control and will. Trust his choices.

Sheri Rose Shepherd Rose knew she had to forgive her mother. She knew that if she didn't, she would remain in bondage. She wrote, "That day I experienced a pain I could not escape. Through a bucket of tears, I sat down and wrote her a real letter—a letter that cut through the bitterness and loneliness that I know we both felt for years. It was a letter asking forgiveness and it paved the road to healing."[193]

Reflection: What one step will you take immediately to move forward in the forgiveness process? How can you model God's forgiveness toward you?

~ I will remember that what hurts today will pass in time. I can speed its departure by forgiving and refusing to indulge in self-pity. ~

Anonymous

Day 204: MileStone

Steps To Overcome Negative Emotions

Move Forward

More lives are spoiled by bitterness and a lack of forgiveness than anything else. The longer we carry a grudge, the heavier it becomes. Jesus is saying today to you, "My dear child, I've washed it all away with my blood. Forgive as I forgave you."

Remember, our forgiveness does not depend on them. All we can do is the right thing—obey God. As God's Champion Girl, we have hope that through our faith in Jesus we can overcome anything. You'll uncover the champion in you! Think about how fear, anger, unforgiveness, any negative emotion, has stopped you from moving forward, and begin to put these new steps in place, one at a time.

Matthew 5:23–24 tells us not to procrastinate or make excuses, as it makes matters worse. In conflict, time heals nothing; it only causes hurts to fester.

Reflection: Ask God for direction and understanding. Learn to let God be God. Accept his judgment. Thank him for all that you do have, even when life is difficult.

~ This is how I want you to conduct yourself in these matters. If you enter your place of worship and, about to make an offering, you suddenly remember a grudge a friend has against you, abandon your offering, leave immediately, go to this friend and make things right. Then and only then, come back and work things out with God. ~

Jesus (Matthew 5:23–24, Msg)

Day 205: Challenge the Old Way of Thinking

Six Biblical Steps To Restoring (Rebuilding) A Relationship

Pray. Take your problem to God and tell him exactly how you feel. The apostle James noted that many of our conflicts and quarrels are caused by prayerlessness. God says, "Come to me first" (James 4:2).

Take the lead. It doesn't matter whether we are the offender or the offended; God expects us to make the first move. Jesus commanded that it even take priority over group worship.

Confess your part of the conflict. If we are serious about restoring a relationship, we begin by admitting our own mistakes. Honestly own up. Agree with God that you are hurting, or have hurt another, and need his cleansing power in your life.

Be sympathetic. Paul taught that we look out for one another, not just for ourselves. We shouldn't try to talk the person out of how they feel. Just listen and let them unload. Then you say, "I value your opinion. I care about our relationship." After we have listened, then we get our chance to unload.

Attack the problem, not the person. Let's choose our words wisely. We're never persuasive when we are abrasive. In resolving conflict, *how* we say something, along with our body language, is as important as *what* we say (Proverbs 16:21). Paul said not to use harmful words but positive words that build up.

Reconcile. Reconciliation means focusing on the relationship. Those who were enemies become friends or acquaintances. Not everyone will always agree about the situation. This doesn't mean we give up finding a solution. Or we agree to disagree and drop the issue.

Day 206: Pray and Meditate

Find a quiet place to be with God. Ask him to bring to your mind any people you have not forgiven in order that you may do so. You may be thinking, *This doesn't apply to me*. I would ask you to consider any feelings of fear, resentment, bitterness, or jealousy.

Ask God to bring names to your mind. Confess them. Place your unforgiveness and your trust right now in God. If you have never placed your trust in Jesus Christ, you can do it right now.

> Dear Father, I want to live the victorious life you intended for me. Help me to focus on the future, not my past mistakes, and grant me the courage to pursue the joy, health, and peace that you promised for me. I acknowledge my sinfulness. I believe that Jesus died on the cross for me and he rose again. I put my trust in you right now. In Jesus' name. Amen.

Self-Soother

Practice one random act of kindness.

Day 207: Kimberly's Choices

The stick is blue! I'm pregnant! My gut imploded. I had a major life choice to grapple with—to bring this baby to term or abort it. There is no issue more troubling than abortion. There was no doubt in my mind that abortion was the answer. After all, I wasn't married, I had an established lifestyle, and I would have brought embarrassment and shame upon my parents. After I had the abortion, I chose to bury this experience like a wrecked ship, on the bottom of an ocean.

Two years later Jesus Christ became my Lord. I became keenly aware of the sin I had committed, a sin that God in his grace and mercy forgave me for. However, I still chose to never bring up that baby or the abortion again. One day I was navigating through a women's Bible study, and my abortion experience surfaced. Again I felt intense pressure to make a choice. I could keep this traumatic experience on the ocean floor, or I could step out in faith and embrace what Jesus wanted to show me.

The first time around, I declined his offer. *I'm fine! I know abortion has traumatic repercussions, but not in my case.* I was living in denial. The abortion incident surfaced again! *Okay, what are you saying, God?* I chose to reopen this old wound. I knew God had forgiven me, but I also knew he had something more to show me; there was a different kind of healing that needed to take place. With God's guidance I began to retrieve the painful memories from the bottom of my ocean.

Reflection: What have you buried on the ocean floor (the darkness) that needs to come to the surface (the light)?

~ *As children of God we don't have to be depressed or defeated in life.* ~

Bob George [194]

Day 208: The Pride

I began to question the choices I made to abort this baby some nineteen years earlier. *Father, show me, what was I feeling when I was pregnant for those eight weeks? I don't have any memory. What was on my mind and heart. Please show me.* I got my answer, an answer I wasn't prepared for.

At the time of my pregnancy, bingeing and purging was my way of life. When I chose abortion, I was really choosing to purge my baby like the food I ate. I could clearly see that at that time in my life I didn't value myself, so how could I value my baby's life? You could say the monster bulimia took two innocent lives. And I hurt God deeply.

The truth is I was just plain selfish, more concerned about my body and what other people would think of me than for a human life. I took my baby's life while following my independent, prideful heart. Then I became angry, satiated with guilt. Often the most difficult work is forgiving one's self. I needed someone stronger than myself to press through this. God did not leave me alone in this self-built cocoon of angst.

God in his mercy revealed that my son (I believe the fetus was a boy) was safe in his loving arms. The Bible has many references to God's unfailing love for children and his assurance of their eternal safety. Life as I knew it was changed forever.

Reflection: Pray about any buried situation: "Show me your ways, O LORD, teach me your paths; guide me in your truth and teach me, for you are God my Savior, and my hope is in you all day long" (Psalm 25:4–5).

> ~ *A proud heart keeps running the same obstacles, and is defeated again an again. But a broken heart victoriously conquers new ground daily.* ~

Barbara Wilson [195]

Day 209: God's Girl Mary of Nazareth

My story, like David and Bathsheba's (Days 86–90), illustrates there are harmful consequences for one bad choice. Every day the media reminds us of our moral decline. In my case, I did not have the faith to believe that God would bring beauty from the dust and ashes. One of the most incredibly faith-filled statements in the whole Bible is Mary of Nazareth's response to the angel Gabriel when he tells her that she will become pregnant by the Holy Spirit with God's son, Jesus (Luke 1).

What if that were you? Would you argue, cry, flip out, or consider an abortion? This didn't seem like a good fit for Mary's life at the time. Her world surely was turned upside down. Mary's response is one of complete submission. *"Mary said, 'I am the Lord's servant. May it be to me as you have said'" (Luke 1:38).*

What courage it must have taken to face people's stares and accusations! Even Joseph had his doubts until the Lord spoke to him in a dream. Joseph could have denied Mary, and most likely she'd have been stoned to death. Mary and Joseph's response is one of complete submission. God was Mary's hope because she knew he was the God of the impossible. Often we avoid doing what is right because we're worried what others may think. It's hard to completely submit to the Lord's will, to give him complete control in faith, but that's what we're asked to do.

Reflection: Managing our own lives has failed. Are you ready to cry, "I quit?" Once we admit our powerlessness, a door opens to the solution to our problem.

~ *A man who has his Bible at his fingers' ends, and in his heart's core,
is a champion in any conflict; you cannot compete with him.* ~

Charles Spurgeon[196]

Day 210: The Courage to Surrender

God's Champion Girl, desiring change, forges ahead displaying courage. Courage means releasing control, allowing God to begin the powerful transformation process. *Surrender, in this case, is not a sign of weakness, but courage.*

You may be saying, "Surrender implies so much! I have had so much pain and suffering. There is so much of my self-will remaining. I can't entirely give it up, because I know it will cause too much trouble and agony." God accomplishes our surrender.

God does not ask you to surrender in your strength or by the power of your will; God is willing to work it in you.

You are very important in the kingdom of God. The purposes of God will prevail in your life once you have surrendered your depression, anger, addiction, bitterness, and selfishness. Or do you want to wait until something else changes?

Look at Abraham in the Old Testament. Do you think it was by accident that God found him? Or that it was Abraham himself, apart from God, who had such faith and such obedience? No. God raised him up and prepared him as an instrument for His glory.

Reflection: Ask yourself, *Am I really willing?* Begin each new day with a simple prayer: "Lord, I surrender my life to you. I choose your will be done, not mine. Give me grace to be a surrendered child today. In Jesus' name. Amen."

~ All my life I labored for success, wealth, acceptance, and power. The more I obtained, the less I discovered I had. Surrendering everything in absolute brokenness; however, was the beginning of finding the identity and purpose for which I had battled so hard. ~

Charles Colson, Founder, Prison Fellowship[197]

Day 211: Never Surrender

Never Surrender! *What? That's not what you said yesterday!* Let me explain. Today when we turn on our televisions, we're quickly reminded that Christian values and virtues are disappearing. But there is one virtue that should never be laid down: the virtue of hope. Regardless of how bleak your circumstances may look, hope can continue. Hope cannot be taken from the Christian, but it can be put off.

Hope is an emotion that holds us steady. It's an anchor keeps us from drifting into deeper water. Hope is the joy of tomorrow. When we lose hope, we lose our freedom and joy. There is no anchor. When you have hope, you can change. You can heal. Someone once said: *hope is a memory of the future.* Therefore never surrender your hope!

Whenever we pray with hope, we give ourselves completely to God, surrendering to his love. The more we surrender, the more we heal, and the more his love fills us. Up to now, believing in God did not always mean accepting his power. As Christians we know God but do not necessarily invite him into our lives. Jesus said in John 14:26 that the Holy Spirit would be sent in his name to teach us and remind us of all he has said. Our situation is not hopeless. Our hope lies outside of us. Jesus is the answer. Proverbs 16:3 tells us to commit to the Lord whatever we do, and our plans will succeed.

As long as God exists, there is reason for the Christian to hope. After all, God is in charge of the present and future, not society. Refuse to surrender your hope in God. Praise him another day. He is our glory and joy!

Reflection: How will you find the courage to go on and fight?

~ *What oxygen is to the lungs, such is hope for the meaning of life.* ~

Emil Brunner[198]

Day 212: Olympic-Sized Faith

Called, the *favored few,* the Olympians prepare harder than any other athletes. They train longer, sacrifice more, and endure more pain and fatigue. That is the cost. To become an Olympic-caliber athlete requires more than skill. It takes dedication, determination, and patience. It takes an "I can do it" and "I can wait" attitude.

It takes a willingness to shake off past failures and defeat. When there's no strength left, the athlete regroups and tries again until she succeeds. If she misses this year's Olympics, she waits four more years. For all great athletes, the grind precedes the glory. Spectators only see them cross the finish line. They don't see the discipline, work, and exercise. Only then comes victory. Similarly, the Christian life is training and work.

Speaking of his own strivings, Paul said, "Forgetting the past and looking forward to what lies ahead, I strain to reach the end of the race and receive the prize for which God is calling us up to heaven because of what Christ Jesus did for us" (Philippians 3:13–14, TLB). The word *race* is from the Greek *agon,* from which we get *agony.*

Most people protect themselves from any form of discomfort, but our race is demanding and grueling. Some days it takes minute-by-minute effort to finish strong. Paul's efforts to grasp the fullness of joy in Jesus Christ were obtained by grasping a hold of him. Jesus' strength enables us to let go of the past and finish the race. This is security.

Reflection: Are you training your mind to think present-tense godly thoughts?

> ~ *There is an art of forgetting, and every Christian should become*
> *skilled in it. Forgetting the things which are behind is a positive*
> *necessity if we are to become more than mere babes in Christ.* ~
>
> A. W. Tozer[199]

Day 213: Faith that Perseveres

Sometimes for seasons, or days, or hours, our faith seems invisible. Nothing is worse than when God feels distant. Instead of feeling like the King's daughter, a Cinderella at the ball in the arms of a handsome prince, we feel like Cinderella, the maid, pushing a dirty, wet mop around and around.

When I feel like this, I remember what Jesus said, "If you have faith as small as a mustard seed, you can say to this mountain, 'Move from here to there' and it will move. Nothing will be impossible for you" (Matthew 17:20).

All of us have made mistakes and experienced devastating setbacks. Regardless of your past defeats, you are not disqualified from competing in the race of life. Yes, you may have missed plan A, but God has a plan B, C, D—all the way to plan Z. God promises to help you get across the finish line and onto the winner's platform.

In his last days, Paul said, "I have fought the good fight, I have finished the race, I have kept the faith" (2 Timothy 4:7). I want to say those words when my race is over. Make it your single purpose to forget what is behind and reach for what's ahead.

Pray: "Lord, I am going to put my past behind me and start today fresh. My mistakes, my regrets, my disappointments do not define me. I am going to press toward the goal to win the prize. In Jesus' name. Amen."

Reflection: Write out what a fresh start looks like in your life today.

~ *Courage is the price that life exacts for granting peace. The soul that knows it not, knows no release from little things.* ~

Amelia Earhart Putham[200]

Day 214: The Resilient Champion

I am awed by what some women will do to pull themselves out of a pit. They have an ability to overcome adversity many of us could only imagine. What do these women have that we don't have? Resiliency, which is the ability to recover readily from illness, depression, adversity, or the like.[201]

The resilient champion girl *learns* to adapt in the face of trauma, significant loss, tragedy, and stress. We often think of it as bouncing back. Anyone can learn and develop resiliency. It is forged through, not despite of, adversity.[202]

Our difficulties can either transform or destroy us. We have seen through the lives of other women that God can use adversity to refine our character and hone our understanding of him in our lives. We bounce back because he extends us grace. Clinical social worker and nurse Marian Eberly affirmed:

> It is in suffering that we experience the conflict of knowing God has allowed it and not knowing how we will make it through apart from His mercy and grace. In suffering we have the opportunity to discover the dialectic of suffering hardship as we explore God's personal gifts of resiliency.[203]

Reflection: You can rebound from your situation. Pray and ask the Holy Spirit for guidance and resiliency to get over the forthcoming hurdle.

~ Consider it a sheer gift when tests and challenges come at you from all sides. You know that under pressure, your faith-life is forced into the open and shows its true colors. ~

James (James 1:2–3, Msg)

Day 215: Pressing On

As we continue to press on in the fight for joy, we will find, and enjoy, the glory of God. If God is for us, then who can be against us? God says, "I will give you a new heart and put a new spirit in you" (Ezekiel 36:26). He does just that. But we have to allow him to take us through the process, however long it takes.

When I completely surrendered my will to God, I began an incredible new journey to clean up the emotional damage that led to my depressive behavior. It was an extensive process. My heart and soul were like a smelly onion, layered with rejection, hurt, fear, deception, and shame. Before God could start peeling away, I had to take the first step and admit that I sincerely needed him in my life.

The enemy will tell you what's done is done; you can't change the past. He'll tell you that no one cares to hear your complaints. He'll tell you that talking about your pain won't take it away. That's a lie. I brought my issues into the light and refused to believe these lies anymore. Satan was defeated and the healing began.

We refuse to be a perpetual victim of the past or present. We refuse to be secretive about any issues any longer. Satan is darkness. Jesus is the light. "God is a sun and shield" (Psalms 84:11).

The prophet Hosea said, "Let us press on to acknowledge him [the Lord]. As surely as the sun rises, he will appear; he will come to us like the winter rains, like the spring rains that water the earth" (Hosea 6:3).

Reflection: What do you want God to begin to peel away first? Pray about this, as he might have a different onion layer in mind.

~ *God says, "I put to death and I bring to life, I have wounded and I will heal, and no one can deliver out of my hand."* ~

Deuteronomy 32:39

Day 216: He Will Put It Right

As I became firmly grounded in my identity in Christ, God assisted me, as he will you. He will help you in time (be patient) to resolve conflicts of the past. He will give you the perseverance and strength you need to complete the journey. Let go of the scorecard if there is one. Set aside your picture of the perfect world. Accept that there are things out of your control. We can't right all wrongs because we are not God. When we put our issues and trust in God's hands, then we truly become conquerors.

> No, in all these things we are more than conquerors through him who loved us. For I am convinced that neither death nor life, neither angels nor demons, neither the present nor the future, nor any powers, neither height nor depth, nor anything else in all creation, will be able to separate us from the love of God that is in Christ Jesus our Lord (Romans 8:37–39).

Reflection: Ask God to help bring to your mind different situations in these areas and write them down. Confess them in prayer. Then ask God to help you fight them going forward through the Holy Spirit.

~ *Wisdom and transformation lie not in finding an answer to all of ones questions, but rather in the encounter with the living God.* ~

Anonymous

Day 217: God's Girls Naomi and Ruth

Rosie became depressed when she moved across the country to take her dream job. She was so excited about this job that she didn't expect to miss her family and friends so much. Rosie walked into a battle of the blues. So much of life is about making transitions. Often that transition requires losing something we value. When we move, we lose daily contact with the familiar. When we live somewhere for so long, we can take people in our lives for granted, which reminds me of Naomi in the book of Ruth.

We meet two women who had Olympic-size faith: Ruth and Naomi. Ruth, a virtuous woman who lives above the norm of her day, and Naomi, a woman whose dreams completely shatter. The events take place during a period in Israel's history that is depicted as rebellion and immoral. The story's emphasis is usually placed on either their friendship or Ruth's love interest, Boaz. This book is the story of Naomi's despair.

Because of famine Naomi, her husband, and two sons moved to Moab from their home of Bethlehem (Ruth 1). There is no warm welcome, most likely because the Moabites were in conflict with the people from Naomi's home, the Israelites. Despite that, her two sons found Moabite women to marry, Ruth and Orpah. Then tragedy strikes. Naomi's husband dies followed by the death of her two sons. Is it any surprise Naomi felt alone and desolate? The dreams Naomi once had for her future seemed shattered.

Reflection: What transition has had a profound effect on you? How did that event change your life?

~ *Never assume God's silence or apparent inactivity is evidence of His disinterest.* ~

Dr. James Dobson[204]

Day 218: Naomi's Losses

Transition creates stress, and stress can lead to the blues or full blown depression. In Naomi's days the sons provided for widows. There was no other way a woman could provide for herself. Women were totally dependent on their men to care for them. Naomi lost her family and financial support. She had no further stake in Moab and decides to return to Bethlehem where she could reconnect with relatives and friends.

Thinking of what is best for her daughters-in-law, Naomi tells Orpah and Ruth to stay in Moab. Naomi was pessimistic about her future and pretty sour. "It is more bitter for me than for you, because the LORD's hand has gone out against me" (Ruth 1:13). All these losses would affect anyone's spirit, and now the anxiety of moving again. Orpah eventually agreed, but Ruth refused to leave Naomi and accompanied her to Bethlehem.

The journey back to Israel is not described, but the reception of the two widows by the women in Bethlehem is. When they arrived the people that knew Naomi didn't recognize her. The women exclaimed, "Can this be Naomi?"

"Don't call me Naomi," she told them. "Call me Mara, because the Almighty has made my life very bitter. I went away full, but the LORD has brought me back empty. Why call me Naomi? The LORD has afflicted me; the Almighty has brought misfortune upon me" (19–21).

We find two women struggling with grief, with nothing to look forward to except difficult times, at least that is how it appears at this point.

Reflection: What one experience do you have in common with Naomi or Ruth?

~ *Press on. Nothing can take the place of persistence.* ~

Calvin Coolidge (1872–1933)

Day 219: The Mood Changes

God guided Ruth to the field belonging to Boaz (the hero of the story), who showed special concern for her. Naomi's mood began to change. "Praise the Lord for a man like that! God has continued his kindness to us as well as to your dead husband!" Naomi cried excitedly (Ruth 2:20, TLB).

The following scene takes place at the threshing floor. Ruth expressed her desire to marry Boaz, according to the custom of the kinsman-redeemer. The hope of an Israelite woman was that the nearest kin to her dead husband would take her as his wife—termed a kinsman-redeemer. But Boaz told her that another man had prior claim. The other relative renounced his claim, and long story short, Boaz married Ruth.

Two things can be said: God must feel at least as compassionate toward all the Ruths of Moab, and every other outcast land, as Boaz felt toward Ruth. God is the God of redemption, with the desire and the power to redeem all into fellowship with himself.

God's plan is to incorporate all people into his plan for blessing. In the end, God provides for Ruth's needs and Naomi realizes that God is not against them. She cheerfully tells Ruth, "He has not stopped showing his kindness to the living and the dead" (2:20).

Reflection: When have you felt that God was against you or unavailable, only to later realize he was there all along?

> ~ *O Lord our God, grant us grace to desire you with our whole heart; that so desiring we may seek and find you; and so finding you may love you; and loving you, may hate those sins from which you have redeemed us.* ~

St. Anselm[205]

Day 220: A Dream Come True

The epilogue in the book of Ruth relates Naomi's joy at this turn of events. Ruth bears a son, Obed (Ruth is the great-grandmother of King David), but the author shines the spotlight on the response of the townswomen toward Grandmother Naomi. Can't you picture Naomi holding her grandson close on her lap? The author appears to ignore the fact that Ruth gave birth and is Obed's mother, most likely because of her Moabite heritage. There's nothing worse than feeling snubbed or not receiving credit where credit is due!

On the surface, the book of Ruth tells us that no matter how bad things are, goodness can exist if we are willing to make the effort. God's compassion shines through as he looks upon two women who are empty and makes their lives full again. Ruth, like Rahab and Bathsheba, was a foreigner who joined God's plan for Israel.

In the last chapter, Ruth moves from widowhood and poverty to marriage and wealth. Boaz brings a Moabite woman into the family line of David and eventually of Jesus Christ. Would you have thought this story would end this way?

Reflection: How will you begin to use this story to build Olympic-sized faith in your life today?

> ~ *Every day you may make progress. Every step may be fruitful. Yet*
> *there will stretch out before you an ever-lengthening, ever-ascending,*
> *ever-improving path. You know you will never get to the end of the journey. But*
> *this, so far from discouraging, only adds to the joy and glory of the climb.* ~

Winston Churchill[206]

Day 221: MileStone

Steps To Overcome Negative Emotions

Move Forward

We have shed another layer of that old, ugly, smelly onion. We're moving forward and taking responsibility for what God has given us. You have probably figured out that being a Champion Girl takes not only courage but discipline. We cannot change successfully if we're not disciplined.

Challenge the Old Way of Thinking

"And now, my daughter, don't be afraid. I will do for you all you ask. All my fellow townsmen know that you are a woman of noble character" (Ruth 3:11).

We, too, are called to change our thinking so we can live a life of noble character—of excellence:

We trust God's provision: shattered dreams are necessary for spiritual growth. We return (repent) to God. When we hurt we often turn away from God, especially if we feel he could have intervened.

We make a commitment to others (God's people) by showing mercy and compassion.

Day 222: Pray and Meditate

The Serenity Prayer

God grant me the serenity
to accept the things I cannot change,
the courage to change the things I can,
and the wisdom to know the difference.
Living one day at a time,
enjoying one moment at a time;
accepting hardship as a pathway to peace;
taking, as Jesus did,
this sinful world as it is,
not as I would have it;
trusting that You will make all things right
if I surrender to your will;
so that I may be reasonably happy in this life
and supremely happy with You
forever. Amen.[207]

Self-Soother

This week has been pretty heavy. Today let go of your inhibitions and do something fun and silly.

Part Twelve

The Victorious Girl

Encouraged by God's Word

"When the angel of the LORD appeared to Gideon, he said, 'The LORD is with you, mighty warrior.'" (Judges 6:12)

Gideon was a warrior who argued with God's choice of leadership. He was so terrified of his enemies that he was hiding! *Yet* the Lord called him a valiant warrior.

Day 223: Mercedes's Story

Mercedes froze when she heard the news. The love of her life, her dad, had just died unexpectedly from a heart attack. Of all the siblings Mercedes had been the closest to her dad, depending on him for guidance and support. Her experience of grief, anger, fear, confusion, and sadness was more intense than anything she'd ever experienced before. The grief and anger were intensified because she felt her mom and sisters were taking his death too lightly.

This vulnerable moment in Mercedes's life opened the door to an enemy named Ed: the eating disorder. She was depressed and didn't want to deal with this loss, so anorexia and bulimia offered her a way out. It preoccupied her mind so she wouldn't have to think about what her dad's death really meant.

"The dieting and throwing up feels like a way of letting my pain and feelings out," she admitted.

In her senior year at college, Mercedes gazed in the direction of an unknown future. Her expectations about adulthood weighed heavily on her heart. She had planned to go to medical school and become a physician like her dad, but he was no longer available to guide her. Unsettling questions began to abound.

"Am I smart and good enough to succeed and forge ahead? Do I have any strength left to stand up for myself? Will I measure up to what is expected of me?"

Ed whispered to Mercedes, *You don't have what it takes to do it on your own ... but everything's possible through me.* Does this sound familiar (hint: the serpent to Eve)?

Reflection: What do you have in common with Mercedes?

~ We are inclined to believe those whom we do not know
because they have never deceived us. ~

Samuel Johnson[208]

Day 224: Mercedes Meets Jesus

Mercedes met Jesus through a Christian group at her college. Jesus helped her see that her enemy, Ed, was the devil disguised as an eating disorder: "a skeleton with a knife, little red eyes, and a black cape."

She recalls, "Ed, took over my life. He even had the audacity to offer to do for me what I imagined my father doing for me. I see that Satan has told me lies over the years. How God really sees me has brought me into a deeper relationship with him."

"I realize that I can't overcome the temptation to binge and purge on my own; I have to trust God's Word and not Satan's lies. I've given Satan practically my whole life through this disease; but no more. I've started to write down the lie I believe and putting the truth from God's word next to it. I'm memorizing God's wonderful verses to transform my mind and heart. It's amazing how quickly I'm changing from the inside out. I've begun to see life outside of my inner struggles. God is building joy inside of me."

Previously Mercedes thought that she could do everything through her dad. Then her thinking said she could do everything through her eating disorder, but she fought back and found the truth; *I can do everything through Jesus Christ!* She became God's Victorious Girl. In the Scriptures God supplies the essentials for discovering our true significance and worth.

Reflection: What one lie do you now recognize you have believed for years? Pray for a verse or passage that will replace that lie with God's truth.

~ *Sadly, we would rather believe a lie than venture into
unfamiliar territory—even into freedom and truth.* ~

Barbara Wilson[209]

Day 225: The Warrior Draws Strength

Like Mercedes, many of us question who we really are. Our culture says, "Be strong, be thin, be self-sufficient, be successful, and be the perfect wife and mother." When stressful situations or people enter our lives, often we feel weak, dependent, and insufficient and think, *I'm not normal! What's wrong with me?*

Our culture has embraced a definition for strength that excludes any feeling of neediness. No one talks about being made in the image of God and what that really means. We give up. We admit defeat. Most role models say, "When life gets tough, just grit your teeth and bear it. Don't let anyone see your angst."

We do just that, grit our teeth harder and harder until we can't take the stress anymore (and have to wear a night-guard because we're grinding our teeth in our sleep).

Instead of wanting to climb the mountain, we lack the mere motivation to even put on our mountain boots. Fear and doubt settle in. Maybe we begin to overeat, not eat, isolate, or have a glass or two of wine to de-stress and forget. Mental and emotional strength are the name of the game, and our image and self-worth are the prize. If you look strong and are in control, you're the woman!

Dr. Robert McGee wrote, "As Christians, our fulfillment in this life depends not on our skills to avoid life's problems but on our ability to apply God's specific solutions to those problems. An accurate understanding of God's truth is the first step toward finding our significance and worth."[210]

Reflection: How close is this description to your present circumstances?

~ *It often seems that unsuspecting believers are the last to know this battle is occurring, and they don't know that Christ has ultimately won the war.* ~

Dr. Robert S. McGee[211]

Day 226: The Warrior Knows Her Enemy

The Victorious Girl starts her journey in the battlefield! In every battle there is an enemy. We call ours the enemy, devil, Satan, the adversary, the tempter, or Lucifer. The Bible tells us the devil is real. He is powerful and incredibly subtle. He seeks to thwart any momentum toward fulfilling God's will. Understanding as much as we can about our enemy is important because his mission is to deceive, tempt and destroy us, which is why we must learn his strategy and how to fight him.

Satan doesn't hate me personally. He hates the image of God in me. Because he hates God, and all that God loves, he hates me. Satan's intent is to confuse me spiritually, darken my heart and encourage me to hide secrets. He was successful for more than twenty years of my life. He would remind me over again that I was dirty and worthless, so I erected more invisible walls to guard from more pain.

Many of you have done the same, eventually losing the ability to feel anything. Satan will use our temperaments and physical condition to further our blues.

Jesus warned that Satan is a thief that comes only to steal, kill, and destroy (John 10:10). He said the devil was a murderer from the beginning, not holding to the truth for he is a liar and the father of all lies (John 8:44). If you don't believe he is real, that means he can come in under your radar screen. As long as we maintain our status quo or disbelief, Satan will leave us in peace. When we seek Christ, he will go on the attack, and we need a strategy to fight back!

Reflect on what you have just learned and this quote.

> ~ *The devil's one object is to depress God's people so that he can go to the man of the world and say: Do you want to be like that?* ~
>
> D. Martyn Lloyd-Jones[212]

Day 227: The Warrior Fights Incapacitating Lies

You are entering enemy territory—the battle zone. Satan wants to keep you out. He's got a "Do Not Enter" sign posted at the entrance of your dungeon named *Secrets*. His power is in your secrets. Satan tried to keep me from confronting dozens of lies, one being the disgrace I felt for engaging in premarital sex. That kind of secret follows you into your marriage. Jesus instructed, "For whatever is hidden is meant to be disclosed, and whatever is concealed is meant to be brought out into the open" (Mark 4:22).

What? I can't do that! Scripture also promises that we are never left to fight our battles alone. As God's Victorious Girl, you have the power of faith within you to overcome. Call upon that power. Secrecy prevents us from hearing the truth, and Satan uses secrets to rob us of the joy and peace and healing that God wants us to give us.

The Victorious Girl listens to the Word of God and stores it in her heart, and her faith grows stronger each day. She fights for truth in her life. You say, "I can't! I've been sick too long. I can't get well." Clear your mind of I can't! God says that you can do all things through Christ who will strengthen you (Philippians 4:13). Remind yourself today and every day: *I am a child of the Almighty God! I can fight back.*

Reflection: Are you ready to commit to a new pattern of thinking and talking? If yes, what are your immediate expectations? If no, what are your fears?

Satan knows that you will be more vulnerable to deception if you are not regularly meditating on God's Word. What things will keep you away from consistent study of the Word? What can you do to change that?

~ Try Jesus. If you don't like Him, the devil will always take you back. ~

Bumper sticker

Day 228: The Strong Need for God

God wants to turn us, the wounded, into warriors. For a moment, close your eyes and imagine yourself fully clad as a warrior.

We all handle stress differently. Therefore the path to wholeness will be different and unique to each person because that is how God has built each one of us. What we have in common is the strong need for God.

In the Bible (Judges 13) Samson was a good-looking guy with an eye for beautiful women. Today he'd most likely be competing in body building contests enthroned by groupies. Yet, Samson violated God's law on many occasions. He was controlled by sensuality, confided in the wrong people, and used his gifts and abilities unwisely. What Samson didn't realize is that he needed God to meet him in his weakness.

He needed God's Spirit to supply the power to resist temptation. Temptation can be much bigger than sexual temptation as in Samson and King David's case. It is often associated with self-desire, gossip, anger, or yielding to feelings of unworthiness. These things separate us from God and are evidence of the tempter's handiwork.

Each one of us is vulnerable, but no one has to yield to temptation. Each Christian has God's Spirit living within, a force more powerful than any attack from the tempter's hands. We have a choice. We can draw from God's strength, then pull out our sword, wield it about strongly, and say no!

Like Samson, we need to ask God to meet us in our weaknesses so we can fight.

Reflection: What difficulties or weaknesses are you facing today that could tempt you to use your own methods in seeking an escape rather than God's?

~ *The* LORD *is a warrior; the* LORD *is his name.* ~

Exodus 15:3

Day 229: Debilitating Deception

The Bible likens Satan to five different animals: a serpent (Genesis 3:1; Revelation 12:9); a bird trying to spoil God's harvest (Matthew 13:5, 19); a wolf (John 10:12; Matthew 10:16); a lion, and a dragon trying to destroy Jesus Christ (Revelation 12:1–9).

Today he's selling his message—the deception—through romance novels, magazines, music, movies, soap operas, ads, and television. Living in an age of advertisement, how better to subtly assault us!

The two most powerful men in the Bible said this about deception. Jesus said, "Many false prophets will appear and deceive many people" (Matthew 24:11). Paul warned, "Let no one deceive you with empty words" (Ephesians 5:6). Satan may also pose as someone giving sincere counsel, which is why it is imperative we know God's Word on particular subjects.

Satan is merely a fallen archangel who received his name because he opposed God. He is our adversary. We must consider him to be that—no more and no less. Satan is a created being with limitations. John 12:31 tells us that Satan shall be cast out. He has already been defeated through the death and resurrection of Jesus.

Then why are we talking about him? Because his destruction is not finished. Our challenge is to recognize his strategies and tactics, and then resist those tactics.

Reflection: Are you up to the challenge? Why or why not?

~ *Never let yourself succumb to feelings of divine betrayal, which is Satan's most effective tool against us. Instead, store away your questions for a lengthy conversation on the other side, and then press on toward the mark.* ~

Dr. James Dobson[213]

Day 230: The Warrior Fights Giants

I love the story of David and Goliath (1 Samuel 17). A brave boy approaches this giant with only a shepherd's sling. Without armor or a shred of fear, little David announces God's victory. The ogre has a demonstrative attitude, but David is optimistic. He has absolute belief in God's strength. He knows he will conquer this giant with spiritual weapons.

Today countless giants take us on—depression, fear of failure, feelings of unworthiness or inadequacy, which becomes our self-talk.

The Israelites spent forty years in the desert. It was a trip that should have taken about eleven days. It wasn't distance that stood between them and the Promised Land; it was the condition of their hearts. We do somewhat the same thing because we take our eyes off God and have a pessimistic heart condition. I heard it once said, "The pessimist may be right in the long run, but the optimist has a better time during the trip."

The optimist has Jesus in her life. It is Jesus that helps her get around the mountain. Pessimism may be part of our life experience because of our circumstances. The pessimist probably doesn't rely on Jesus, because if she did, she would know that when faced with any difficult situation, Jesus would walk her through it.

Reflection: Do you consider yourself an optimist or a pessimist? If you say pessimist, how's that working for you (as Dr. Phil says)?

> ~ *What do we do when life is piling on top of us? Many times we bury our optimism, our hope, and our joy and react with fear, anger or weariness, allowing overwhelming circumstances to knock us flat ... we can choose to intentionally respond to any circumstance with optimism, hope and joy.* ~

Dr. Gregory Jantz[214]

Day 231: Our Mind is Like a Computer

It's been said that a pessimist sees the difficulty in every opportunity; but an optimist sees *the opportunity in every difficulty*. How do you talk to yourself when you make a mistake or walk into negative circumstances?

Each of us have years of rejection, hurt, deception, and anger programmed in our minds, much like a computer. We made a choice: to believe the data or not; to delete the data or not. One way we promote and sustain optimism and joy is to intentionally fill our brain (our computer) with positive self-talk or positive data. Unfortunately, like a computer's hard drive, the negative data can be recovered, which again, is the reason we must chose to learn new ways of thinking and talking.

Pastor Lloyd-Jones wrote:

> It is because we listen to the devil instead of listening to God that we go down before him and fall before his attacks. That is why the psalmist keeps on saying to himself: 'Hope in God for I shall praise Him.' He reminds himself of God because he was depressed and had forgotten God.[215]

When I sense these fears and doubts (negative data), I pull up positive data like David's story. David used a stone. God tells us to use the power and knowledge of the Bible, our faith, and prayer to fight. His good conquered an evil giant bent on destruction. As God did this for David, he will certainly do it for you and me—if we believe.

Reflection: The Bible says, "For as he thinketh in his heart, so is he" (Proverbs 23:7, KJV). So, how are you? Choose today to focus on optimism, hope, and joy.

~ *When there is room for doubt, the optimist fills the gap with hope.* ~

C. Peterson[216]

Day 232: God's Girl Deborah

Judges 4 and 5 are two of the earliest passages that portray women in roles other than victims or villains. Deborah was the only woman in Israel to become a judge or a leader. She was called the mother of Israel, loving her people as her own children. They came to her for guidance. And she was a prophetess. What is your image of Deborah?

Unlike other leaders, Deborah was not power hungry. She was able to plan, direct and delegate effectively. Deborah's relationship with Barak (the male military commander who, with Deborah, destroyed the Canaanite army under their leader, Sisera) says a lot about this woman as a leader. Deborah was a woman who respected the people God put in authority, notably, Barak.

Often it is assumed that Deborah was given a leadership position because men failed to do so. Because Deborah is a prophetess, her words are identified with God's words, and this is her authority for leading Israel: she knows God's mind. Barak may not have initiated the campaign or destroyed the enemy, but he does what he is called to do, letting others have the glory. Barak trusts more in Deborah's relationship with God than in his own relationship. Deborah calls Barak in her role as a prophet, an envoy of God.

On Mount Tabor, Deborah announces the victory. She herself does not go down to the battle. Her role is to inspire, predict, and celebrate in song. God fought the battle. After the victory over Sisera, Deborah sang a song of praise to the Lord. When it would have been tempting to take personal credit, she didn't.

Reflection: How often do you try to take credit for what God has orchestrated?

~ There is only one thing that makes a dream
impossible to achieve: the fear of failure. ~

Paulo Coelho

Day 233: God's Girl Jael

As Deborah and Barak (Judges 4 and 5) led their men into battle against the Canaanites, a mysterious woman took center stage in the history of God's people, Jael. With the battle won, fleeing on foot, the Canaanite leader Sisera fell into a trap laid by this woman. Jael's husband, Heber, a Midianite, was on good terms with the Canaanites, so Sisera thought he had found safe haven when he arrived in their camp.

Jael unassumingly hid Sisera in her tent, gave him a drink, and covered him. Then ... surprise! "Jael acts with callous efficiency. She picked up a tent peg and a hammer and went quietly to him while he lay fast asleep, exhausted. She drove the peg through his temple into the ground, and he died" (4:21).

Oh my! Were you expecting that ending? Deborah's song of praise depicts Jael a heroine (5:24–27). Through Jael God fulfilled Deborah's prophecy: "for the LORD will hand Sisera over to a woman" (4:9). She, too, was part of God's plan.

I'm thinking of two farm girls—one fiction, one not. Dorothy in the *Wizard of Oz* stumbled upon Oz, not because she was looking for adventure but because her feelings were hurt. Yet she's the one to bring the Wicked Witch down! Joan of Arc, an illiterate, receives a vision from God and ends up leading armies to war! There is glory to your life that the enemy fears. Your life story is one of assault by the enemy because he knows what you could be ... and fears it. Be courageous! Be encouraged! Be victorious!

Reflection: How does this story encourage you about God's plan for your life?

~ Courage doesn't always roar. Sometimes courage is the quiet voice at the end of the day saying I will try again tomorrow. ~

Anonymous[217]

Day 234: Gifts and Competencies

What impression has Deborah left on you? Deborah does not immediately believe that God called her alone to free Israel. She realized that God would do much of the work through Barak.

Deborah trusts God. She knows he's already taken care of business. She kept perspective, versus thinking about her position, herself. This is probably the reason she was used. She gave God control, and he gave her a way to serve.

Deborah challenges us in several ways. She reminds us of the need to be available to both God and others. She wanted only to serve God. Her story shows how God can accomplish great things through people who are willing to be led by him. I could have easily felt unworthy to serve with my past, but then the enemy would have won the battle.

Deborah used her gifts and competencies to give her people forty years of peace. Under Deborah's inspired leadership, the poorly equipped Israelites defeated the Canaanites. The flooding of the Kishon River evidently interfered with the enemy's impressive chariots (5:21–22), and the Canaanites retreated to the north. They never reappeared as an enemy within Israel. The Song of Deborah (Judges 5) is a poetic version of the account recorded in Judges 4.

Like Esther, Deborah and Jael were called to do a special job at a special time. Each woman was patient and willing. They impacted their world.

Reflection: What has God asked you to do that may be atypical?

~ *If not now, when?* ~

Jewish scholar Hillel (30b.c.- 10a.d.)

Day 235: MileStone

Steps To Overcome Negative Emotions

Move Forward

Moving forward is the process of recognizing defeated thinking. When (not if) negative thinking and painful emotions surface, remind yourself who you belong to and that you have moved on. Breaking free of toxic feelings empowers us to live more productively. It means encouraging ourselves and then deleting the negative data daily. Nothing is wasted by God and he is using your experiences to change you.

Challenge the Old Way of Thinking

Lack of joy literally distorts our perception so that good becomes bad, and bad becomes disaster. The more we frame things negatively, the more unhappy we feel.

Let's see where you are today:

Exercise 1: If you've just rear-ended someone, what three things would you say to yourself? First, write them down, and then finish this exercise. We will explore the possible scenarios:

One: I magnify my blame and say, "I'm sooo stupid." This crushes me as an individual and leaves no room for forgiveness.

Two: I minimize my responsibility and say, "I'm not responsible. It's not my fault!" I don't learn from the situation and become a better person. Neither option allows me to experience truth or grace and grow.

If we carry on these types of conversations with ourselves multiple times a day, can you see that the cumulative effect can be significant? Our self-talk gets out of balance. I either become a victim of my own perfectionism, or I hold myself captive to my own mistakes. If we want a healthier relationship with others and ourselves we learn to engage in more realistic and truthful self-talk. In this auto accident, truthful self-talk says, "I acknowledge accidents happen. I am grateful I have car insurance and that no one was injured." Did you notice I did not beat myself up or let myself off the hook either?

Exercise 2: Your teenager gets poor exam results. Do you see your reaction style in this list?

> I'm such a lousy mother. He's obviously feeling neglected at home and is trying to draw attention to himself.

> His life is ruined; he'll end up on the scrap heap without good grades.

> He won't get into college now. When his finals come up and he does just as badly again, it'll be a disaster. He's doomed to being one of life's failures.

Write a positive counterbalance if your answer was one of these.

Someone once said that if you can't have the best of everything, make the best of everything you have!

Day 236: Pray and Meditate

Life is risky business. We have many reasons to distrust people and situations in our life. Unwavering confidence in God is our antidote for fear and loneliness. We chose to trust God for wisdom and protection. Meditate on, or rewrite, these verses as they speak to you.

> The LORD is my light and my salvation–whom shall I fear? The LORD is the stronghold of my life–of whom shall I be afraid? When evil men advance against me to devour my flesh, when my enemies and my foes attack me, they will stumble and fall. Though an army besiege me, my heart will not fear; though war break out against me, even then will I be confident (Psalm 27:1–3).

Self-Soother

Brian Wilson (of the Beach Boys) said, "I can hear music ... sweet, sweet music."

Music lifts our spirits, engages our minds, and relaxes our bodies. Put on some soothing or upbeat worship music. Sing and dance—loudly! Let yourself go!

Day 237: God's Girl Anne

When I became a Christian, I expected all my negative thoughts would *Poof!*
Disappear! The Bible said that when I was born-again I became a new creation!
However, I found myself in the desert asking, *If I've changed so much, why do I*
still compare myself to other people? I didn't feel particularly transformed. *Shouldn't*
my old mind tape be wiped out and replaced with a new Christlike one? Why do I still have
these old negative thoughts? God's Girl Anne had a similar experience.

Excerpt From *Released From Bondage* by Dr. Neil Anderson:

> Dr. Anderson: I have struggled through my whole Christian experience
> with bizarre thoughts that were so embarrassing I usually never told any-
> one. I tried once to honestly share part of what I was struggling in a
> Christian group. People sucked in their breath, there was stiff silence, and
> then someone changed the subject. I could have died.
>
> I didn't know what it meant to take every thought captive. I thought
> all those thoughts were mine. There has always been a terrible cloud
> hanging over my head because of these issues. I never could accept the
> fact that I was really righteous because I didn't feel like it. Praise God it
> was only Satan—not me. I have worth! The problem is so easy to deal
> with when you know what it is.[218]

Reflection: How similar are your thoughts?

~ There is always a struggle, and sometimes there is a pitched battle with our
own nature where the lines are so confused that it is all but impossible to locate
the enemy or to tell which impulse is of the Spirit and which of the flesh. ~

A.W. Tozer[219]

Day 238: The Battles Rages On

I have a wonderful relationship with God, yet I still sin and think negatively. The battle continues to rage—my flesh against my spirit. Believe it or not, God is not surprised. I've known many righteous women whose lives fell apart because they got so frustrated with sin and falling short of their own high expectations.

Oswald Chambers said, "If you are not right with God, you can never turn your mind anywhere but on yourself."[220] If we want victory in our lives, we must clearly take the focus off ourselves and identify our enemy. Scripture is clear the enemy isn't one demon but an entire legion of evil spirits (Mark 5:1–20).

As you have seen from my story, my wilderness mindset, or wrong way of thinking, kept me from dealing with those areas God wanted to touch and heal. I was going around and around the same mountain. God showed me the way out of the desert! He helped me identify and change those wrong mindsets.

I am God's Girl, which means I have a new way of thinking. I've been rescued from the desert and I will show you the way out!

Reflection: These feelings and questions are common, and answering them is part of our healing journey. Ask God in prayer today to show you your wilderness mindset and help you make the necessary changes.

~ *The way to triumph over adversity is to use it for the good of others.* ~

Dr. Gregory Jantz[221]

Day 239: The Enemy's Beatitudes

An old fable tells the devil offered his tools for sale. He displayed these tools—malice, hatred, jealousy, deceit, guilt, and several others, with the prices marked on them. One of them was set apart, marked with a higher price than the others. When asked why, he said, "Because that is my most useful tool; it is called depression; with that I can do anything with people."[222] Recognize his tools and tactics, which often lead to depression.

This is a powerful illustration called *Satan's Beatitudes (Satan's Sermon):*

> Blessed are those who are too tired, too busy, too distracted to spend an hour once a week with their fellow Christians in church ~ they are my best workers. Blessed are those who wait to be asked and expect to be thanked ~ I can use them in my business.

> Blessed are those who are touchy. Soon they will stop going to church ~ verily, they shall be my missionaries. Blessed are those who sow gossip ~ they are my beloved children. Blessed are those who have no time to pray ~ for they are my prey. Blessed are those who cause trouble ~ for they are my secret agents. Blessed are you when you hear this and think it has everything to do with other people, and nothing to do with you. ~ I've got room for you at my inn. [223]

We have all fallen for Satan's tactics. He is a discourager and pulls us down emotionally, spiritually, and financially—any way he can. Don't stress. We have hope! Jesus is our encourager. He came to give us peace, joy, and the tools to fight this battle.

Reflection: Do you see yourself in any of the beatitudes?

~ No one ever told me that grief felt so like fear. ~

C.S. Lewis[224]

Day 240: The King of the Jungle

One of the most erroneous images in our culture is the picture of a little devil dressed in a red bodysuit and holding a pitchfork. This cute little caricature couldn't be further from the truth. Peter tells us the truth: "Be self-controlled and alert. Your enemy, the devil prowls around like a roaring lion looking for someone to devour" (1 Peter 5:8).

Lions are beautiful animals and described as kings of the jungle. As magnificent as they are, the fact is lions stalk their prey and destroy it. A lion sets his own rules. Just as a lion is the king of the jungle, Satan is the prince of *this world* (do not confuse with our Prince of Peace).

There is no love or mercy or forgiveness in his jungle. He has been around for a long time, prowling like the lion, stalking his prey, and waiting for the precise moment to attack. The lion defends his territory, as does Satan. Satan's territory is doubt, accusation, temptation, deception, and delusion, which create strongholds in our heart and mind and soul—an area of dominance.

Peter said, "Be self-controlled and alert," which we can't be when our lives are out of balance. Today Satan is much more subtle. It seems he likes to prey on our self-image and our relationships with his tools called deception, shame, and fear.

Reflection: How aware have you been of the king of the jungle in your life and the effect he has on the balance?

~ *We have nothing to fear from truth; only ignorance can hurt us.*
New truths always challenge old opinions. But new truths never
destroy old truths; they merely separate truth from falsehood. ~

William LaSor

Day 241: Deception, Shame, and Fear

Most of us didn't plan for our life to turn out this way. I'd be a millionaire if I received a nickel every time I said, "If I could do this part all over again." You know most of my story by now. The one part I always hesitate to talk about is how I tried to satisfy my need for love in the arms of men. With each man there was the dream of love and commitment, but most of the relationships ended with brokenness and pain.

One of the many consequences was getting pregnant. When I aborted that baby, he arrived in heaven safely in the arms of God while I continued to retreat into my dungeon. I had to hide down there because I was so ashamed.

Although I became the perfect Cover Girl, choosing just the right mask to wear that particular day, I was still imprisoned. The more I hid, the more I feared coming out. *No one can know! If they find out my secret I will be ostracized. I just can't take any more rejection!* Whenever I thought about what I did, the more I was thrust myself further down into the quicksand of isolation and secrecy.

Barbara Wilson, author of *The Invisible Bond,* writes, "Whether we enter into it voluntarily or have it forced upon us, sexual sin causes severe wounds and scars that need more than forgiveness. They require healing."[225]

Healing requires breaking those sexual bonds. Healing of any sin requires breaking those invisible bonds—the bonds of deception, shame, and fear.

Reflection: Talk with God in the area of deception, shame, and fear. Ask God to help bring to mind different situations in these areas.

~ *The* LORD *is with me like a mighty warrior.* ~

Jeremiah 20:11

Day 242: The Perpetrator of Lies

There's a joke that goes, "If you want to make people angry, lie. If you want to make people livid, tell the truth." Lies are Satan's biggest weapon. A lie is a false statement made with deliberate intent to deceive, an intentional untruth.[226] Satan is the perpetrator and the propagator of lies.

Satan has been telling us for years that God could never love someone like us or could never use us, and if we work hard enough at being good enough and showing others how to be good, then he might have mercy on us. Satan aggressively sells his lies to every Christian. He knows that if we catch just a tiny glimpse of God's grace and his truth, then we will be on fire for Jesus.

It's not easy to hear Jesus' voice in a world that shouts, "You're no good." "You're ugly." "You are worthless." "You are appalling." "You are a loser." These voices (these lies) can be so loud and persistent that they become believable. That is Satan's tactic, the trap of self-rejection.

Jesus completed his intended work on earth, and the enemy can do *nothing* to change God's plan of salvation. What he can do is keep people from hearing the truth of the Gospel message and alienate us from God. Truth is powerful. Jesus said, "You will know the truth, and *the truth will set you free*" (John 8:32). The soul will not be healed without truth.

Reflection: What negative voices do you struggle with? In what ways do you find yourself agreeing with them?

~ *God's my strong champion; I flick off my enemies like flies.* ~

Psalm 118:7 (The Message)

Day 243: The Antidote: Truth

God loves you just the way you are. Not because you're good enough, pretty enough, smart enough, or work hard enough. He loves you for just being you. Satan doesn't sell that message. His sales pitch spells discouragement, deceit, and destruction.

Satan works in harmony with the flesh (mankind's born nature and inner tendency to sin). If a person struggles with lustful thoughts, Satan will take advantage and exploit this tendency. He will stimulate the natural inclination and introduce new thoughts and ideas. He will nudge the person into acting on the fantasies.[227]

It is important to recognize that Satan alone can't destroy things like your self-confidence, marriage, finances, but it is his lies that have the power to destroy. His voice doesn't roar, "I'm going to lead you into an affair." He'll quietly whisper, "Doesn't that man seem interesting? Get to know him better!" See how subtle he is? We actually spend more time believing Satan's lies than believing what God says—the truth.

We all fall into the temptation trap, which is why we must learn the truth about God. Then we are set free. God is whispering, *I have called you by name from the very beginning. You are mine, and I am yours. You are my beloved. On you my favor rests. You belong to me.* Each time we choose to listen to God's Word, we discover a desire to listen more and more to his still, quiet voice.

Reflection: What two specific things can you do starting today to begin separating truth from deception?

> ~ *Success, popularity, and power can indeed present a great*
> *temptation, but their seductive quality often comes from the way they*
> *are part of the much larger temptation to self-rejection.* ~
>
> Henri J.W. Nouwen[228]

Day 244: The Temptations of Jesus

Giving into temptation has been a serious problem for centuries and is part of our lives today. Jesus told his disciples that hard trials and temptations were bound to come (Luke 17:1). He understands how you feel under the weight of temptation. He has faced the tempter, Satan, and overcome the darkness and adversity associated with Satan's fiery trials. Matthew 4:1–11; Mark 1:12, 13; and Luke 4:1–13 record the events.

After the baptism at the Jordan River, when God's voice spoke from heaven and said, "This is my beloved Son," Jesus was led into the lonely wilderness for forty days. Satan found Jesus all alone in the wilderness, so he tempted him.

The first temptation was in regard to food. Satan intended to thwart Jesus' dependence on his Father by causing him to use his own resources to meet his need for food. *If you have a desire, it deserves to be fulfilled!*

The second temptation Satan hoped to lure Jesus into testing God's Word. Satan quotes the Bible accurately. The third temptation was in regard to power and wealth. Satan knew about God's plan to save people from their sins through Jesus. He tried to spoil that plan by tempting Jesus. *You can achieve your goal through me!* All three temptations were virtuous temptations versus sinful (or vice).

Reflection: Jesus faced what you face—temptation by Satan. How will use this knowledge to move forward?

~ *Lord, always remind me that while I have no control over being tempted, I can avoid thoughts, situations, people, and desires that I know will harm me.* ~

Fletcher Spruce[229]

Day 245: Satan's Tactics

Satan tried to get Jesus to listen to his cunning plans, to open his heart to sin, just as Adam and Eve did, but Jesus would not listen. When the forty days ended, Jesus grew very faint and hungry, for he had eaten nothing. Satan remembered how he had tempted Eve to eat pleasant food and how this temptation had caused her to listen to his words. Adam and Eve were deceived. Perhaps the Messiah (the second Adam) could be.

Satan said, "If you are the Son of God, command that these stones become loaves of bread" (Matthew 4:3). He thought Jesus would surely yield to this temptation and try to prove that he was God's Son. But Jesus answered, "It is written: Man shall not live by bread only, but by every word of God" (4:4).

Jesus retaliated by quoting Scripture (God's Holy Word). Although he was hungry and faint, Jesus would not use his great power to please himself. Satan soon saw that he could not cause Jesus to yield to such a temptation, so he tried another tactic.

Taking Jesus to the uppermost part of the temple in Jerusalem, he said, "If you expect people to believe that you are really God's Son, you must show some great sign. Now cast yourself down to the ground and trust God to protect you and keep your bones from being broken; for in the Scripture he has promised that angels will bear you up and not allow any harm to befall you" (4:5). Jesus answered, "It is also written ... " (4:6).

Reflection: Satan uses Scripture to tempt Jesus. Do you think he would do that to you? If you said yes, you are correct. How do you fight back?

~ Faith will not stop temptation, but it will stop you from yielding.
Faith will not hold back trouble, but it will get you through it. ~

Douglas Connelly[230]

Day 246: Never Give Up

Even though Satan used Scripture to push Jesus to do this foolish deed, Jesus would not obey him. For Jesus knew that the Scriptures had forbidden any one to tempt God in such a foolish manner. The third time Satan brought out his greatest temptation. He took Jesus to the top of a high mountain and caused him to see all the kingdoms of the world. "These great kingdoms are mine," said the tempter, "and I can give them to any one I choose. Now I will give them to you if only you will fall down and worship me" (Matthew 4:8–9). Jesus knew that Satan's words were not true.

Jesus said, "Get away from me, you evil one! For it is written in the Scriptures that the Lord God is the only being who should be worshiped" (4:10). Jesus tells Satan to go away and leave him alone. You can do the same thing. Say it out loud. You have the power and authority to send away Satan and his demon army.

Then Satan left Jesus alone (4:11); for he could find no way to crowd sin into the pure heart of the Son of God. When he went away, the angels came from heaven and supplied Jesus' needs. How they must have rejoiced at the Savior's victory over the evil one! I believe the angels rejoice when we are victorious. Just as Jesus warred with Satan while on earth, we also are at war with him. Our power is the same Jesus relied on—the power coming from God's Word and our filling of the Holy Spirit.

Reflection: Write in your journal about your most recent victory.

~ To avoid temptation, remember HALT. Don't get
too • Hungry • Angry• Lonely • Tired ~

Dr. Charles Stanley[231]

Day 247: Our Temptation

Luke 4:13 says, "When the devil had finished all this tempting, he left him until an opportune time." Satan would be back. He always comes back. He waits for just the right moment. Even Jesus was tempted by Satan to turn away from God but saw through the enemy's schemes. Jesus remained firm in his love and devotion to the Father.

Jesus was tempted in every way we are tempted. He responds by pushing Satan away using Scripture and verbally telling Satan to get lost. That means Jesus understands how we feel when Satan whispers into our hearts and urges us to sin or do something that is over-virtuous (Hebrews 4:15). He knows how to help us when we call upon him in prayer. We need to recognize that one of Satan's most powerful tactics is temptation because it strikes at our points of weakness.

Temptation (that which has been labeled off limits) often means you are distracted and have desires for something or someone. That person or circumstance suddenly aligns into an attractive opportunity. There is a difference between temptation and sin. Being tempted is not a sin, as in Jesus' case. It is not sin until we give into the temptation and it turns into action.

Often we wonder what we did wrong to invite temptation. As Jesus demonstrates, the answer is often nothing.

Reflection: What has been your most recent temptation? What is your strategy for fighting back?

~ *Right is right, even if everyone is against it; and wrong*
is wrong, even if everyone is for it. ~

William Penn[232]

Day 248: Avoiding the Hole

Autobiography in Five Short Chapters by Portia Nelson[233]

Chapter I: I walk down the street. There is a deep hole in the sidewalk, and I fall in. I am lost. I am helpless. It isn't my fault. It takes me forever to find a way out.

Chapter II: I walk down the same street. There is a deep hole in the sidewalk. I pretend I don't see it. I fall in again. I can't believe I am in the same place, but it isn't my fault. It still takes a long time to get out.

Chapter III: I walk down the same street. There is a deep hole in the sidewalk. I see it is there. I still fall in. It's a habit, my fault. My eyes are open. I know where I am.

Chapter IV: I walk down the same street. There is a deep hole in the sidewalk. I walk around it.

Chapter V: I walk down another street.

Too often we're told just to stop a sinful behavior. We don't stop to examine and free ourselves from the root cause. *Why do I keep walking down this street?* Moving forward requires understanding why and how we fall into the hole—the enemy's trap.

First, we give the enemy access, access in the form of a potentially toxic or fearful situation. Satan plants the lie. We listen to the lie: "You're going to botch that up because she's better than you." We think about the lie, dwell on it, and begin to follow what has been placed in our mind. We contemplate that the message feels or sounds right, so we believe the lie. The lie looks attractive. We rationalize the lie and then consent and act on it. Beliefs that produce negative behavior (fear, jealousy, etc.) get stronger.

Reflect on both of these scenarios and how each applies to your life today.

~*Temptation usually comes in through a door deliberately left open.* ~

Anonymous

Day 249: Enduring Temptation

Temptation is the classic way Satan operates by enticing believers into sin, which is why he is called the tempter (1 Thessalonians 3:5). He watches for distraction, fatigue, hunger, weakness, and then attacks with a tempting offer. It is at that point that we make a choice—to let him in or shut him out. To be tempted is not to be dominated or controlled by Satan. Every Christian is tempted. To succumb to the temptation and fail to appropriate the power of the indwelling Spirit of God is to surrender one's heart and mind to the devil, giving him a foothold.

Why would God allow temptation? Through Jesus' example we know it is to strengthen our faith and spiritual muscles. If we never had to stand against temptation, we might never know our own spiritual strength. Facing temptations will bring out either the best or the worst in us. Temptation is an opportunity for obedience, leading to blessings.

To resist temptation we need to: 1) Recognize the temptation, the lie; 2) Stand firm and say no when confronted with what we know is wrong; 3) Pray for the strength to resist and are sensitive to God's Spirit when we feel the attack of the enemy.

The apostle James gives us confidence: "Blessed is the man who perseveres under trial, because when he has stood the test, he will receive the crown of life that God has promised to those who love him" (James 1:12).

Reflection: Think about how you can raise your awareness of the enemy.

~ *I find that if I seek God first, it saves so much time, worry, and uncertainty.* ~

Fiona Castle[234]

Day 250: The Tactics: Fear, Doubt, & Guilt

Some of the Satan's most powerful weapons are psychological. Past crises and problems have translated into present worries, doubts, and anxieties. Fear is one. Fear of a failed relationship. Fear of isolation and despair. Fear of disease or death. Fear of feeling this way forever. We say, "If only things were different, I could relax." Yet even when everything is going fairly well, we still get anxious that something is wrong.

Then there is his powerful gun called guilt. Long-standing guilt is hard to shake off; an uneasy sense of self-condemnation hangs over many of us like smog. If we constantly feel guilty, we can never be completely free. Because calamity is not always the result of wrongdoing, we must guard against assigning or accepting blame for every tragedy we encounter.

This is the key: God only holds us accountable for what we do, not what other people do. As long as we are following God's way of life (called obedience), we needn't worry or feel guilty about other people's opinions or responses to us. Think about how much of your guilt is unnecessary? How often has something you fretted over *not* come to pass? When we lean on God for strength and peace, there is often a quiet awareness in the midst of the chaos. We sense the Lord is with us ... and in control.

Reflection: I hope you feel like you are beginning to get to know yourself better. Start to get in the habit of focusing on the present and recognizing your strengths. Ask God to use your weaknesses (and your past, if it's for his glory).

~ *Never stop because you are afraid - you are never so likely to be wrong.* ~

Fridtjof Nansen (Norwegian explorer, scientist, and diplomat)

Day 251: What If? If Only!

For years Satan never stopped playing with my mind, the "what if...what might have been" game. I believed my life would have been different if I hadn't fallen into the dungeon of depression and addiction. I felt I threw away my perfect American Dream.

Two more powerful words are "if only." Two words that say, "If only my circumstances were different, I would be different." "If only I had (you fill in the blank), I'd be happy!" "If only my family was different, I'd have turned out functional!" (By the way, there is no completely functional family.) "If only I followed Jesus starting as a teenager, my life would have turned out like a princess's!"

What we are saying is that something or someone made me the way I am. If our circumstances make us what we are, then we are all victims. *I'm not responsible!* We ask over and over why God keeps piling on problem after problem. It's easy to take on the victim role and assume that people will just accept us this way because we've had such bad luck. That's the enemy's tactic and he wins!

The trouble with "if only" and "what might have been" is that nothing changes. We move backward instead of forward. These thoughts are road blocks for not trying. The key is to recognize these thoughts as lies and stop our minds from even going there.

Reflection. Think about what "if only's" and "what if's" have gotten in the way of the change and direction God has called you? Realize that while we're bemoaning our past, we're crippling ourselves from living in the present and future.

~ *Form the likeness of your Son in me by transforming my fears to courage, my struggles to conquests, my frustrations to faith, my losses to hope, my suffering to health.* ~

NBW [235]

Day 252: Busting Lies, Shame, and Fear

When I speak at women's retreats, each woman is given a balloon and marker. She draws her face on the balloon and then blows it up. I ask each woman to stand up, think about the biggest lie she has been believing, and share the lie with God. Her marked balloon represents that lie in her life. Then I tell them, on the count of three, sit down and bust the balloon—bust the lie. "One-two-three! Satan's domain over this lie has now been broken!" We rejoice ... and have a good laugh. I encourage you to try it!

This journey you are on is about exposing the lies, shame, and fear. We all battle these debilitating forces. Our only alternative is to fight back. March on, Christian soldier! Our battle plan consists of five parts:

Recognize Satan's lies, which means understanding how we develop our negative self-talk.

Reject negative and distorted thinking.

Replace, or reprogram, negative thinking with truthful thinking (God's Word).

Renew your mind, aiming for a Christlike mind.

Resist, as in fight back and pray for strength.

The Victorious Girl fights back by choosing to believe God's promise: "For everyone born of God overcomes the world" (1 John 5:4).

Reflection: What lies do you now recognize as enemy contraband?

~ *A lie gets halfway around the world before the truth has a chance to get its pants on.* ~

Winston Churchill[236]

Day 253: MileStone

Steps To Overcome Negative Emotions

Move Forward

Oswald Chambers wrote, "If the Spirit of God detects anything in you that is wrong, He does not ask you to put it right; He asks you to accept the light, and He will put it right. You will never cease to be the most amazed person on earth at what God has done for you on the inside."[237] This is hope!

Talk with God in the area of lies, shame, and fear. Draw three columns and name them Lies, Shame, and Fear. Ask God to help bring to mind different situations in these areas and write them down. Confess them in prayer. Then ask God to help you fight them through the Holy Spirit and go forward.

~ All growth that is not towards God is growing decay. ~

George MacDonald [238]

Day 254: Challenge the Old Way of Thinking

We are God's Girls—beautiful, wonderful, and capable, worthy of love and joy. We each have a gift to give the world that no one else can duplicate because no one else is made exactly like us. We are fearfully and wonderfully made!

The problem is we don't believe it because we have never recognized our negative self-talk as enemy contraband. When we have a negative attitude, only two people can change it: the Holy Spirit and us. However, the Holy Spirit won't act if we don't ask and work our battle plan. You have the power to choose to change your thinking today.

Are you committed? Ready to fight back? Let's go!

Instead of saying "if only," replace those two words with "next time." You say, "If only I went to that women's retreat, then I'd know more women—stupid me!" This is a whisper from the enemy!

Instead say, "Next time there's a women's event, I will go and not be afraid they will reject me."

~ A thousand voices clamor for our attention, and a thousand causes vie for our support. But until we have learned to be satisfied with fellowship with God, until he is our rock and our fortress, we will be restless with our place in the world. ~

Erwin W. Lutzer[239]

Day 255: Pray and Meditate

In Psalm 21 David praises God after victory in battle. When God answers your prayer for victory, thank him. Mediate on this psalm and thank God for your victories.

How the king rejoices in your strength, O Lord! How he exults in your salvation. For you have given him his heart's desire, everything he asks you for! You welcomed him to the throne with success and prosperity. You set a royal crown of solid gold upon his head. He asked for a long, good life, and you have granted his request; the days of his life stretch on and on forever. You have given him fame and honor. You have clothed him with splendor and majesty. You have endowed him with eternal happiness. You have given him the unquenchable joy of your presence. And because the king trusts in the Lord, he will never stumble, never fall; for he depends upon the steadfast love of the God who is above all gods. Your hand, O Lord, will find your enemies, all who hate you.

When you appear, they will be destroyed in the fierce fire of your presence. The Lord will destroy them and their children. For these men plot against you, Lord, but they cannot possibly succeed. They will turn and flee when they see your arrows aimed straight at them. Accept our praise, O Lord, for all your glorious power. We will write songs to celebrate your mighty acts! (TLB)

Self-Soother

List five things you would do differently with your life if you could.

Day 256: LaTanya's Story

Recently LaTanya attended a women's retreat. During the last session, the leader asked for prayer requests. LaTanya stood up reluctantly and confided in a small voice that her husband (who was an elder in the church) was having an affair. She had confronted him and he admitted it. She began crying as she disclosed that he was more than likely going to leave her for this woman. She sat back down, slumping in her chair like a limp, well-worn rag doll, embarrassed that she had revealed this secret.

When LaTanya got home from the retreat, her husband had moved out. In the days to come, what hurt LaTanya even more was that none of these women followed up with her or offered to pray with her.

A voice whispered in her head, *You idiot! Why did you tell them? Think of the gossip that's going to start now. Everyone will be pointing fingers at you. You did something to make him run into the arms of another woman! Stupid loser!*

No one expressed understanding or support. In fact, some women expressed the opposite—they avoided her. She wondered why the church was treating her like a piranha. The voice got louder. *See, I told you! You're insignificant! Those women don't care about you!* LaTanya's value as a person was under attack because the very place she looked for acceptance wasn't radiating with love or forgiveness.

Reflection: When have you ever felt a similar attack?

~ *I wanted a perfect ending. Now I've learned, the hard way, that some poems don't rhyme, and some stories don't have a clear beginning, middle, and end.* ~

Gilda Radner[240]

Day 257: LaTanya's Pity Party

LaTanya, whose husband was leaving her for another woman, prayed and mustered up enough courage to meet with the pastor to discuss this dreadful event. She hoped for some answers, but after their discussion she realized he didn't understand the pain she was in. His advice was to join a women's Bible study. How could she? She had fallen into depression and couldn't concentrate long enough to make a grocery list.

The voice said, *I told you. He thinks you are a whiney housewife who deserves what she got. Just forget talking to anyone else about this. Don't bother to even go back to church.* LaTanya agreed with the voice. She felt degraded and was too humiliated to go back there. She wallowed in self-pity and depression for six months. The hate, bitterness, stomachaches, and insomnia were taking their toll on LaTanya.

Through the honesty of a true friend, LaTanya realized she held a pity party on a daily basis. She agreed she needed counseling, in addition to rekindling her relationship with God. Her journey to wholeness began.

King David often entered God's sanctuary. As David listened, he got a proper perspective on things. He meditated on God's Word and saw by way of contrast how blest he really was. David's pity parties changed to praise and worship. That is the key: to meditate on God's Word day and night, allowing it to penetrate our spirit and soul.

Reflection: What sort of thoughts have you had lately causing you to arrange a pity party? Explain.

~ *Self-pity is our worst enemy and if we yield to it, we can never do anything good in the world.* ~

Helen Keller[241]

Day 258: The Warrior Resists

Pity parties are the enemy's orchestration. Paul teaches us to resist going to the party. We learn to set our minds on things above, not on earthly things or false emotions (Colossians 3:2). Wrong or wilderness mindsets affect our circumstances and our spiritual life. One of miracles of the mind is that once we learn something it becomes automatic and unconscious. For example, when you first learn to drive a car, you learn to steer, brake, and judge distance. It requires all of your attention. Eventually driving a car becomes automatic. You pay little attention because it has become unconscious.

Our thinking processes are automatic and unconscious. We develop automatic thinking patterns in childhood. Some of those patterns are distorted, which we bring into adulthood. Distorted or negative thinking is any reasoning process that distorts God's reality. It is blindness to the truth. That's Satan's strategy: to blind our minds to the truth.

When I became a Christian, I expected all the corrupt data in my mind to be instantly deleted. I thought the old mind tape would be replaced with a new one. I became somewhat confused. *Does this mean I'm not a real Christian?*

Satan was planting seeds of doubt in my mind. But I am also reminded that God is in control, not Satan.

Reflection: In what way does this compare to how you are presently living?

~ A woman is like a tea bag—you never know how
strong she is until she gets in hot water. ~

Eleanor Roosevelt[242]

Day 259: Kimberly's Mindset

When I was twelve I wanted to be a supermodel, despite the fact that my nickname was Bozo. My mind said that beauty is the road to being accepted, successful, being loved, and getting a husband. What I ended up learning was if you place a high value on beauty (or maybe it's possessions), the devil points out how you don't have it; he plays on your desire to have beauty (or possessions), which may become an obsession, as it did with me.

I believed in God, but I worshiped the gods and idols of plastic perfection, which ultimately made me feel worthless and humiliated because I couldn't measure up to their standards.

Paul said that he wanted to do, think, and be the best; however, he still had those stinky thoughts and made mistakes. Today I would love to be the perfect wife and teacher, and I try to follow this great plan. But I'm human; therefore I fall for the lies and negative emotions. I still enjoy life, despite the fact I have such thoughts and make mistakes, because I walk by faith. I have been given a new heart, and I believe what God's Word says not only about God, but about me, and so I get back up.

Part of our battle plan is digging deeper into the subject of mind renewal and learning how to get back up after we fall into the hole by deprogramming corrupt data.

Reflection: Where do you see a similar parallel in your life?

~ *The Lord gets His best soldiers out of the highlands of affliction.* ~

Charles Spurgeon[243]

Day 260: Our Incredible Mind

I listened to a woman describe her experience of living within a religious cult community for twenty-four years. She said the leadership dictated how she should think, act, and feel. They induced feelings of fear and guilt in order to control her, and their mission was to make a lot of money. I took this all in and thought to myself, *This doesn't sound much different from the way I was living!*

Cults usually use a three-point process, which ironically correlate to our lives.

Control information in order to limit one's choices. A parent or spouse is often labeled a controller. They have a domineering and manipulative effect on how we think and act. They take our ability to make choices away from us and violate our boundaries.

Use deception. In America the media, music, novels, and the Internet control what we see and hear. We are told that if we make enough money or have enough "stuff" or seek a cosmetologist or are famous, then we will be secure, important, significant, and confident. Life will be easy!

Use group pressure. We all face peer pressure to conform, regardless of our stage in life—some negative, some positive.

The fact is we're all vulnerable to powerful influences of mind control.

Reflection: How does your life or present situation relate to a cult's three points?

~ There is no neutral ground in the universe; every square inch,
every split second, is claimed by God and counter-claimed by Satan. ~

C.S. Lewis[244]

Day 261: The Warrior Girl Rejects

When we hear the word religious cult we think "brainwashing." My brainwashing was like a cake mix with three ingredients. One, I saw "perfect" women modeling what I should look and be like. The supermodels, super moms, super business women. Two, add to that the messages from my family, peers, boys, and teachers, which formed my self-image. Three, add to that thousands of daily media messages. Mix them together and bake. *I'm fat, ugly, and can't do anything! I hate life. No one will ever love me because I don't fit this mold!* Putting on frosting called a mask won't even help.

That's Satan's plan, to make us feel like a failure so we won't even try anymore. Isaiah 35:8 tells us that our own natural way of thinking, even as Christians, is not only different than God's, but it's usually totally opposite from God's.

My personal search for happiness and acceptance railroaded me into that battlefield. Not with fighting soldiers, but a battlefield full of invisible land mines, disastrous and disguised weapons belonging to the enemy. That is Satan's method. He subtly gains access to our thought processes by planting that land mine called a lie, but when we stop that lie from exploding, we witness a change in ourselves, and it becomes a positive habit. *I like thinking this way! I'm going to work at doing it more and more!*

Reflection: What one new thing will you begin doing to stop the lies from exploding? (One strategy: Review Day 248, Avoiding the Hole)

~ *Being confronted by our thoughts and feelings isn't*
necessarily negative. The source can be promptings from the Holy Spirit
leading us into truth ... or the enemy's attempt to throw us off course. ~

Yvonne Martinez[245]

Day 262: The Warrior Girl Renews

Our culture doesn't always think of the mind when it thinks of devotion to God or loving others. The heart is equated with love, but the Bible is emphatic that we use our mind to love God and others. Therefore we need to take a closer look at what is filtering through our minds and why. Quite often we don't like what we see. When we begin the process of mind renewal, we find it plays out in the battlefield.

Without a renewed mind our lives remain as they've always been, no matter what we do or what we try. No matter how many retreats we attend or how many books of the Bible we read or how often we go to church, if we don't have a mind change, we will still have the same problems and failures and defeats. Let God transform you into a new and different person. Not the television version of an extreme makeover, but by changing the way you think. Mind renewal is our key to freedom and joy.

How do we begin to renew our mind? It is a process. The apostle Paul gives us instructions in the epistles. Romans 12:2: "Do not conform any longer to the pattern of this world, but be transformed by the renewing of your mind."

In other words, *submit* your heart and mind to God. Don't be molded or copy the behavior and customs of this world because they are selfish and corrupting. Let God transform you into a new and different person by changing the way you think. This is a picture of *submitting* to the will of the Father and to the character of the kingdom.

Reflection: Pray. Ask God to begin opening your mind to the renewal process.

~ *Yesterday, we did the best that we could. Yesterday is over. We have slept. We think we know some of what today will hold.* ~

Anonymous

Day 263: The Warrior Recognizes & Confesses

Have you ever bought a new car? When you do, suddenly you notice the same car everywhere. Before you purchased the car, in your mind there were zero. Those cars were always there; you simply didn't notice them before. Because you put thought and effort into selecting this particular car, your mind now tends to notice this type of car wherever you go. The same thing happens when you identify negative thinking and lies.

The key is to recognize the negative thought, confess it, then reject it. That means catching the thought, talking about it with God and asking him to show you *why*, starting a process that allows God to change the way you think through the Holy Spirit.

You say, "That's too hard!" You're right! But I have exciting news. Paul said that, as Christians, "we have within us a portion of the very thoughts and mind of Christ" (1 Corinthians 2:12–16). When transformation begins in the mind, God gives us part of Christ's mind.

The enemy will try to discourage us from putting these steps in place, but we move forward, drawing from the power of Jesus Christ. And Paul encourages us, "Let us not become weary in doing good, for at the proper time we will reap a harvest if we do not give up" (Galatians 6:9).

Reflect on this incredible revelation!

> ~ *Some persons grumble because God placed thorns among roses. Why not thank God because He placed roses among thorns?* ~
>
> Benjamin Franklin

Day 264: MileStone

Steps To Overcome Negative Emotions

Move Forward

Negative thoughts are indirect attacks by the enemy, which often lead to guilt, fear, doubt, anxiety, "if only," and low self-esteem. Each toxic thought has the power to shackle us, in spite of great experiences and our faith and knowledge of God. Do you recognize your negative thinking arising out of one or more of these everyday attacks?

Strife and disharmony often disrupt my family life.

Someone has treated a person I love unjustly, and I am angry, bitter, cynical—unforgiving.

I have anger issues. I get defensive.

I suffer from guilt because I feel I'm inadequate.

I fear others will see the "real" me.

I struggle with envy by comparing my life to
friends' or other families' life styles.

I struggle with insecurity, worry, and anxiety over the future.

My prayer life is inconsistent, and I feel God
doesn't want to listen to me anyway.

When these thoughts rear their ugly faces, stop them and go to prayer. Give yourself a pat on the back for recognizing they are from the enemy. Then confess them to God. Poof! That negative thought has been destroyed … for now. Remember, the enemy always comes back.

Day 265: Challenge the Old Way of Thinking

We have a choice: keep acting on the lies, or close down the field containing the land mines. In other words, we recognize and then reject the lies. How? We feed ourselves God's Word—Bible food. As we dwell on the truth, we begin to act on what God says and not what the enemy says. We change our negative self-talk into God-talk, disabling the enemy.

Pray and Meditate

Lord Jesus, we are on the lookout for You today.

We know that You will come in ways we least expect You,

In answers we never hoped we could find,

In love we do not deserve.

Lord, keep us surprisable by Your innovating power.

Amen.

- Lloyd John Ogilvie[246]

Self-Soother

Think of one nice thing someone did for you recently.

Say thank you every chance you get, to God and to others. This is a wonderful pick-me-up!

Day 266: No Place for Stupid

There is a popular novelty T-shirt slogan that says, "I'm with stupid" with an arrow pointing in both directions, insulting the person standing next to the wearer. Books, songs, Internet forums, and television programs have been created around the theme "I'm stupid" or "I'm with stupid." Who hasn't felt stupid? Even Mother Teresa confessed in prayer to an archbishop, "I am so stupid."[247] That's corrupt data!

God's Word says *you have a portion of the mind of Christ.* Believe it! As you recognize a lie, defend yourself out loud: *I'm not stupid!* Replace the lie with God's thinking, the truth. Say, "I am [verse] ... " Truth sets us free from the bondage of thinking we're dumb.

Paul wrote in his letter to the Philippians, "Make my joy complete by being like-minded ... Each of you should look not only to your own interests, but also to the interests of others. Your attitude should be the same as that of Christ Jesus" (Philippians 2:2–5).

Paul is saying that our mind and our attitude should be same that Jesus had. That doesn't come naturally, does it? Some days don't you feel like screaming, *If you want breakfast in bed, sleep in the kitchen!* Don't fret. The good news is simple: if you have given your life to Jesus, Jesus has given himself to you. He has made your mind his home. Just having this knowledge is one weapon you have against the enemy.

Reflection: How does that make you feel to learn this? Fearful or humbling?

~ Anger is a blocked goal to fulfill a need in my own way. ~

Unknown

Day 267: Developing Humility

Sometimes we develop humility the hard way. It is our human nature to do and say things that put the spotlight on us. At seminary I was first accepted into a short-term certificate program. At orientation I met another woman who was in the master's program. I thought, *I want that!* I didn't get any information about the master's program. I definitely didn't ask God his opinion, the one person who destined that I go to seminary in the first place! I filled out the paperwork and then registered for classes. I immediately started bragging, "I'm in the master's program at seminary." Basically, *Aren't I hot stuff? Don't you admire me?*

After starting classes I received a letter stating my grade point average from college wasn't high enough to be accepted into the program. If I could get a 3.0 grade point average in the certificate program, I could be admitted later on into the master's program. Moving slowly with my tail, called pride, between my legs, I had to cancel my classes and pay a drop-out fee.

Often the self-confidence we try to portray is only a mask to hide our fear of failure or insecurity. Satan was trying to destroy my future ministry. Maybe he's got you believing this is the best life can be … accept and cope as best you can. Those voices were loud and condemning. They were not from God. His voice isn't prideful and obnoxious.

Reflection: If you've gotten this far today, God has successfully spoken to you. Keep the airwaves open. Your heart and spirit are prepared to receive the truth.

~ A proud man is always looking down on things and people; and, of course, as long as you're looking down, you can't see something that's above you. ~

C.S. Lewis[248]

Day 268: God's Girl Miriam

Recall Miriam, Moses' sister (Day 59). Years later we briefly meet Miriam, now a courageous woman who sought God's will (Numbers 12:10–14). God chose her to be an esteemed leader. The years of slavery had been hard for Miriam and her people. There was abuse, fear, death, anger. Over two million people left Egypt, including Moses, Aaron, and Miriam, with the Lord at their side. Then Pharaoh had a change of mind. He sent his vast army out to capture the Israelites but lost the battle (Exodus 14:21–25).

The party began! Singing! Dancing! With all the women following Miriam, she sang out her song of praise to God. She was also a prophetess, speaking the word of the Lord to the Israelites, *but* Miriam had a critical spirit. One day Miriam and Aaron were criticizing Moses because his wife was an (inferior) Cushite woman.

Her critical spirit landed her in the prison of isolation for a week. Scriptures says she became "leprous, like snow." Moses asked God to heal her. The LORD replied to Moses, "Confine her outside the camp for seven days; after that she can be brought back" (12:10). I'm sure that gave her time to think about her harmful attitude.

Miriam's story is an incredible example of God's willingness to forgive those who sin. She paid the consequences for her actions and returned a humbled and forgiven woman. Miriam was a woman of influence. Despite "falling into the hole," God still used her. We, too, are capable of the same sinful actions, and God will discipline those he loves. But that anger only lasts a moment. His favor lasts forever.

Reflection: When has God put you in a prison of isolation for your critical spirit?

~ *Truth is the most valuable thing we have.* ~

Mark Twain (1835–1910)

Day 269: Absolute Humility

The opposite of pride is humility. Humility is not the same as humiliation (even though it can feel like it). "Absolute humility," said AA co-founder Bill W., "would consist of a state of complete freedom from myself, freedom from all the claims that my defects of character now lay so heavily upon me. Perfect humility would be a full willingness, in all times and places, to find and to do the will of God."[249]

God has designed a *will* for every one of us. Our personality, abilities, vocation, marital status, everything is built into his plan. We each have enormous value. God invests himself in our lives through the indwelling Holy Spirit. He calls us to fulfill his will and commits himself to working for our very best. However, Satan wants us to live a life of EGO: Edging out God.

On the other side of the coin, humility is also acceptance of ourselves. Paul told us that our mind should reflect a servant's attitude, thinking of others, not self. That's counter-cultural! I'll be honest with you. I think of myself quite a bit. It's my sin-nature. I have to work at a mindset of humility. Someone once said, "Humility is not thinking less of yourself; it's thinking of yourself less." It is work, but it is doable, as you will see.

Reflect and pray: "Deliver me, O God, from a false humility that denies your gifts and from an assertive pride that denies your lordship. Help me to see myself as you see me, to accept my limitations and use my abilities to the glory of your name. Amen." (Eugene H. Peterson)[250]

~ *Swallow your pride occasionally, it's not fattening.* ~

Frank Tygard[251]

Day 270: Is Your Mind A Sewer?

An unknown movie critic wrote, "The plot moves rapidly down the sewer. It would not be so damaging to those who watch such trash if the mind could be equipped, like your kitchen sink, with a garbage disposal. Then you could flush away all the filth and be done with it, but the mind does not work that way. It stores up impressions for a lifetime. The only way to protect the mind is to expose it to only the best!"

> Brothers, whatever is true, whatever is noble, whatever is right, whatever is pure, whatever is lovely, whatever is admirable–if anything is excellent or praiseworthy–think about such things. Whatever you have learned or received or heard from me, or seen in me–put it into practice. And the God of peace will be with you (Philippians 4:8–9).

Paul tells us to program our mind with thoughts that are *true, honorable, right, and pure*. Add to that: *dwell on the fine, good things in yourself!* No doubt you've heard the saying, "garbage in, garbage out." What goes into our mind comes out in our words and actions.

Saturate your mind with God's truth. Instead of garbage, tell yourself truths such as, *God made me and loves me as much as anyone else on this entire planet! What I think is important! I don't have to be perfect...I just have to be me! I am a good person—a classic, one of a kind—no one on earth is exactly like me.*

Reflection: Do you think about what is true, good, lovely, pure, and right, or do you think about what is depressing, frustrating, unfair, and wrong?

~ *It is not only what we do, but also what we do not do for which we are* accountable. ~

John Baptiste Molière (1622–1673)

Day 271: The Warrior Girl Replaces

When was the last time you examined what you put into your mind? Are you buying the devil's message through romance novels, soap operas, gossipy conversations, movies, magazines? Perhaps you need to re-examine, because God calls us to live (and think) in purity. As Christians we hear that word a lot—purity. There are several definitions that fit in this context: freedom from anything that debases or contaminates; freedom from guilt or evil or sin; physical chastity or virginity; the absence in speech or writing of slang or other elements deemed inappropriate to good style.[252] But how?

"You were taught, with regard to your former way of life, to put off your old self, [old thinking] which is being corrupted by its deceitful desires [from the enemy] and be made new in the attitude of your minds; and to put on the new self [renewed mind] created to be like God in true righteousness and holiness" (Ephesians 4:22–24).

Don't beat yourself up. *No one* is immune from thinking a negative or sinful thought. Consciously we are learning now to replace or put on the good thoughts and to immediately release the lies, or put off the bad or negative thoughts, by recognizing, confessing, and repenting our corrupt thoughts. Then we can put on the mind of Christ through the Holy Spirit. It takes work, practice, and time, but it is worth it.

Reflection: I hope you feel more confident of being able to recognize (put off) and replace (put on) God-thoughts. As thoughts crop up, pray: "Lord, I take this negative thought and give it to you. I put it off, down the garbage disposal. Lord, please replace this thought with your Word. I put on your truth." That toxic thought has been destroyed!

~ *She who is humble is confident and wise. She who brags is insecure and lacking.* ~

Lisa Edmondson[253]

Day 272: Deprogramming the Data

I was indoctrinated to believe my worth was in what I did, what people thought of me, who I was married to, what I looked like, how much money I made, and whom I associated with. This was deceptive thinking because it was not consistent with the Word of God. What we read or hear may sound, feel, and seem right, but if it is contrary to the Word, it isn't right. It is the enemy. In order to move forward, I had to begin to deprogram. Deprogramming means to counteract the effects of an indoctrination.[254]

Deprogramming requires exposing the effects of deception. It means replacing all lies, deception, and hurt with truth and love. We must give God time to delete the negative programming his way, in his time. "Do not be afraid or discouraged . . . for the battle is not yours, but God's" (2 Chronicles 20:15). We'll never win if we're fighting our own battles. God has his own battle plan, and those who follow it win.

Proverbs 14:12 says, "There is a way that seems right to a man, but in the end it leads to death." If we continue thinking based only on our feelings, we'll end up squashing God's Spirit and not experiencing our purpose and destiny. That's why he is constantly nudging us to put off our way of thinking and put on pure and truthful thoughts. In other words, go the opposite direction and fight for heart and mind renewal.

Reflect on what Oswald Chambers said:

> A saint's life is in the hands of God like a bow and arrow in the hands of an archer. God is aiming at something the saint cannot see, and He stretches and strains, and every now and again the saint says, "I cannot stand any more." God does not heed, He goes on stretching till His purpose is in sight, then He lets fly. Trust yourself in God's hands.[255]

Day 273: Breaking Strongholds

American civil rights leader Frederick Douglass said, "If there is no struggle, there is no progress."[256] God knows that a good way for us to see our true condition is to trip, fall, and break. It's not fun to fail, but that's how God can expose our real self. Once exposed, transformation can begin. Transformation begins with breaking strongholds.

> For though we walk in the flesh, we do not war according to the flesh (for the weapons of our warfare are not of the flesh, but mighty before God to the casting down of strongholds), casting down imaginations, and every high thing that is exalted against the knowledge of God, and bringing every thought into captivity to the obedience of Christ (2 Corinthians 10:3–5, ASV)

Paul mentions three things: strongholds, imaginations, and a thought. A thought unchecked becomes our imagination, which is the action or process of forming images or concepts. Imagination is also the power of forming mental images or concepts of what is not actually present to the senses.[257] Those images we form become our self-talk.

When the thought says *failure, loser, fat,* that image becomes the picture you see of yourself. An image can become a stronghold. A stronghold is the inability in our own strength to break a pattern of habitual sin. Lies are strongholds that can imprison us. Strongholds over my life were food, diet pills, alcohol, and cosmetics because my image was that I had to be beautiful, successful, and youthful in order to be accepted.

Reflection: Name your strongholds (such as food, working out, or approval).

~ *Logic will get you from A to B. Imagination will take you everywhere.* ~

Albert Einstein

Day 274: The Cosmic Battle Front

Yesterday we were told to take captive every thought to Jesus and pull down the strongholds of our minds, those areas dominated with distorted thinking and sin, and to *consciously* putting aside our personal feelings. This is called a battle strategy.

If you are like me, you are often tempted to turn a conversation around so it becomes about you. Try, "Even though I feel like it, I choose not to talk about myself (pride)... I choose not to focus on what she's thinking about me (people-pleaser)... I choose not to worry about the car payment right now (fear)... because God knows my situation and has everything under control! This is a battle for our mind.

This is not a war such as our world fights, but a spiritual war. Every soldier knows that the time to put on armor is before being attacked—not after the fight begins.

> Put on the full armor of God, so that you will be able to *stand* firm against the schemes of the devil. For our struggle is not against flesh and blood, but against the rulers, against the powers, against the world forces of this darkness, against the spiritual forces of wickedness in the heavenly places. Therefore, *take up* the full armor of God, so that you will be able *to resist* in the evil day, and having done everything, to stand firm (Ephesians 6:11–13, NASB, author's emphasis).

This elaborate metaphor conveys that we need protection because there is a dangerous struggle in the spiritual realm.

Reflect on what Skip Toomaloo said: "The Christian's battle is against anyone and anything that efforts offense against the true God. We have been given the tools and the armor to withstand the most violent and evil assaults of the unfaithful."[258]

Day 275: Our Dress Code

We are at war. Are ready to dress up for victory? This is our new dress code for battle—the clothes of Jesus Christ (sorry, you can't find it at the mall):

> Stand firm then, with the belt of truth buckled around your waist, with the breastplate of righteousness in place, and with your feet fitted with the readiness that comes from the gospel of peace. In addition to all this, *take up* the shield of faith, with which you can extinguish all the flaming arrows of the evil one. *Take* the helmet of salvation and the sword of the Spirit, which is the word of God (Ephesians 6:14–18).

Notice the action words "take up." When you do something new, it is a powerful step in the change process. The armor against Satan's strategies is to put on the Lord Jesus Christ. Each piece of armor is a characteristic of the Lord Jesus. Anything I do to make myself more like Jesus is putting on the armor of God. Then I am victorious!

The Belt of Truth

Satan equals lies. Jesus equals truth. It is *so* important that we hold fast to the truth, that we know the truth of who we are *in Christ*. Truth must be the filter for all our perceptions, ideas, and even dreams. We throw them out if the message and feelings don't line up with God's Word, the truth. The truth reminds us that our past, the darkness, is under the blood of Jesus and has already been paid for.

Reflection: Pray, "Guide me in your truth and teach me, for you are God my Savior, and my hope is in you all day long" (Psalms 25:5).

~ *Rather than love, than money, than fame, give me truth.* ~

Henry David Thoreau[259]

Day 276: Breastplate of Righteousness

Our heart is the enemy's target, and we must guard it. By ourselves we have no righteousness; we are only clothed in righteousness when we are in Christ. Righteousness means, "In accordance with virtue or morality; without guilt or sin."[260] Righteousness is the worthiness to stand in God's presence. The moment we accept Jesus Christ, God declares we are no longer condemned sinners. Instead we are forgiven, and we receive Jesus' righteousness. We are now fully pleasing to God Almighty!

We realize our status before God as one who has been acquitted of all guilt and shame. When we put on righteousness, we bring into our life things that are pure—nothing polluting. We acquire personal holiness and develop an upright character.

When Satan whispers you are not worthy of God's love, that you can never get better, or that you are a loser, come into God's presence in the name of Jesus, and refute him, because you are the daughter of the king and clothed in righteousness.

Boots of Peace

The Gospel is about us making peace with God, a person previously at war with the world and Satan. We choose to move forward because God gives us the motivation to continue. We have peace with God through Jesus, and that gives us victory in this war, which drives the believer to share the gospel wherever God calls her.

Reflection: In what areas is Satan attacking you right now?

~ *Peace I leave with you; my peace I give you. I do not give to you as the world gives. Do not let your hearts be troubled and do not be afraid.* ~

The Apostle John (John 14:27)

Day 277: The Shield of Faith

Our faith in God is our protection against those fiery darts, the ugly thoughts and lies that Satan ignites. When Satan lies, tempts or accuses us, we hold up the shield the faith to deflect each fiery dart (1 Peter 5:8–10). We cannot do this on our own. God will keep us strong, firm, and steadfast when we demonstrate faith.

There is an unnamed Canaanite woman in Mathew 15:21–28. She came to Jesus, crying out, "Lord, Son of David, have mercy on me! My daughter is suffering terribly from demon-possession." She was told that she did not qualify for Jesus' help. But this woman had undeniable faith. She believed Jesus was powerful enough to help and compassionate enough to care. Humbly she said, "But even the dogs eat the crumbs that fall from their masters' table." Then Jesus answered, "Woman, you have great faith! Your request is granted." And her daughter was healed from that very hour" (15:28)

Faith is a two-sided weapon. When we step out to do something, it is our faith and our belief that God has called us to do it. Without the shield of faith, the rest of the armor will not work. Without faith we don't have a real relationship with God.

The Gloves of Love

I have my own piece of armor that I try to wear daily—the gloves of love! Foundational to Paul's work was a heart full of unconditional love and a commitment to be with the people God called him to share the Gospel with.

Reflection: Describe how your faith has grown since you started this journey.

~ The smallest seed of faith is better than the largest fruit of happiness. ~

Henry David Thoreau

Day 278: The Helmet of Salvation

A helmet protects our brains and our minds. Paul wrote: "So then, let us not be like others, who are asleep, but let us be alert and self-controlled ... putting on faith and love as a breastplate, and the hope of salvation as a helmet" (1 Thessalonians 5:6–8). Satan will say we don't deserve salvation because he wants to separate us from God. God has promised us that we do belong to him, which changes the way we think.

Being a child of the Almighty God means we put on the characteristics of Jesus Christ every day to fight Satan. These qualities belong to us, but Satan will subtly try to bring us back down to the world's level. We resist, which means we oppose, we rebel and fight back for our position as a child of the Most High God.

Prayer

The bottom line is pray! Paul tells us: "And pray in the Spirit on all occasions with all kinds of prayers and requests. With this in mind, be alert and always keep on praying for all the saints" (Ephesians 6:18).

It is through prayer we build our relationship with God, but the enemy will do what he can to get in the way of that relationship. He'll say, *You don't need to pray about this! You don't have time to pray!* Another lie!

When you pray in Jesus' name, Satan is forced to leave (Matthew 4:10). He will come back so stand firm in prayer. *Christian soldiers fight best on their knees.*

Reflect on what Andrew Murray said: "All the powers of evil seek to hinder our prayer life because prayer, by nature, involves conflict with opposing forces. May God give us grace to strive in prayer until we prevail." [261]

Day 279: The Sword of the Spirit

Evil and sin assert their influence in three different, but related, ways: the *flesh*, through the *world*, and directly through *Satan* and his army. These negative influences commonly work together to lead people away from God. Satan, himself, will target the influences of the world and our flesh as a means to break us down.

The sword of the Spirit is the Word of God. It is living, powerful, and the hope we have against evil and sin. God's Word also functions as a mirror, enabling us to see ourselves as we really are—daughters of the king. It also exposes our real heart conditions and sin. Speaking the truth stops Satan from running rampant in our lives.

When we walk and talk in truth, we make decisions according to God's plans, not Satan's. The enemy will strike! It's not a matter of "if." It's "when." When we put the full armor of God on, we put on the nature of Christ, which means we are dressed to kill!

You say to Satan, "You have to go through Jesus to get to me!" Shout out loud to the devil, "In the name of Jesus, I demand you leave. I will no longer believe your lies or accusations. I choose to believe the truth of the Word of God."

In time the battle will get easier. The reason we fail is because we wait until the hour of the battle. Those that succeed gain victory in prayer long before the battle begins.

Reflection: How has your battle gotten easier as you have started reading the part on spiritual warfare?

> ~ *If I could hear Christ praying for me in the next room, I would not fear a million enemies. Yet distance makes no difference. He is praying for me.* ~
>
> Robert Murray McCheyne[262]

Day 280: MileStone

Steps To Overcome Negative Emotions

Move Forward

God does not ask us to devise our own battle strategy and then ask his help in carrying it out. Moving forward means we ask him what his plans are before the battle begins. We must wait on God so he can reveal his plans to us.

Tell God honestly about your current battle. Then ask him to show you his plan, asking for wisdom in how you should carry it out.

Challenge the Old Way of Thinking

Exercise #1: Speak It Out!

2 Corinthians 10:5 tells us to take captive *every thought* and make it *obedient to Christ*. Do you want to control your thoughts (making them obedient to Christ), or do you want your thoughts controlling you (making them obedient to Satan)?

As you recognize a lie, defend yourself out loud. *Truth changes our thinking, and thinking changes our behavior.* Examples:

Corrupt Data: Nothing I've tried works. I am weak and a lost cause.

Speak it out: I am strong! (2 Corinthians 12:9; Joel 3:10)

Corrupt Data: I am a victim of my past and will never be able to overcome that.

> *Speak it out:* I am a victor! (Psalm 60:12; 1 Corinthians 15:57)
>
> Corrupt Data: I am nothing–worthless.
>
> *Speak it out:* I am treasured! (Deuteronomy 7:6)
>
> Corrupt Data: I can never be healed. I don't deserve to be healed.
>
> *Speak it out:* I am healed! (Isaiah 53:5)
>
> Corrupt Data: No one likes me. You wouldn't like me.
>
> *Speak it out:* My worth is in who God says I am! (Psalm 8:5–8)

Get into God's Word every day. You will find that over time your spiritual muscles of resisting Satan will grow, and the battle will get easier.

Exercise #2: Polishing God's Monuments

In his book *Polishing God's Monuments*, author and pastor Jim Andrews describes pillars of victory and hope for those of us going through punishing times:

> Sometimes our faith may be under such heat from the friction of afflic-
> tion that we may find ourselves at risk of spiritual meltdown. Long before
> that happens it is time to practice preventative maintenance. Whenever
> you pray, polish your personal monuments ... the active memory of those
> demonstrations and confirmations of God's goodness, wisdom, power,
> and faithfulness that we have stored up from our past. Monumental faith
> is a faith trained to look away from the confusion of the moment to find
> security and confidence in the past evidences of God's character and
> faithfulness. The scriptures are replete with illustrations of monument
> building and polishing in the midst of the travails of God's people.[263]

Day 281: Pray and Meditate

The Bible says, *"The effective, fervent prayer of a righteous man avails much"* (James 5:16). The next time you find yourself in the battlefield of life, remember that there is safety within the trench walls of prayer. Victory can be yours when you bring your battle before the Lord in prayer. In times of temptation and trials, when the enemy whispers lies in order to confuse, defeat, and discourage, take your stand against him by clothing yourself in the mighty armor of God (Ephesians 6:10–18). *Pray this every day:*

"Lord, help me to remember as I face life's challenges that an unseen battle is going on for my thought life and heart. Send your Holy Spirit to give me the wisdom to recognize what is the truth and what is a lie. Remind me that the best way to win the battles of my mind is in prayer and by reading your Word. To prepare myself for the battle ahead, by faith I put on your armor and cover myself with your blood as protection.

"Help me to be more like you today—full of truth, righteous, peace, and honor. I surrender all to you today and let you fight for me. Thank you for assuring me of victory. If you are with me, I know nothing can hurt me, and I can be transformed. So, by faith, I claim victory over my life! In Jesus' name. Amen."

Self-Soother

Have you had a desire lately to makeover your hair, makeup, or wardrobe? Do it!

Part Thirteen

The Loving Girl

"For God *so loved* the world [*loved you*] that he gave his one and only Son, that whoever [*that is you*] believes in him shall not perish but have eternal life. For God did not send his Son into the world to condemn the world, but to save the world [*save you*] through him." (John 3:16–17, author's emphasis)

"Love is patient, love is kind. It does not envy, it does not boast, it is not proud. It is not rude, it is not self-seeking, it is not easily angered, it keeps no record of wrongs. Love does not delight in evil but rejoices with the truth. It always protects, always trusts, always hopes, always perseveres." (1 Corinthians 13:4–7)

Day 282: The Adjustments

For six years my husband traveled extensively for his job, and I had a lot of time to myself. A lot of women couldn't handle the separation or the loneliness (no kids were living at home), but my job kept me busy. The days flew by, and I had a handful of critters to chat to, so this arrangement seemed acceptable. Then we both got lay-off notices—at the same time! My husband decided to accept an early retirement package.

Retire! He's too young to retire! No! He was simply too excited...oh, he couldn't wait. My whole being began kicking and screaming, my feelings imploding further and further inside. Not only did we have to deal with huge financial adjustments, but now we had to be around each other 24–7. *Oh! No! I've lost my space!*

My imagination said: *I have to plan and prepare dinners every night now... lunches too. I can't handle this stress! What does this thinking say about* me *as a wife? I'm a terrible person!* And it didn't help that I was peri-menopausal. The self-silencing became self-criticizing, and it was killing me.

What was in his imagination did not match up with my imagination, and the more bitter I became. I began to look at our life together and thought we really didn't have anything in common anymore. Was divorce inevitable? We didn't talk about that. I managed to suppress all the angry thoughts and feelings. It was all about me!

Reflection: What are the current stressors in your marriage that you feel you can't talk about? Start by talking to God about them.

~ A quarrelsome wife is like a constant dripping on a rainy day;
restraining her is like restraining the wind or grasping oil with the hand. ~

Proverbs 27:15–16

Day 283: The Lie Flourishes

In yesterday's story did you see what I did? I gave Satan access. He planted the lie. (We listen to the lie then dwell on it.) The lie was: we have nothing in common anymore. (Our thoughts trigger our emotions, and we develop that image.) My image was that my husband was a different man now. (We think and begin to follow what the enemy places in our mind.) I looked at each negative thing about this situation and my husband.

I started to believe that divorce was inevitable because we were thinking in two different directions. This is exactly what Satan wanted. The next step was action. However, I got smart. I began praying every day, renouncing and pulling down each conscious destructive thought. It wasn't easy. It was a very rocky year, but my Battle Commander was always there, in control.

Someone once said that men are not broken, just different. God kept my marriage out of the divorce courts because he helped me replace negative thoughts and actions with his Word. I put steps in place to renew my mind and started to replace criticism with praise. I love and respect my husband. Today, when I bring out my list of complaints about him, God brings out his list of things I need to work out about myself.

If our depression is treated with only medication, but our root issues and relationship problems are not addressed, statistics say the depression will return. Don't ask God to merely fix your marriage. Ask God to heal and transform you. Most often, your marriage will be healed as a result.

Reflection: If you are married, or even divorced, what lies has Satan planted in your marriage? Can you presently pinpoint one of those lies?

~ *Wives: Be to his virtues very kind. Be to his faults a little blind.* ~

Anonymous

Day 284: God's Girl Loves Others

We may think our lives would be far smoother and more productive if only other people lived up to our standards and changed, or better yet, if we didn't have to deal with people and all their messes. The irony is, if we got our way we wouldn't experience the growth we need. God created us to be in relationship with others and then tells us to love one another just as he has loved us. Others enable us to know him more fully.

> Jesus said: "Love the Lord your God with all your heart and with all your soul and with all your mind and with all your strength." The second is this: "Love your neighbor as yourself." There is no commandment greater than these (Mark 12:30–31).

Life is not about receiving. I know that's not usually accepted. Life is about knowing the heart of God and anchoring ourselves in him. When the scribe approached Christ, asking him to identify the greatest law, he explained, it is to love God so without fail that it produces an ability to love others.

God gave each individual life for the purpose of becoming conduits of his love. Many other variables, of course, go into the making of a successful life, but all pursuits are secondary to the notion of love. We need to be mindful that we are here for the purpose of loving others.

Reflection: When a family member angers or disappoints you, do you address the problem for the purpose of rebuilding love, or does some other priority lead you toward a lesser goal?

~ A man who lives right, and is right, has more
power in his silence than another has by his word. ~

Phillip Brooks[264]

Day 285: Intentionality

Jesus can teach us the essentials to loving others. First, Jesus loved the disciples *realistically*. Being human as well as divine, he was completely realistic about his earthly limitations and chose twelve individuals into whom he poured out his love.

Secondly, Jesus loved intimately. For three years he and the disciples did everything together. He was intentional about being in fellowship with the disciples. He planned it and chose to make time for it. Jesus carved out time, gave up other things, to be with the disciples on a regular basis. He made himself available to them in a way he was not available to others. Was he being insensitive to the rest of the world or showing favoritism? No! He was just being realistic, intimate, and intentional with his love.

The decision to love someone unconditionally, like your spouse, is often simply made, yet it takes daily persistent effort and prayer. Christian psychologists Gary Smalley and John Trent coined the phrase "Love is a decision. Contrary to popular belief, love is actually a reflection of how much we 'honor' another person—for at this core genuine love is a decision, not a feeling."[265]

The nature of God's love is called agape love. It emphasizes more desire to give than to receive, more to save than condemn. The Loving Girl not only loves God, her husband, and family, but others, whether they deserve love or not. She loves herself and loves life. "*[She] loves because he first loved us*" (1 John 4:19). Our faith and love is our response to him, not the other way around.

Reflect on Drs. Trent and Smalley's statement.

~ *While we are focusing on fear, worry, or hate, it is not possible for us to be experiencing happiness, enthusiasm or love.* ~

Bo Bennett[266]

Day 286: Love and Humility

Having loved his own who were in the world, he now showed them the full extent of his love (John 13:1). In the Gospel of John, Jesus shocked his disciples at the Last Supper by wrapping a towel around his waist and washing their feet in a basin (John 13:1–17). "I have set you an example," he said, "that you should do as I have done for you." Jesus' example is one of both love and humility. Jesus replied, "You do not realize now what I am doing, but later you will understand."

"No," said Peter, "you shall never wash my feet." Jesus answered, "Unless I wash you, you have no part with me."

What do you think Jesus meant when he said, "Unless I wash you, you have no part with me?"

Throughout his ministry Jesus resisted outward status. He refused to pull rank. God gave each individual life for the purpose of becoming conduits of his love. We, too, can be Christlike in love and humility, as in washing one another's feet.

As we place ourselves under God's control and submit to his will and plan for our lives that will happen. We will soon find that once our fear and despair lessens and we accept God's care and control, we begin to experience love and joy in our lives, just as Jesus did. Many other variables, of course, go into the making of a successful life, but all pursuits are secondary to the notion of love.

Reflection: Jesus said, "Do you understand what I have done for you?" (13:12). What has Jesus done for *you?*

~ It is not by chance our lives are intertwined. Loving someone today will heal two wounds, ours, and possibly theirs. ~

Unknown

Day 287: God's Girl Loves Herself

For many women our greatest love is the amount of time we spend taking care of our children. We provide emotional support and comfort, as well as coordinating everybody's activities every day. Dads are least likely to provide care for babies and school-aged children because what these little ones need, Dad isn't usually expected to provide. So it follows that Dad's status is not equal to that of Mom's.

The flip side of this love is blame. When things go wrong with the children, like when they're sick or struggling, we blame ourselves, not our husbands or the kids. Our roles are so demanding that we feel we can never do motherhood (or whatever role we're called to) well enough. There's nothing worse than believing we're a bad mother.

The Bible teaches us that God fashioned each one of us with a wonderful and unique design. The emphasis is not on re-shaping other people or our environment or becoming someone else; instead the emphasis is on who we are as God's creative expression. As you discover who God created you to be, you learn to love yourself.

It takes time to learn to love ourselves, especially if we're trying to dig out from under a load of negative garbage, or we've done things that seem unforgiveable. Hopefully we have family and friends who love us, sustaining us as we put the pieces of ourselves back into proper focus. It's okay to be who we have been, but now we have Christ's Spirit within us, and we are now a new valuable creation.

Reflection: How do you constantly put others' needs ahead of yours?

~ *Women's gender roles involve excelling at an unending task that*
is not highly valued. Some researchers believe that is why
married women with children are at risk for depression. ~

Dr. Valerie Whiffen[267]

Day 288: God's Creative Expression
Part 1

Dr. Gregory Jantz, *Hope Newsletter, February* 2006, *featured lesson:* [268]

Sometimes it's easy to focus on the negatives, the mistakes, the missed opportunities. Even when the damage is not through any fault of our own, we can still accept the blame. Shame and guilt don't need to be earned to be debilitating. The blame, shame, and guilt can whisper to us that we are not worthy of love, that we are unlovable.

That, of course, is a total lie. We are lovable—and loved. If I had no husband, no kids, no family, no close friends, I would still be loved by a compassionate, caring God. And that same compassionate, caring God, who loves me, *expects me to love myself.*

As a small child, this was expressed as the Golden Rule: *Do unto others as you would have them do unto you* (see Matthew 7:1).

Or, put another way:

If you are judgmental with yourself, you probably are to others.

If you focus on your own weaknesses, you expect others to let you down.

If you expect perfection in yourself, you're probably hard to live with.

If you look for the worst in yourself, you tend see it reflected in others.

If you're unable to forgive yourself, you have a hard time letting go of resentments toward others.

Reflection: Do any of these statements describe you? How?

~ *You must do the thing you think you cannot do.* ~

Eleanor Roosevelt (1884–1962)

Day 289: God's Creative Expression
Part 2

Loving yourself isn't selfish, because love, truly expressed, isn't selfish or self-serving. Rather, loving yourself serves as a model for you to love others.

Let's continue discussing loving yourself (Dr. Jantz's featured lesson):[269]

If you're comfortable with who you are, you're more accepting of others.

If you forgive yourself and learn from your mistakes, you allow others the same.

If you love yourself, you're able to experience and share joy.

If you expect a better tomorrow, you're able to let go of today.

If you know you're loveable, you make yourself available to be loved.

Now, some of you may say, "Well, you just don't know me." That's true, but I know God. And I know that he loves you, even knowing you better than you know yourself. He finds you lovable and worth dying for. See yourself through his eyes. No matter what you've done or what has happened to you, believe in his love for you.

Loving yourself allows you to see yourself as God does, to believe in his plans for you, to be open and accepting of love. "But in all these things we are more than conquerors through him who loved us" (Romans 8:37).

Reflection: This journey called self-acceptance isn't instant. It's a journey that takes time. Begin your journey tonight. When you are getting ready for bed, in your bathroom, stand in front of your mirror and smile at God's creation. Love yourself! (This doesn't mean singing "How Great Thou Art.")

~ I pray that I may respect myself enough to listen to my real feelings. ~

Anonymous

Day 290: God's Girl Loves Her Life (for Singles)

When I was single I was convinced my identity came from the prefix "Mrs." Many of us are indoctrinated to believe that if we're thirty-something and unmarried, we're a loser. Or maybe you're a single parent despairing or grieving over the loss of your soul mate. Perhaps you chose singleness. The apostle Paul said:

> I'm not saying you must marry, but you certainly may if you wish. I wish everyone could get along without marrying, just as I do. But we are not all the same. God gives some the gift of a husband or wife, and others he gives the gift of being able to stay happily unmarried. So I say to those who aren't married and to widows—better to stay unmarried if you can, just as I am (1 Corinthians 7:6–8, TLB).

Sherri Langton, the associate editor of *Bible Advocate* magazine, wrote, "The word *single* sounded like a disease. Sometimes, the Bible's support for the single life helped me feel less weird. But if being single was so great then why did most of my friends constantly date in an effort to head toward the altar? Why did the few single women I know seem like miserable misfits? I concluded marriage and motherhood equaled "success"; singleness branded her a failure. God challenged my notion that a woman's worth is based solely on her marital status. He's opened my eyes to the ways he considers me a success—even single. God can help change your definition of success, too."[270]

Reflection: In what ways do you relate to Sherri's story?

~*God has wonderful things in store for us singles when we let go and get involved with the richness and rhythm of life.* ~

Luci Swindoll[271]

Day 291: Successfully Single

Singleness is a gift. One advantage of being single: the potential of a greater focus on Christ and his work. God's keys to being successfully single can be found in:

Holding fast to God's Word and standards. I believed the lie that in order to be accepted I had to "trap" not only a guy, but a good looking guy. And I also believed that I had to give into his needs in order to attract and keep him. My promiscuous behavior backfired, causing my self-esteem to plummet further into that dark pit. Holding fast to your values, no matter how counter-cultural, is a huge success in God's eyes.

Influencing other lives. Like me, you may not be blessed with your own children, but if you have a heart for God he can use you to influence and teach others. Passing on biblical truth to others is a fulfillment of Deuteronomy 4:9 and Titus 2:4, another mark of a woman's worth.

Giving away our gifts. We've talked about the many gifts and a talents God has bestowed upon each one of us. Others need our gifts. These are opportunities for us to talk about our faith and transformation. What an example we have in the single lives of the apostle Paul and God's Girls Mary Magdalene, the prostitute Rahab, widows Naomi and Ruth, and sisters Mary and Martha (we will meet them later).

Leaning on God. No matter what your needs are today, turn to God, the lover of your soul. In those lonely times, hang onto his Words: "No one will be able to stand up against you all the days of your life. As I was with Moses, so I will be with you; I will never leave you nor forsake you" (Joshua 1:5).

Reflection: In your journal describe why singleness is a gift to you.

~ *I will not abandon you or leave you as orphans in the storm.* ~

Jesus (John 14:18, TLB)

Day 292: God's Girl Loves God

"Teacher, which is the greatest commandment in the Law?"

Jesus answered, "Love the Lord your God with all your heart and with all your soul and with all your mind" (Matthew 22:36–38).

Often we are tempted to look elsewhere for love and approval. Many of us bought into the lie that pre-marital sex brings true intimacy. I let that landmine of a lie explode because I want to feel close to someone. Soon I became hurt and disappointed. Communication through sex wasn't real intimacy. I needed to return to my first love. He can be the only source for true love, approval, intimacy, and inner joy.

We each have been given the gift of choice. More than anything God desires our love. Real love can't be forced. That is why God will never coerce us into relationship with him. Faith allows us to choose God.

Jesus teaches us to love and honor family but asks us to love him more. It's not a commitment to be taken lightly nor in ignorance. It may even mean rejection by others. Nonetheless if we choose to follow and love him first, the rewards will be abundant. Paul said, "No eye has seen, no ear has heard, no mind has conceived what God has prepared for those who love him" (1 Corinthians 2:9). What an awesome promise!

Reflect on his Word and what it means to you personally.

~ How great is the love the Father has lavished on us, that we should be called children of God! And that is what we are! ~

The Apostle John (1 John 3:1)

Day 293: God's Love Story

If you're like me you enjoy a good love story. We can find love stories for every mood and occasion, ranging from fantasy to real life. Today I'm going to share the greatest real-life love story ever told.

When Moses officiated the covenant ceremony between God and the Israelites at Mount Sinai, it was a wedding, and they were pronounced man and wife. An entire nation of blood relatives, composed of twelve tribes (large families), became the bride and wife of God, known collectively as Israel. God loved the descendants of ancient Israel, but they became, as Jesus called them, lost sheep.

Our ancestors lost their identity as Israel when, as the wife of God, they went searching after idols and other gods, similar to adulterers. As a result the Israelites divorced God. (Knowing the pain of divorce, you can imagine how God was grieved.)

Due to their disobedience, they were deported to Assyria and held in bondage for so many years that they could no longer remember the original covenant made. God expected to be loved, honored, and obeyed. He defines love as, "If you love me, keep my commandments" (Exodus 20:6).

A crucial aspect of love is its volitional element. Love involves an act of the will—a choice, a commitment. God created humans without restraint and freely bestows his love upon them. He seeks a free response of love in return. This drama of love between God and humans is the ultimate source of the meaning of life.

Reflection: Meditate on this. In your own words, define your love for God.

~ *Life's greatest tragedy is to lose God and not to miss him.* ~

F.W. Norwood[272]

Day 294: Marriage with God

Fast forward four hundred years to the New Testament. God made himself into the man Jesus Christ, and now there was a new covenant. Jesus ordered his disciples to find the lost sheep. They found them. It was the nations of Europe who fulfilled prophecy as the people returning to their former lover and husband.

Think about this historical fact. We would not have Christianity today were it not for these lost sheep of the house of Israel, a long lost love being found again in the Gospel of Jesus Christ. They promised to love, honor, and obey God.

The enemy doesn't want this love story told. The beautiful part of this story is that God so loved the world that he gave his only Son for you and me. "Greater love hath no man than this, that a man lay down his life for his friends" (John 15:12).

How do we prepare ourselves for marriage with God? By believing in his love and the sacrifice he made for each one of us. "We know how much God loves us because we have felt his love and because we believe him when he tells us that he loves us dearly. God is love, and anyone who lives in love is living with God and God is living in him" (1 John 4:16, TLB).

God's Loving Girl knows that nothing can separate her from the love of God found in Jesus Christ. She lives her life seeking to share this knowledge and his gift of eternal life with others who are lost. Jesus said, "As the Father has loved me, so have I loved you. Now remain in my love" (John 15:9).

Reflection: What is Jesus saying specifically to you in this verse (John 15:9)?

~ *Death leaves a heartache no one can heal, love leaves a memory no one can steal.* ~

A headstone in Ireland[273]

Day 295: MileStone

Steps To Overcome Negative Emotions

Move Forward

There is a wonderful saying that "A life with love will have some thorns, but a life without love will have no roses."[274] Does love just show up at our front door? Usually not. It's when we reach out and show love ourselves that love taps us on the shoulder.

Whether that love comes in the form of a lover, a child, a parent, a best friend, or God, we have to work to cultivate that relationship. A garden tended by loving hands reaps succulent fruits. This is moving forward.

Challenge the Old Way of Thinking

We are nearing the finish line! We will begin focusing on taking charge of our life and setting goals—an exciting adventure! A goal is the purpose toward which an endeavor is directed, an objective. [275] We are free to do the will of God!

Pray and Meditate

Help me, O Lord, to be more loving. Help me, O Lord, not to be afraid to love the outcast, the leper, the unmarried pregnant woman, the traitor to the State, the man out of prison. Help me by my love to restore the faith of the disillusioned, the disappointed, the early bereaved. Help me by my love to be the witness of your love. (Alan Paton)[276]

Self-Soother

Do something you have put off doing...and enjoy it!

Day 296: Taking Charge & Setting Goals

First, I want you to imagine you have an incurable disease and have been given less than six months to live. After coming to grips with the diagnosis, you say, "I am going to spend the last months living life to the fullest, doing things that are truly important to me." Now imagine yourself living out those six months in the manner you have just decided.

Scripture encourages us to trust God for our needs. Some people think that means we should not set our own goals because it means a lack of confidence in God. This interpretation fails to acknowledge trust as an important discipline. Goal setting helps us determine where to focus our energy to accomplish the work God has for us to do (which is scriptural, Ephesians 2:10). Our goal is simple: to stand before God with a prepared and willing heart, and then we let him do his work in and through us, claiming all glory.

You may be afraid to set your hopes on a bright future for fear the darkness will once again overtake. I hope you have realized that you have a person on your side much greater than the darkness. God's Girl can begin to take charge and set goals for her future, which you will achieve with God's counsel.

Taking charge means we recognize that there are areas of our life that require decision and control, which belong to us. Goals are things we can control, like completing this book in less than 365 days. Setting goals is the most basic step toward achieving anything worthwhile. No matter what you've been through or are facing, realize that God has a plan for your life.

Reflect on goal setting. What is your commitment level today?

~ It is when things go hardest, when life becomes most trying, that there is greatest need for having a fixed goal. ~

B.C. Forbes (1880 - 1954)

Day 297: Taking Charge of Your Time

Taking charge of our life means taking charge of our time, rather than time taking charge of us. In seeking a more meaningful life, we must preserve and schedule time for personal spiritual growth. We need to schedule in time with God. That is how we find out what God's plans are for our life. Your goal is to develop for yourself your own method of self-renewal and budget that into your daily and weekly schedule.

I remember my first day at seminary I met another student who said, "God told me ... I heard God say ... God wanted me to do ... " I thought, *God doesn't talk to me! How can she know him like that?* Haven't we all heard someone tell their conversion story, or some other experience, and thought, *I've never felt or had that! I must not be a real Christian.* That's the enemy. He'll do whatever to keep us from spending time with God.

I learned God didn't actually audibly talk to this student, but she had a designated time of day that was solely dedicated to praying and meditating with God. I began to practice similarly and grow spirituality, and I too heard from God ... not audibly!

We begin by prioritizing our life. You may want to enlist the aid of someone else to help you. Be as up front as possible about what is truly important and significant in your life. *What am I willing to sacrifice? To what will I give my next hour of life? When that hour is gone, was it worth it?*

Reflection: Designate a goal of spending a specific amount of time with God on a daily basis, at a specific time, taking into consideration what works best for you.

~ *Never give in, never give in, never, never, never.* ~

Winston Churchill

Day 298: Gifts for the Kingdom

Life is a matter of priorities and choices. As we get older, we will look back and see where we wished we had spent more energy and time. Time is our gift from God to the world. Jesus regularly called the disciples back to their priorities, "How does a man benefit if he gains the whole world and loses his soul in the process?" (Mark 8:36, TLB).

Most of us waste huge quantities of time each day and each week. When we add up the hours that weren't creatively used, we become either appalled or depressed. Someone once said that our life, and our temple, is God's gift to each one of us. What we do with our life and our temple is our gift to God.

We each play out various roles daily, and we each have tasks to accomplish. Certainly it is God's will that we prove to be trustworthy with what he's given us to do. Daily decisions are likely to produce the best results when we keep our hearts and minds focused on the one who brought us into this world.

The Scriptures encourage us to be honest about our emotions, but they never tell us to live solely by them. Biblical truths are the only reliable guide for our lives. Our emotions may reinforce these truths, but our emotions may also reflect Satan's lies. The truth of God's Word is our sole authority, not our emotions.

Reflection: What gift(s) has God given you to use for the kingdom? I would suggest you also take a spiritual gifts test. A pastor, or someone in ministry leadership, can tell you how to go about doing this. Once you recognize your gifts and talents, list them. Then you are ready to set goals.

~ *Start by doing what is necessary, then do what is possible, and suddenly you are* doing the impossible. ~

St. Francis of Assisi (1182–1226)

Day 299: Expressing the Desire of Your Heart

If you were asked to pinpoint one desire of your heart, what would that be? The desire of our heart can also be termed *passion*. How long would it take to articulate your deepest, most genuine desire or passion? I believe we can know God's will and plan for our life if we look deep within and ask ourselves what we are passionate about doing.

Let me backtrack for a moment. Yesterday I suggested we not rely on our emotions but on God's Word. Was I saying you should repress your feelings? No, because then you most likely couldn't feel what your heart is saying. We need to express our emotions to God and look to Scripture to determine what he would have us to do.

Back to our lesson: What are your heartfelt desires? There are things that we want and things that we truly need, but this isn't what I'm driving at. If you've never taken the time to prayerfully meditate on this issue, then you may not even know your heart's desires. Dr. Charles Stanley wrote, "Not knowing our true desires leads us to offer a string of prayers for random, inconsistent wants rather than genuine, heartfelt desires. Sometimes, the Lord graciously answers these requests. Other times, He even more graciously protects us by saying no. But if our requests are not grounded in prayer and heartfelt sincerity, we may never understand why they go unanswered."[277]

Reflection: Dedicate prayer time to this subject this week. First, ask the Lord to open your eyes to his desires for you. Then request that he make his desires your own.

~ When we do the best that we can, we never know what
miracle is wrought in our life, or in the life of another. ~

Helen Keller[278]

Part Fourteen

The Friend Girl

Encouraged by God's Word

"This is the case of a man who is quite alone, without a son or brother, yet he works hard to keep gaining more riches. And to whom will he leave it all, and why is he giving up so much now? It is all so pointless and depressing. Two can accomplish more than twice as much as one, for the results can be much better. If one falls, the other pulls him up; but if a man falls when he is alone, he's in trouble. Also, on a cold night, two under the same blanket gain warmth from each other, but how can one be warm alone? And one standing alone can be attacked and defeated, but two can stand back-to-back and conquer; three is even better, for a triple-braided cord is not easily broken." (Ecclesiastes 4:8–12, TLB)

Day 300: God's Girl Crystal

Crystal recounts, "I remember it was a Thursday, and I didn't feel any brighter than I had the previous month or so. My friend Julie would call me at least once a day. "'If you need anything, call me, and I'll be there in a flash.' Precious Julie. She tried so hard to bring me out of my funk. I don't need anything or anyone. I just want to sleep.

"One day the doorbell rang. There was Julie with an arm full of cleaning products.

"'I bet you haven't cleaned your house in days. I'm your Merry Maid!' Before I could say anything she darted into the kitchen, and I heard cupboards slamming.

"'No, I'll call you Jewel Julie,' I yelled. A friend like Julie was a gift from God, no doubt about it. If only I could be that kind of friend to her. I guess I'm just not made to be a Jewel Julie.

"Eventually I became my own version of Jewel Julie to a friend, who was terribly unhappy ... but let me reiterate, it was only through God's strength, comfort, and healing touch I was able to do so."

The question is not, "What can I give you?" But, "Who can we be for each other?" Healing from depression means we cannot go it alone. From her years of counseling the depressed, Dr. Laura Roberts said that in today's busy, overbooked world, many women have few, or no, friends. And others are often too busy to respond to the depressed woman's feeble attempts to be included.[279]

The fact is we need God and other people in our lives to support us.

Reflection: List the people who are supporting you today?

~ You'll notice that a turtle only makes progress when it sticks out its neck. ~

Anonymous

Day 301: The Warmth of Loving Friends

No question, intimacy is risky. *If I reach out to another woman, there's a fifty percent chance she may reject me. It's risky. If I trust my deepest, darkest secrets to another woman, she may pull back in shock, or even worse, tell others.*

We don't have to have a lot of friends, but we need at least one person we can count on. If a woman has just one person she can count on, she is protected from depression when she experiences significant life stress.[280]

Why would I want to set myself up for hurt? Like Ruth we each need the warmth of loving friends to help us walk through the valley of the dark and rejoice in the valley of the light. Taking these kinds of risks as Ruth did ignites our flame for connection. An English publication offered prizes for the best definitions of a friend. The prizes went to:

"One who multiplies joys, divides grief." "One who understands our silence." "A volume of sympathy bound in cloth." "A watch which beats true for all time and never runs down." "A friend is the one who comes in when the whole world has gone out."[281]

Often our sense of worth may be tied to our relationships. We may at first try to ignore those reaching toward us, but with the Holy Spirit's guidance, we will soon feel and welcome their presence. Once we embrace friendship, then we become that much-needed genuine friend to other women, helping them out of the dark valley into the light.

Reflection: When have you been willing to risk reaching out to someone you were drawn to? Was that a positive or negative experience? If negative, what do you need to do to risk again?

~ The trouble with doing something right the first time is that nobody appreciates how difficult it was. ~

Unknown

Day 302: The Need for Friendship

Only your real friends will tell you when your face is dirty. "Wounds from a friend are better than kisses from an enemy!" (Proverbs 27:6, TLB) A friend is a person one knows, likes, and trusts; a person with whom one is allied in a struggle or cause; a comrade; one who supports and offers sympathy.[282] A friend loves at all times and brings out the best in you.

Is it any wonder that isolation depresses and being in the company of dear friends relaxes and restores us? Women care about friendships, and that makes them vulnerable to depression when those relationships go wrong. Sociologist Pat O'Connor says that women who are rich in friendships enjoy better physical health, live longer, and are less prone to alcoholism, suicide, and mental illness than those who are lonely and isolated.[283]

We have learned through this book that connecting to others is very important. God designed life for intimacy, not isolation. As we learn to reach out to God and others, they will meet us, and new friendships will take root and grow. I call these *divine appointments*. We open our eyes and ears and heart, and we are willing to become vulnerable. Vulnerability hastens connecting. When someone else confides in me, I am honored that she would trust me, and in turn I feel at ease confiding to her. When I become transparent, other hurting women are drawn to me.

Reflection: What did you learn from your mother or another woman about being a friend?

~ Friends are the support players who usually require fewer emotional supplies than family members and who help us with our problems. ~

Brenda Hunter [284]

Day 303: The Greatest Gift

The greatest gift we can give another person is the gift of ourselves—of friendship. Liane Cordes, author of *The Reflecting Pond,* wrote:

> When we can share our deepest convictions and failures, our ideals and disillusionments, our hopes and frustrations, our dreams and despairs, our answers and our questions then we are loving our neighbors as ourselves as well as loving our enemies. A friend put it this way: If I share the whole of me with you, I share the good as well as the bad. I don't hide anything of myself from you, not in a deep friendship, or a deep marriage for that matter. By sharing some things I hate about myself, I'm loving my inside enemy. I'm telling you I'm still human and have a lot of growing to do. I'd love to tell you only about all my good points: it would make me feel a lot better, but it wouldn't be sharing all of me with you.[285]

To find someone who is willing to share both tears and laughter with you is a rarity. It's a gift from God. I believe God has someone for you who can help and guide you. Pray about it. Look for the divine appointment. Trust God. If you've been disappointed or hurt in the past, with God's strength you can risk again. He has carefully selected that special woman and has a specific purpose that only that woman can fulfill in his appointed time. These are special girl friends who have a divine purpose.

Reflection: Think back to the first time you met a friend who is now very special in your life. What makes her so special?

~ *Alone we can do so little; together we can do so much.* ~

Helen Keller[286]

Day 304: God's Girls Mary & Elizabeth

A wonderful example of God setting up a divine appointment is the story of Mary and Elizabeth. This is a case when God knew the needs of these two women better than they did themselves. It is a story about faith and an intimate friendship (Luke 1:26–45).

The angel Gabriel visited Mary of Nazareth and told her she would bear a son, Jesus. We are also told that the barren and elderly Elizabeth will finally bear a son. God made sure that Mary knew about Elizabeth's pregnancy when the angel said, "Even Elizabeth your relative is going to have a child in her old age, and she who was said to be barren is in her sixth month. For nothing is impossible with God" (Luke 1:36–37).

Mary must have seen God's hand in the situation because she hurried to see Elizabeth and ended up spending the last three months of her pregnancy with her.

Elizabeth lived quite a distance away. Despite great obstacles Mary was determined to follow through on God's leading despite the fact that she was pregnant herself. Her trip must have been a long, uncomfortable, and perhaps difficult one. Despite the distance and her pregnancy, Mary knew she had to see her friend Elizabeth. Elizabeth, now six months pregnant, came to the door and saw her niece, Mary. She didn't expect her. Scripture says that Mary encourages Elizabeth with her greeting. She's excited to see her; so much so her womb leaps for joy!

Reflection: Why do you think God wanted this included in this passage? Has your womb ever leaped for joy? My friend's fetus did somersaults when she was pregnant.

~ *A true friend never gets in your way—unless you
happen to be going down a wrong way street.* ~

Anonymous

Day 305: The Intimate Friendship

We don't know the exact greeting Mary brought to Elizabeth, but it had an effect so powerful that Elizabeth was filled with the Holy Spirit. It was John the Baptist in Elizabeth's womb—his tiny fetus responded to Mary's greeting. And why not? The Messiah was inside of Mary.

In the next chapter, the angel says, "I bring you good news of great joy that will be for all the people" (Luke 2:10). That's what a friend brings us—great joy. Elizabeth said, "Why am I so favored, that the mother of my Lord should come to me?" (1:44).

God provided Elizabeth to Mary as a kind of pregnant spiritual grandmother who would nurture and encourage her in the Lord. Elizabeth was everything to her: her instructor, her teacher, her friend and confidant, her mentor, and her advocate. God gave Elizabeth to Mary for a special period of time and a special purpose.

Did you also notice that Elizabeth welcomed Mary in her home for three months? She didn't even know Mary was coming! I don't know about you, but that would have left me a little miffed. Elizabeth showed unwavering hospitality.

Let's not forget that Jesus calls us his friend as he did the disciples (John 15:15). How comforting and reassuring to be chosen as Jesus' friend!

Reflection: Like Mary, how sensitive have you been to God's divine appointment(s) upon meeting people?

~ Close friendships require a sense of self, an interest in other people, empathy, loyal commitment … and letting go of our fantasies of ideal friendship. ~

Judith Viorst[287]

Day 306: Yoked Versus Unyoked Friendships

Different friends bring different elements. For example, women marry Mr. Wrong all the time. They choose an alcoholic, an adulterer, or an abuser, instead of remaining single. These are toxic relationships. The same applies with girlfriends.

The Bible tells us to be "equally yoked." The apostle Paul tells us what that means: "Don't be teamed with those who do not love the Lord, for what do the people of God have in common with the people of sin? How can light live with darkness?" (2 Corinthians 6:14, TLB).

If we're enmeshed in a toxic relationship (those that enable and encourage us to live in darkness), we need to cut those ties because they are poisonous. As you grow in Jesus Christ, you may find that unyoked or toxic friends begin to reject or ostracize you. It's hard not to hurt, but they are not personally rejecting you; they are rejecting Jesus Christ (whose Spirit is living within you).

Reflection: How has the story of Mary and Elizabeth changed or added to your perspective about the friendships of women? About being yoked?

~ *Friendship is born at that moment when one person says to another, "What! You too? I thought I was the only one!"* ~

C. S. Lewis[288]

Day 307: The Unmasked Friendship

If you really knew me, you wouldn't like me! Sound familiar?

Without a viable connection to God and others, we can't be that woman God created us to be. Several things can happen. We become independent, believing we can manage our life on our own. *I don't need anybody else!*

We can isolate. *I don't have any friends because no one likes me, and that's fine with me!* We can be the super-mom or the super-businesswoman, too busy to make any friends. *I don't have any time for friends!*

In other words, we can't be our real selves. When we're not our real selves, then we tend to put on a mask(s). Not the fruity cosmetic kind, but the kind of masks that are toxic and pure poison to our friendships. We become Cover Girls, which is the opposite of God's Girls.

The intimate friendship, like Mary and Elizabeth's, gives us the confidence to discard our mask. An equally yoked friendship allows us to begin opening up and exposing our real self. *I can be me!*

Reflection: How does this resonate with you?

~ *Satan hath his devices to destroy the saints; and one great device is by working them first to be strange, and then to divide, and then to be bitter and jealous, and then to bite and devour on another.* ~

Thomas Brooks[289]

Day 308: The Mask of Jealousy & Envy

Have you ever tried to be like someone else? Maybe not their personality, but maybe you tried to dress like them or decorated your house like theirs or clothed your kids similarly. What happened? It didn't work. In school and then in the workplace, I was jealous of anyone who was thinner or prettier or smarter than me. Jealousy told me to aim to be someone I wasn't. I fell on my face because I tried to change myself into someone I wasn't created by God to be. It's stupid to be jealous! We each have *different* gifts and purposes and need what God's given each one of us.

Then there's envy. I lived many years in Chicago and loved to drive around and admire the multi-million dollar homes. Seething with envy I'd think, *Why can't I find a rich husband and live this grand dame life!* We are the losers in the envy game.

We are never satisfied. We feel sorry for ourselves for what we don't have. God knows possessions never make anyone happy for long. William Shakespeare referred to envy as the "green sickness." When we envy what someone else has, we have judged ourselves and found something defective or faulty, which says to God, "You goofed up!" God created each one of us unique, and he wants us to reflect our own style.

Envy, like jealousy, is a toxin to our relationships and more so our relationship with God. Proverbs 14:30 says, "A heart at peace gives life to the body, but envy rots the bones." That's spiritual osteoporosis! Let's ask God to show us our own gifts and talents instead of looking at what others have. Then we're ready to use those gifts according to his purpose, and God gets the glory, which is what it's all about.

Reflection: How is jealousy and envy presently affecting your relationships?

~ *It is better to fail in originality than to succeed in imitation.* ~

Herman Melville

Day 309: The Mask of Judgment & Comparison

Typical of the people pleaser, I constantly compared myself to others and usually came up short. I'd go from *I'm fatter than you* (low self-image) to *I'm thinner and better than you* (defensive pride). *Why not? Others judged me.* I had to stop that! The Bible told me why in Romans 2:1: "You, therefore, have no excuse, you who pass judgment on someone else, for at whatever point you judge the other, you are condemning yourself, because you who pass judgment do the same things."

A saying goes, "One good thing about being wrong is the joy it brings to others."[290] That is not a friend. Looking back I realize just how much of my life has been spent dwelling upon the faults of others. It gave me satisfaction. By dwelling on their faults, I avoided looking at my own. Stop playing comparison games with your friends, neighbors, and others in your life. While their feelings are certainly important, what they think of you really isn't. What you think of yourself is far more important.

I would add that the only person we should worry about pleasing is our Lord. Remember, we are called to be witnesses, not lawyers or judges. The bottom line is, if we know who we are in Jesus Christ, we will not try to become someone else in order to have meaning and value in our lives.

Reflection: What do you think of yourself today? Pray and ask God to help you remove any mask of judgment and comparison.

> ~ *When we struggle for the approval of others, we disregard the unconditional acceptance of God. Essentially, we tell Him His love is not good enough and we need the regard of others first. Jesus told His disciples to seek the kingdom of God first and all their needs would be met.* ~
>
> Charles Stanley[291]

Day 310: The Mask of Dependency & Control

Angelina writes, "Due to my self-esteem problem, I'm a smothering type of person. I know this. Friends tell me I'm a very controlling, suspicious, and jealous person. I don't want my best friend going out with other girl friends, co-workers, or anyone that might take her away from me permanently."

Some women look to another woman friend to fill that void or have a lust to acquire a friend like a possession. That friendship becomes poisoned. I, too, managed to kill several friendships by trying to control that special friend.

These masks represent sinful ugliness, which is why it is important to ask God to help us unmask. When we really believe that we are loved and accepted, no matter what, we no longer feel the need to be perfect, to compete for attention, or look for love in the wrong places. Those are the devil's games, which only produce anxiety and unhappiness.

Say out loud: *My Father loves me and takes pleasure in me no matter what I've done or will do!*

Reflection: Are you willing to share your special girlfriend(s)? Why or why not? Or do you need to begin seeking out a special girlfriend?

~ No one can wear a mask for very long. ~

Lucius Annaeus Seneca

Day 311: Drawing Strength from One Another

No one chooses to suffer. But when we hurt, we should remember that friends and family are more important than things or pills. We can make an effort to draw strength from God and one another. Ecclesiastes 4:9–10 says: "Two are better than one, because they have a good return for their work: If one falls down, his friend can help him up. But pity the man who falls and has no one to help him up!"

I'll tell you from firsthand experience that the healing process begins when we bring our story (our past, our secrets) into the light among friends. Then we bring it out of exile. When I shared my hurts, trials, and shame with another friend, the healing began.

I am created in the image of God, and he is the God who speaks. He has given me a voice. He has given you a voice.

The Israelites in speaking of their bondage to the Egyptians said, "Then we cried out to the LORD, the God of our fathers, and the LORD heard our voice and saw our misery, toil and oppression. So the LORD brought us out ... " (Deuteronomy 26:7–8).

Reflection: God gave you a voice. Next time you have an opportunity to talk about your exile, share something that's changed since you met him. Tell of how you once were blind, but now you see.

~ A thief with a stocking over his head held a gun at a frightened victim, and yelled, "Give me all your valuables." The victim began stuffing the sack with all his friends. ~

A Comic

Day 312: First We are the Baby Lamb

When I was a baby lamb in need of a shepherd, I had to risk being vulnerable. When I began to speak up and make quality connections, then God provided that much needed comfort and peace. I was able to let down my defenses and not feel exploited. Slowly I started bearing fruit of love, joy, peace, and humility. I could feel love and love others. I was no different (no better, no worse) than any other woman.

Being a friend means that we share our life and burdens with each other. We ask to be cared for. We share words of blessing and encouragement, using examples from our own lives and God's heartfelt promises in Scripture. However, most of us are reluctant to ask for help. Don't we tend to do the opposite— send people away when we need them the most? *I don't want to burden or inconvenience anyone*, we think. *Could they really like me if they knew this about me?*

Keeping secrets can make us fearful, and the enemy wins. Sharing our experiences helps us understand how very similar we all are. We feel profound relief when we share our most intimate and shameful secrets and the women listening don't blink an eye.

Finding the right words can be slow and terrifying. At the same time there's a desire to speak out, and to speak the truth. Counselors will tell you that giving voice to our stories and the depth of our suffering can be a major vehicle for healing.

Reflection: Begin thinking about how you can give a voice to your story.

~ *Treat your friends as you would a bank account.*
Refrain from drawing too heavily on either. ~

Samuel Johnson

Day 313: Being a Shepherd Friend

Each time we discover God's comfort in our own suffering, our capacity to help others is increased. The apostle Paul had that in mind when he wrote, "Blessed be the Father of mercies and God of all comfort, who comforts us in all our tribulation, that we may be able to comfort those who are in any trouble, with the comfort with which we ourselves are comforted by God" (2 Corinthians 1:3–4).

Paul tells us to carry one another's burdens (Galatians 6:2). That means learning to be empathetic, willing to share in one another's emotions, thoughts, and feelings.

"Rejoice with those who rejoice; mourn with those who mourn" (Romans 12:15).

We are now responsible to pass God's comfort to others. Being a shepherd may mean initially spending more time with this friend because she is in great pain and in need of short-term intensive help. Keep this in mind: when a friend is in trouble, she doesn't necessarily want you to solve her problem. She is seeking a compassionate listener. If she asks for advice, give it to her. Don't try to fix her problems. That's God's job. Most professionals will tell you that it is unhealthy to become a rescuer in a relationship. If practical help is needed, like meals, child care, car pool, extend that to her, and she will know you love her and have heard her cries. If she is struggling emotionally, refer her to a pastor or counselor.

Reflection: Are you willing to step out in faith as a shepherd friend? If you said no or are unsure, what are the obstacles?

~ It is not by accident that the happiest people are those who make a conscious effort to live useful lives. ~

Ernest Fitzgerald[292]

Day 314: MileStone

Steps To Overcome Negative Emotions

Move Forward

Dale Carnegie, author of *How to Win Friends and Influence People, classically said,* *"You can make more friends in two months by becoming interested in other people than you can in two years of trying to get other people interested in you."*[293]

Move forward by reaching out to someone new; someone you feel is a divine appointment. If you can hold someone's hand, hug them, or even touch them on the shoulder, you are blessed because you can offer God's healing touch. If that person does not respond or rejects you, pray for her. She most likely is feeling some type of pain.

~ Whatever you can do or dream you can do, begin it now. ~

Goethe[294]

Day 315: Challenge the Old Way of Thinking

Abraham Lincoln, the sixteenth president of the United States, said, "You cannot escape the responsibility of tomorrow by evading it today." Keep going. You have a vision and dream for your future.

My vision for this healing devotional study was a clear image of what God wanted to accomplish through my writing and personal experience that would give him the glory. I had a dream the study would be published and you would be reading it.

Write down your vision. This may seem overwhelming, so start small. Begin with everyday events before taking on the big ones. What is your plan for tomorrow? What would be possible obstacles that would stop you from making those plans for tomorrow?

When preparing your list work in this order:

First, prioritize your commitment to your home and family.

Second, fulfill your responsibilities to your employer.

Three, donate your time, money, or resources to the work of the Lord.

You may feel it's too late to fulfill a dream. That's another lie from the enemy. I have been motivated by women in their seventies that have such a heart for God and are driven in their particular area of ministry.

What are your goals? Begin to define them in these areas: Spiritual. Personal. Career. Educational. Ministry. Financial.

Once we get in the habit of meeting smaller daily goals, then long-range goals become more realistic.

Day 316: Commit Your Goals to God in Prayer

You are beginning to visualize and talk about your goals. Do you want to go back to school? I did in my late forties! Let me tell you, I was far from the oldest. There is no retirement in God's kingdom. God will use you until he takes you home.

Often it's hard to discern whether God's will is actually coming from God or us or the devil. The Word of God will answer those questions. God's Warrior Girl learned that if her thoughts were contrary to the Word of God, then those thoughts were most likely from the enemy. We apply the same principle to goal setting. Test your goals against Scripture.

Pray and Meditate

Oh the inexpressible comfort of feeling safe with a person,

Having neither to weigh thoughts,

Nor measure words—but pouring them,

All right out—just as they are

Chaff and grain together

Certain that a faithful hand will take them and sift them

Keeping what is worth keeping

And with the breath of kindness, Blow the rest away.

(Dinah Maria Mulock Craik)[295]

Self-Soother

Do one thing you've been afraid of doing, like signing up for a new class.

Part Fifteen

The Honorable Girl

Encouraged by God's Word

"He picks up the poor from out of the dirt, rescues the wretched who've been thrown out with the trash, Seats them among the honored guests, a place of honor among the brightest and best." (Psalm 113:7–8, Msg)

Day 317: Kimberly's Diagnosis

Still a newlywed, I began to have physical problems I'd never experienced. I awoke each morning with stiff, achy hands and forearms. Simple tasks such as loading the washing machine became increasingly difficult. My extremities were so achy that I could barely turn a doorknob. I'd push doors open with my shoulder. It was like sludge running through my hands and forearms, limiting all physical movement.

Anti-inflammatory medications didn't help. I consulted an orthopedist who ordered different therapies, but they didn't work either. He referred me to a rheumatologist to be tested for rheumatoid arthritis. The fact that I had lost my vision in my left eye ten years earlier made me wonder if this was a sign that something else was going on that was not confined to muscles or bones. The rheumatologist ran a series of tests. The one that clinched the diagnosis was the antinuclear antibody (ANA) test. The results were unmistakable—positive for systemic lupus erythematosus!

Lupus! I can't believe it. My life has just started! This is a death sentence, I thought. *Will this be painful and agonizing?* I was grieved and depressed. As a new Christian I didn't know what to think. I didn't blame God. As usual I thought it must have been something I had done to myself—a result of my sinfulness. However, in the midst of grief and despair, I had one optimistic thought: *surely with modern drug therapy I will have a normal life again.*

Reflection: When was the last time you were given despairing news? How did you react? With optimism or pessimism?

~ *Trust in the* LORD *with all your heart and lean not on your own understanding.* ~

King Solomon (Proverbs 3:5)

Day 318: Honoring What God Has Given

I took the news and medical plan one day at a time. My husband soon realized I wasn't going to turn into a vegetable either. I praise God that the medication eventually worked. The side effects were not pleasant, but the inflammation and painful stiffness subsided. I know that many women with lupus have allergic reactions and other debilitating side effects. Some have to quit their jobs. Yes, I was very blessed!

It is God who guides the doctors and pharmacists. He gets the glory. The most important lesson I learned through this experience was that the lupus and the accompanying grief and despair weren't God's punishment for my past sins. I heard a psychologist recently say that autoimmune diseases and problems are at an all-time high because we are wearing out our bodies (mentally and physically). I believe that's just what I did. My present-day autoimmune disease, which does flare up from time to time, and lack of vision in my left eye (which God restored), are side effects of living in a fallen world. It is our responsibility to use our circumstances to glorify and honor God.

God's Girl honors what God has given her. Instead of being competitive or jealous of those who may have some advantage over us, we should honor and applaud them because we are all members of the same body in Christ. God's Girl honors the people and relationships God has put in her life. She honors her body by taking proper care of it, and honors her marriage and parents. Above all, she honors God.

Reflection: How will you use your present-day circumstances to honor and glorify God as you understand the term honor?

~ *It's not the load that breaks you down, it's the way you carry it.* ~

Lena Horne

Day 319: God's Girl Honors God

Why do you think you are here on earth? *To have a family and make my mark!*

We are here on earth to honor and obey God, enhancing him before a watching world. There is a difference between obeying and honoring. Obey means to do as one is told. Honor means to respect and is expressed in the choices we make. Honoring God is expressed in the commitment of both our life and possessions to the Lord's service. Proverbs 3:9 states one honors God by giving back a portion of what God has given one. Sometimes we may be faced with a decision as to what is the lesser evil or lesser sin, like Bathsheba was. When that happens we mustn't lose sight of what God wants.

We may have to push aside our feelings in favor of what God says is the right thing to do. Oswald Chambers wrote, "God guides us by our ordinary choices, and if we are going to choose what He does not want, He will check, and we must heed."[296]

Doing that right thing may be uncomfortable or even painful, but it is honoring God. It is an example of surrender and obedience.

In all of history only Jesus Christ truly honored the Father by submitting himself totally to God. His submission led him to the cross. God raised Jesus Christ to his permanent position as our King, a significant honor. Jesus also taught that the one who serves him would be honored by his Father (John 12:26); conversely, those who reject him also reject God the Father (John 15:23).

Reflection: Does your lifestyle and attitude today honor God? Why or why not?

~ Men are free to decide their own moral choices, but they are also under the necessity to account to God for their choices. ~

A.W. Tozer[297]

Day 320: Those Who Honor God Will Be Honored

As our ongoing transformation moves us toward wholeness and Christlikeness, we should be grateful to God. We honor him. This truth is seen in this story.

A poor widow is doubly in need. She cries to Elisha, "Your servant, my husband is dead ... But now his creditor is coming to take my two boys as his slaves" (2 Kings 4:1–7). She needs a husband to provide for her because her husband left her with little. This may be your story. Perhaps you both said, "Life isn't fair!"

Elisha replied, "How can I help you? Tell me, what do you have in your house?"

"Your servant has nothing there at all," she said, "except a little oil."

Just a small pot of oil. No doubt she thinks, *How can that save me from the creditor?*

Elisha said, "Go around and ask all your neighbors for empty jars. Don't ask for just a few." He tells her to go into her house with her sons, shut the door, and begin pouring olive oil from her jar into the empty pots, setting them aside as they are filled. When all the jars were full, she said to her son, "Bring me another one." But he replied, "There is not a jar left." Then the oil stopped flowing. I would guess this woman wished she'd collected more empty jars. Perhaps there was a reason she couldn't.

God uses her pot of oil and meets her financial needs in an unexpected way. God is able to do immeasurably more than all we ask or imagine (Ephesians 3:20).

Reflection: When has God met your need in a way you didn't expect?

~ *If God has singled you out to be a special object of His grace, you may expect Him to honor you with stricter discipline and greater suffering than less favored ones are called upon to endure.* ~

A.W. Tozer[298]

Day 321: God's Girl Honors Her Parents

Honoring our parents is important to God. "Honor your father and your mother, so that you may live long in the land the LORD your God is giving you" (Exodus 20:12). This is the first commandment with a promise attached. To live in peace for generations in the Promised Land, the Israelites would need to respect authority and build strong families. It means speaking well of them and politely to them. It means acting in a way that shows them obedience, courtesy, and respect, but not following any commands or advice that means disobeying God, like breaking a law. If they are believers, it means following their teaching and example of putting God first. Even those who have difficulty getting along with their parents are still commanded to honor them.

Secondly, God commands children to obey their parents because it is training for the respect and obedience needed for a healthy relationship with the Lord. Becoming acquainted with submission to loving authority and obedience to a caring parent makes it easier for a child to have a genuine desire to love, serve, and obey God.

Not sure if you are honoring your parents? Pastor David McLaughlin said the test is if you have photos of them displayed. If you are not honoring your parents, you don't exhibit any photos.[299]

Perhaps you are still harboring unforgiveness toward a parent. We've already concluded that if we don't forgive, our life will not be what God intended it to be. That especially holds true for a parent. We need to face the hurt, the unforgiveness, and then move toward reconciliation and forgiveness.

Reflection: Ask God to help you to begin the process of honoring your parent(s).

~ Obedience is the gateway through which knowledge, yes,
and love too, enter the mind of the child. ~

Anne Sullivan[300]

Day 322: The Abusive Parent

Perhaps one of your parents is (or was) physically, emotionally, or verbally abusive to you (and may no longer be part of your life). Does this rescind God's commandment to honor that parent? My friend Lorrie Fulton, director of women's spiritual development, Foothills Community Church, said, "Honoring a parent does not mean that we allow wrong behavior on their part. Forgiveness does not mean forgetting, nor does it mean that we become a doormat that others wipe their feet on as they enter in and walk on our hearts. At some point we must stop letting the offender in.

"To honor one's parent might look like this: the daughter acknowledges her parent's sin (in this case verbal abuse), forgives the wrong, which may be difficult, but is still necessary for the daughter to have emotional freedom and maintain the depth of her relationship with Jesus, and tells the parent that she will not allow herself to be spoken to in that manner. The parent then has to choose to speak respectfully, or the daughter will remove herself from the situation. The daughter does not speak back as she was spoken to (repay evil with evil), nor does she go off and publicly trash her parents. In this manner she continues to honor them. She is not, however, obligated to maintain a relationship with anyone who does not treat her as she should be treated. She can close the relational door. She shouldn't lock it though, as the parent's heart may change, thereby creating an opportunity for the relationship to be restored."[301]

Reflection: If this sounds too difficult, pinpoint your reason(s) and turn them into a prayer to God.

~ A man's children and his garden both reflect the amount
of weeding done during the growing season. ~

Unknown

Day 323: Emotional Release

Most psychologists and pastors recommend dealing with childhood issues, if possible. That may mean re-establishing contact with parents. Obviously you can't if a parent is dead or angry. Discussing the past may provide some parents a much-needed emotional release, but some may deny: "Don't judge me!" "That never happened!" Consider writing a letter about the hurt. Pray whether you should mail it or not.

It was easy for me to find reasons to blame my parents for my past, but as God healed my heart, I realized that my parents did the best they could with what they were given. We have to look back at how they were raised.

Some of us may lack the ability to speak back in our defense to our parents or function as an adult in their presence. Some of us have difficulties setting boundaries with our parent(s) due to other underlying issues that have not been identified yet. We may continue to struggle with the process of forgiveness and boundaries.

We all want our parents to be heroes, not embarrassments, and writing a letter about things they did can bring that hurt to the light. Open the door and thank them for the things they did right, even if it's only a few things.

Reflection: Are you in an abusive relationship with a parent today? What is one thing you can do, with God's help, to move toward closing the door of abuse?

~ *Though my father and mother forsake me, the* LORD *will receive me.* ~

Psalm 27:10

Day 324: God's Girl Honors Her Husband

Children are commanded to honor their parents (Day 321). Today it seems many parents make it difficult for their children to honor them when they do not honor one another or their marriage vows. For love in marriage to survive, we decide to honor our husband's position every day, regardless of how we feel about him at that moment.

Gary Thomas, author of *Sacred Marriage*, wrote, "We have to stop asking of marriage what God never designed it to give—perfect happiness, conflict-free living, and idolatrous obsession." Instead, he says, we can appreciate what God designed marriage to provide: partnership, spiritual intimacy and the ability to pursue God.[302]

Eve's creation gives us some important biblical lessons about our divinely designed role to honor our husband. Even though Eve was spiritually and intellectually Adam's equal with dominion over all other creatures, there was nevertheless a distinction in their roles. Scripture teaches that Adam was the head of the human race, yet Eve remained Adam's spiritual and intellectual equal. She was created to be his helper, not his supervisor or his slave. Scripture stressed the complementary nature of the partnership.

What does that mean for us? We make a conscious decision to honor our husband's decisions, his thoughts, and love him passionately because he is made in the image of God. You will not only become the woman of your husband's dreams, but your legacy may live through your children's marriages and for generations to come.

Reflection: In your words, what is a "good wife?" How do you measure up?

~ Marriage and family are institutions founded by God. They are considered his highest priority next to personal salvation. They are worth defending in battle. ~

Beverly LaHaye[303]

Day 325: God's Girl Honors Relationships

Someone once said that the five most essential words for a healthy and vital relationship are, "I apologize" and "You are right."

Christians are called upon to honor one another. That is, each is to consider his fellow believer more worthy of esteem than himself (Romans 12:10).

In 1 Peter 1:7 Christians are said to possess honor. Showing honor to others should affect one's entire lifestyle. Husbands are to honor their wives by showing loving regard for them.

We can honor others in one of two ways. One involves ulterior motives. We honor our bosses so they will reward us, the wealthy so they will contribute to our cause, the powerful so they will use their power for us and not against us.

The other way involves love. As Christians we honor people because they have been created in God's image, because they are our brothers and sisters in Christ, and they have a unique contribution to make to Christ's church. Love and respect are the most important aspects of all relationships.

I've learned that just because someone doesn't love or honor you the way you like, it doesn't mean they don't love and honor you. You and I can look at a beautiful work of art and see two different things. I've also learned that we don't have to change friends or spouses as long as we understand that people change.

Reflection: Think of a person that you are not honoring today that deserves your honor. What one step can you take to begin to honor her or him?

~ *The first duty of love is to listen.* ~

Paul Tillich (1886–1965)[304]

Day 326: A Reason, a Season, a Lifetime

People come into your life for a reason, a season, or a lifetime. When some-one comes into your life for a *reason,* it is usually to be a shepherd. They have come to assist you through difficulty, to provide guidance and support, to aid you physically, emotionally, or spiritually. Perhaps then quite unexpectedly, this person will bring the relationship to an end. Your need has been met. Their work is done.

Some people come into your life for a *season.* They bring you joy or peace or make you laugh. They may teach you something you have never done—but only for a season. *Lifetime* relationships teach you lifetime lessons, things you build upon in order to have a solid emotional foundation. Accept the lesson, love the person, and put what you have learned into practice in all areas of your life. It is said that love is blind, but friendship is clairvoyant. Still there are seasons God wants us to walk alone. He knows we need him to be our Friend. Billy Graham said, "One with God is a majority."[305]

Whatever the reason or season (long or short, joyful or painful) God's fingerprints will be there, and it up to us to ask him to show us the purpose of that relationship. If our heart is broken, in some mysterious way known only to God, we do grow. To be able to love means that we risk being rejected.

Reflection: Will you risk opening your heart to a new friend only to possibly endure a painful parting scene in the future?

*~ One of the most beautiful qualities of true
friendship is to understand and to be understood. ~*

Lucius Annaeus Seneca[306]

Day 327: God's Girl Honors Her Body

That dreaded mirror! Last week I went clothes shopping. I hate those horrible change room mirrors. As I tried the clothes on, I longed for smaller this and smaller that. I overheard a group of adolescent girls.

"These pants are too tight," a frustrated voice said. "My butt and thighs are *huge*!"

"Come out! I'm sure they look fine."

"No way! I *hate* my body!"

How many times have we wished for the elusive perfect body?

No matter what size we are, we are all confronted with media messages where female role models are underweight. It's no surprise we experience low self-esteem and depression. Eating disorders and depression go hand in hand. A pastor once said that his congregation had many overweight women, but that wasn't their fault. Eating was the only pleasure they were allowed that wasn't a sin.

In her book Silver Linings, Florence Littauer wrote, "So many overweight women try to consider themselves pleasingly plump and rationalize that all chubby people are jolly. But they're not. They are often depressed, and while they may try to laugh a lot in public, they often weep at home when the zipper just won't make it."[307]

Our bodies are temples of God's Holy Spirit, and he expects us to value them. The Spirit of the living God has chosen our bodies as his dwelling place; therefore we honor him with our bodies.

Reflection: What is your perception of your body?

~ *The Lord prefers common-looking people. That is why he makes so many of them.* ~

Abraham Lincoln[308]

Day 328: Are You a Body Hater?

Psychologist Kim Gaines Eckert has a test called *Are You a Body-Hater?*[309] Find out if a poor body image interferes with your daily life:

Are you constantly trying to lose weight, even if you're in the healthy weight range for your height?

When people compliment you, do you find it hard to believe them?

Do you avoid situations that make you feel self-conscious about your body?

Do you compare yourself with other women, taking note of who's thinner or more attractive than you?

Do you avoid looking in mirrors or always find something to critique when you look in a mirror or see yourself in photos?

Is your self-talk filled with critical comments about your appearance?

Do you find yourself thinking that "if only" you just lost ten pounds, you'd feel content and secure?

Does negative body image affect your relationships? For example, do you avoid physical intimacy with your husband because you're ashamed of your body?

Can you list ten things you really like about your appearance? No? What about five things?

Reflection: If you answered yes to a majority of these questions, you're in a battle with your body. Healing means loving your body and treating it with honor.

~ *Today let me realize that respect for my body builds a healing temple in which the rest of my life can grow.* ~

Anonymous

Day 329: Temple Maintenance Plan

Do you love and care for your body as well as you love and care for your home and kids? Do you feel your body deserves attention and a loving maintenance plan?

Taking our body for granted is easy because of its remarkable durability. Self-care takes time and priority planning to be successful. We may find we put off our exercise and nutritional needs, saying, "Tomorrow." Taking care of the body God gave us (our temple) needs to be an ongoing priority.

God expects us to love and nurture our body. When we take proper care of it, God brings rewards. The Bible tells us, "Do you not know that your body is a temple of the Holy Spirit, who is in you, whom you have received from God? You are not your own; you were bought at a price. Therefore honor God with your body" (1 Corinthians 6:19–20).

We have control over our personal health. Wellness is a matter of choice (and good genes don't hurt either). We determine what we put into our mouths and bodies. Many women with symptoms of depression find relief by making better food choices.

Reflection: Write down five things you will begin to do to that will become part of your daily or weekly Temple Maintenance Plan?

~ When your physical body is supported, it can help you find the self-confidence and encouragement to deal with the important emotional, relational, and spiritual issues that need to be addressed in your long-term recovery. ~

Dr. Gregory Jantz[310]

Day 330: MileStone

Steps To Overcome Negative Emotions

Move Forward

In all kinds of relationships, it is unrealistic to expect every minute to be perfect and filled with joy (that fairy tale dream). There will be times we disagree. We may want to do something separate from the other person or simply be in a bad mood. Real life is about experiencing emotions of all kinds. We may experience sadness, frustration, anger, disappointment, and depression. These feelings are all part of life, and we must allow others to have their own feelings too.

There are some days we don't feel like serving our husbands. We move forward by remembering, and practicing, that when we serve our husbands we begin to grow softer spirits and more loving hearts.

Reflect: Think about it this way: we are really serving Jesus, therefore we will be blessed in ways we can't imagine!

~ I'm totally out of shape, so I joined a fitness club and took an aerobics class. I bent, twisted, gyrated, jumped up and down, and perspired for an hour. By the time I got my leotards on, the class was over. ~

Anonymous

Day 331: Challenge the Old Way of Thinking

Eating a Balanced Diet, Including Rich Nutritional Supplements

Many feel discouraged and tired, unable to make dietary or other changes in health habits. Professionals recommend giving a new change anywhere between two weeks and two months, especially if change involves a lifestyle renovation. The good news is that the lift you'll feel in your energy level will be remarkable. That may sound impossible, but remember, the Lord is our strength! He is the God of the impossible. You will receive the strength to keep going with other changes. Let's get going!

Many factors that contribute to depression are created by nutritional deficiencies. I suggest you locate and work with a professional nutritionist and/or a preventative-minded physician who understands nutrition. That person can develop a personal program around your specific needs. There are many books and resources available on eating a balanced diet. Eating healthy is a great start, but overcoming depression will most likely require vitamin supplementations too.

Dr. Maurice Stephens, medical consultant and nutrition expert, explains, "It is no longer possible to get all the nutrients we need by just eating a 'balanced diet.' Our foods are being stored too long. They are altered or irradiated to increase shelf life. Nutrients are damaged by processing and packaging. Sometimes the nutrients just aren't there...recovery from depression can only be more assured when the body becomes healthier, with greater energy and coping strength."[311]

Eating healthy and adding nutritional supplementation are good ways to give your body what it needs to battle depression.

Challenge your old way of thinking by implementing these changes.

Day 332: Reduce Stress & Enhance Mood

I challenge you to begin thinking about exercise. I know, many of us think a dumbbell is an idiot. A female comedienne said every woman should be able to do these exercises: beat around the bush; jump to conclusions; climb the walls; throw her weight around; drag her heels; push her luck; make mountains out of molehills; run around in circles; climb the ladder of success; pull out the stops; put her foot in her mouth; go over the edge; pick up the pieces ... and collapse in a heap![312]

Seriously, exercise is important for our daily health because it releases endorphins, which create a natural euphoria, reducing cortisol levels. You don't have to join a gym. A daily walk to the mailbox is a good place to start.

Experts recommend beginning slowly and working up to thirty minutes, six times a week. Combining some weight-bearing exercise with aerobic activity (like walking or biking) provides the best relief.

In addition, moderate sun exposure year-round is quite beneficial. A real connection exists between vitamin D deficiency and depression. It's commonly known that light exposure, especially sunlight, which stimulates vitamin D production, is a very effective treatment for SAD (seasonal affective disorder). The same with supplements of vitamin D.

Reflection: Make a date with a friend to go walking *at least* twice a week.

~ *Do what you can, with what you have, where you are.* ~

Theodore Roosevelt[313]

Day 333: Sweet Slumber

Getting a good night's sleep may be a challenge for you. Dr. Gregory Jantz says that depression interferes with the healthy production and operation of serotonin and melatonin, neurotransmitters used for the body's sleep-wake cycle. As you work toward wholeness, you will want to assist your body in any way you can to achieve this restful sleep. Try intentionally preparing for rest. This means allowing your body and your mind time to transition into sleep. This winding down could consist of listening to relaxing music, reading, listening to soothing natural sounds, or quiet meditation.

He says to give yourself enough time to get adequate rest. Eight hours, granted is an average, but be aware of when your body might require more sleep. Whenever a body is under stress, physical or emotional, it will require more rest to rebuild and replenish. Five to six hours a night is probably not going to provide what you need. It may require you to make choices about activities so you can establish a healthy routine of getting to bed on time.[314]

Pray and Meditate

Holy Spirit, truth divine, Dawn upon this soul of mine.

Word of God and inward light,

Wake my spirit, clear my sight.

In Jesus' name. Amen. (Anonymous)

Self-Soother

Think of two small things you can do to become more productive. Now do them.

Part Sixteen

God's Girl is Light!

Encouraged by God's Word

"You are my lamp, O LORD; the LORD turns my darkness into light. With your help I can advance against a troop; with my God I can scale a wall." (2 Samuel 22: 29–30)

Day 334: Stepping Out in Faith

When I was laid off from my job, I optimistically thought, *I have years of experience. It won't be hard to get another job.* At the time I didn't really know God too well. I chose to lean on him, asking for guidance and wisdom for specific job positions. I'd get to be one of the top candidates considered, but never hired. I'd take my disappointment to God. He'd place some verse or story in my path as encouragement.

Then I read the book *The Purpose Driven Life* and all the pieces began to fall together. *I have a purpose!* While more and more out of work Americans sunk into depression and gave up on the job market all together, I persevered with God's strength.

The closer I got to God, the more I wanted a career that would allow me to do his work. Naturally, there still was uncertainty. Ministry meant giving up my comfort and all I had known for the last twenty-five years (I thought). I really wanted both, to work for God and man, to have my cake and eat it too. I got my cake: Devil's Food.

The devil planted seeds of doubt like, *You're not qualified to work for God…You're not gifted enough…* I put my armor on and resisted eating that cake. The answer came when I was prayerfully journaling my dilemma: ministry or workplace—or both?

I came upon this Scripture: "Jesus said, 'No one can serve two masters'" (Matthew 6:24). I realized God was asking me to choose between a demanding career and him. I needed to step out in faith and trust God to provide for my financial needs.

Reflection: What one thing have you felt hesitant about doing? Take that step of faith today.

~ *God will not commission you to do anything without ensuring your success.* ~

Henry T. Blackaby[315]

Day 335: Send Me!

I believe most women long to have their lives count for something—much more than their dress size or the square footage of their house or job qualifications. I judged myself by these superficial standards. Going into ministry, I still didn't feel qualified, but I began to see that God likes to use ordinary people to do his extraordinary work.

God delights in doing incredible things through people who simply say, *I'm available!* When the prophet Isaiah saw the Lord seated on a throne (in a vision), and heard the glorious sounds of heaven, his response was, "I am a man of unclean lips" (Isaiah 6:5). His reaction is much like our response. After Isaiah received cleansing and forgiveness, he heard the Lord speak those challenging words, "Whom shall I send? Who will go for us? Isaiah immediately said, "Here am I. Send me!" (Isaiah 6:8).

Like Isaiah, I literally cried, *Send me!* God did. For a long time I bought the enemy's lie that because of my addictions and failures, God could never use me. On the contrary, I'm living proof that God can and does use us despite our past mistakes.

Rest assured God will not allow anyone or anything prevent his children from accomplishing his purposes. Don't believe the lie that God cannot use you because of your past or present circumstances. In fact, God often completes the healing process while we're in his service. He's still working on me!

Reflection: Will you allow God, who has called you to himself and equipped you with his Spirit, to work through you?

~ Everybody can be great because anybody can serve. You don't need a college degree. You only need a heart full of grace. A soul generated by love. ~

Martin Luther King, Jr.[316]

Day 336: Jesus' Ambassador

We've all asked, *What am I here for?* Only time with God will answer that question, but I can tell you every Christian is called to be Jesus' representative. We can't fulfill this important role if we're living in a dungeon. Your bumper sticker says, "Follower of Jesus." If we call ourselves a Christian, *we are* God's living words; we bear his name. Our actions are evidence of God's presence, which means we respond as Christ's ambassador. An ambassador is an authorized messenger or representative, who represents the message, methods, and character of her leader.[317]

Paul said in 2 Corinthians 5:17–20 that our old life *was* centered around ourselves. *Now* we are new creations because the old has passed away. We were changed when we met Jesus. The Holy Spirit gives us new life, and we are not the same anymore.

That light we talked about is ever present in us now. As we encounter people, we may think they should be attracted to our outsides, but not so. It is the light of the Holy Spirit that illuminates from our inside, and that makes us beautiful.

Not only do we have the indwelling of the Holy Spirit (the light), but we have new choices to make and new responsibilities to live life according to God's teachings. Understanding this is God's will and moving forward is spiritual maturity.

God himself has begun the work in each one of us. That takes the pressure off us. Our job is to submit completely so the Holy Spirit can begin his work. Then we find God putting us in places and situations we never dreamed of.

Reflection: Where would you like God to place you? What is your dream?

~ *The problem of modern living is that we're too busy*
to notice that we are being blessed. ~

Henri J.W. Nouwen[318]

Day 337: An Endless Adventure

English teacher and Christian leader Bertha Munro said, "Surrender to Jesus is the first step of an endless adventure with Him."[319] What an optimist! I am where I am (you are where you are) because we were each called to represent Jesus. God uses us to speak to others as though Christ himself were here. However, we can't be successful ambassadors if we're motivated by our own self-interests and negative attitudes.

As his representatives we teach by example, and that compels people toward or away from Jesus. If we are *not* living in a way consistent with God's Word, we're putting his reputation at stake. Our lives either honor or dishonor Jesus. We are called to be light, which means to speak and act as his representative. God's Girl does not live for *self* anymore. She is a portrait of a woman used by God, a woman of light. She reflects the fruit of the Spirit (joy, peace, love, patience, kindness, goodness, and faithfulness, Galatians 5:22), which makes her his beloved daughter.

Paul tells us how we are to do that: "Therefore, as God's chosen people, holy and dearly loved, clothe yourselves with compassion, kindness, humility, gentleness and patience" (Colossians 3:12).

We're given another outfit to put on! The Living Bible says it this way: "You should practice tenderhearted mercy and kindness to others. Don't worry about making a good impression on them."

No doubt you want to make a difference. Jesus pleaded, "Don't hide your light! Let it shine for all; let your good deeds glow for all to see, so that they will praise your heavenly Father" (Matthew 5:15, TLB).

Reflection: List one or more ways you are now reflecting the fruit of the spirit.

~ *What counts is not my ability, but my usability.* ~

E. Stanley Jones[320]

Day 338: The Honor and Privilege

All along we've wondered what God's purpose for us is.

You don't have to be a theologian to understand. We look at Jesus' example: "That is what the Son of Man [Jesus] has done: He came to serve, not be served—and then to give away his life in exchange for the many who are held hostage" (Matthew 20:28, Msg).

Max Lucado wrote, "He [Jesus] spent three decades wading through the muck and mire of our sin yet still saw enough beauty in us to die for our mistakes."[321]

We have been set free! The ransom has been paid! Now it is our turn to reciprocate God's love by speaking and acting as God's delegate. We pray about it. That means we are always asking God what he wants to accomplish through us. When we move forward, we ask, *As I respond to this person or this situation, am I faithfully representing the character of Christ?*

People are watching the way we act more than they are listening to what we say. When we meet Jesus in heaven, don't we want to hear him say something like, "Thank you for letting me use you. Because of your heart, your availability, and your witness, there are others here today."

Looking around, you see those others smiling and waving at you!

Reflection: This is why it is so important to ask God daily to help us speak words of life and love. Pray: "Lord, please anoint my conversations and control my tongue!"

~ Change is the characteristic of all growth. ~

Anonymous

Day 339: God's Girl Huldah

One of God's representatives was a woman named Huldah, a prophetess. The king Josiah sought her out for a word from the Lord. She spoke the Word of God, and her words generated a significant religious reform. As a prophetess, Huldah was privileged to be a messenger of God (2 Kings 22:14–20; Chronicles 34:22–23).

We don't know much about this remarkable woman, but we know God used her to influence this young king. God entrusted her with his word at a time of national crisis. After her prophecy, Josiah led one of the greatest religious reforms in history, purging Judah and even parts of Israel of paganism and idolatry. Unfortunately, the kings that followed Josiah reversed the course. Huldah was a woman so in touch with God that he allowed her to communicate his words to those that would change a nation.

Huldah is one of only four women with a prophetic ministry mentioned in the Old Testament. Miriam, Deborah, and Isaiah's wife are the other three.

We may not be prophetesses, but we are charged with speaking the truth. Being used by God is a great privilege and honor. It is the reason to get up in the morning! It's an opportunity to be part of what God is doing in the lives of others.

Each woman we have been studying believed that God could work through her to make a significant difference ... and you can too!

Reflection: What can you begin to do to remind yourself daily that your life is about living for God as his representative?

~ *Only an experience of deep pain develops our*
capacity for recognizing and enjoying true life. ~

Dr. Larry Crabb[322]

Day 340: The Queen Seeks Wisdom

You have surely heard the phrase, "She thinks she's the queen of Sheba!" We associate that title with someone who is usually spoiled, well kept, and arrogant. What do we really know about the pagan queen of Sheba, and can we learn from her?

According to the Bible (1 Kings 10:1–13; Mathew 12:42), the unnamed queen heard of the great wisdom of King Solomon and his God and journeyed there with gifts of spices, gold, and precious stones, to see for herself if this was true. She was beautiful, rich, and brought 4.5 tons of gold with her to give to Solomon!

Even though her people worshipped many gods, she wanted to hear more about Solomon's God. She decided to take a six-month (each way) 1,400 mile trip across the desert sands of Arabia to visit this man who knew this God personally. Finally, she arrived. This was the grandest palace she had ever laid eyes on. Her purpose wasn't to see the most beautiful archeological place ever built, it was to find a secret treasure—the wisdom of the one and only God.

When she finally met King Solomon, she tested his wisdom using riddles and proverbs, and surely asked him deep questions about God. She found what she had longed for and said, "Praise be to the LORD your God" and pronounced a blessing on Solomon's God. Solomon reciprocated with gifts and "everything she desired." The queen's quest for wisdom was rewarded beyond her expectations.

Reflection: Recall a time spent with a godly person. How did their richness affect you?

> ~ *You can tell a man is clever by his answers. You can tell a man is wise by his questions.* ~
>
> Naguib Mahfouz (1911–2006)

Day 341: Acquiring Wisdom

Forbes magazine is known for its lists: more than twenty lists cataloging people on the basis of wealth and power. Our culture honors this over wisdom. Yet wisdom is a greater asset. Jesus mentions the queen of Sheba in Matthew 12:42. He honors her request for wisdom. She went to a great deal of trouble to hear Solomon's wisdom, yet the wisdom available to her was only the understanding of a man. Wisdom is the ability to see life from God's perspective and know the best course of action to take.[323]

Proverbs 9:10 teaches that to fear of the Lord (respect and honor) is the beginning of wisdom. It comes from knowing and trusting God. When Solomon asked for wisdom in his dream, God promised him riches and honor (1 Kings 3:13).

When you meet someone new, or have guests into your home, what do they come away thinking? *What a beautiful house! She really looked pretty today. I love her landscaped garden.* Or will they be drawn to your insight through the Holy Spirit living in you and feel they were blessed by spending time with you. Ask God for wisdom.

God freely gives spiritual wisdom to those who ask and seek it with all their heart (James 1:5). Ask him to help you remember all that you learn from him and to live it daily. Not only will you be spiritually rich, but also your friends and family will find a treasure that people have traveled the whole earth in search of.

Reflection: Do you spend more time fussing over the outward beauty of yourself or your home than the inward beauty of your soul?

~ *Even the saddest things can become, once we have made peace with them,*
a source of wisdom and strength for the journey that still lies ahead. ~

Frederick Buechner[324]

Day 342: God's Girl Bears Fruit

For most of us, journeying through this book has been a long, intense, and difficult trial. There is a reward. These trials lead to a healthier, more mature you, allowing God to prune away some of the old sin and garbage in your life. We hurt because God is pruning us. He does this because we are a tree worth saving! What do these verses tell us about our garden and about us? Jesus said:

> I am the true vine, and my Father is the gardener. He cuts off every branch
> in me that bears no fruit, while every branch that does bear fruit he prunes
> so that it will be even more fruitful. You are already clean because of the
> word I have spoken to you. Remain in me, and I will remain in you. No
> branch can bear fruit by itself; it must remain in the vine. Neither can you
> bear fruit unless you remain in me. . . . I have told you this so that my joy
> may be in you and that your joy may be complete (John 15:1–4,11).

The term fruit has different meanings depending on the context. In the Bible fruit is a metaphor. You have felt pruned because you have been chosen and appointed to bear fruit (John 15:16). We are on our way to being supernaturally transformed, receiving the ability to bear the ripest and richest fruit. *But* we have to remain "in him," connected, in relationship with God. This is our purpose, to produce fruit, which produces joy!

Reflection: Name two things that God is pruning in your life today? Why do you think he has chosen these two things to prune?

> ~ *Christians who lose God during a period of spiritual*
> *confusion are like a vine cut off from its source. Deprived of*
> *nurture and strength, they cope at first, but soon begin to wither.* ~
>
> Dr. James Dobson[325]

Day 343: The Fruit of the Spirit

God created you in his image. He sees possibilities and potential you can't see. Until God's transformation process begins in us, we live in a state of being continually conformed to this society. If we allow him to, *God changes us from the inside out,* and we begin to bear this scrumptious fruit. He does what you can't do.

When you begin bearing fruit, people will look at you and see a new woman! A woman spewing out God's beauty and love. A renewed woman walking in the light, walking in God-confidence. A woman enlightened by the Spirit, filled with joy and peace and a passion to bless others.

A.W. Tozer said, "The whole purpose is to make us holy and to restore us to the image of God. To accomplish this, He disengages us from earthly ambitions and draws us away from the cheap and unworthy prizes that worldly men set their hearts upon."[326]

God points to the fruit of the Spirit: "When the Holy Spirit controls our lives he will produce this kind of fruit in us: *love, joy, peace, patience, kindness, goodness, faithfulness, gentleness and self-control*" (Galatians 5:22–23). This is God's definition of an *inside makeover*—a transformation that becomes life changing. Did you notice one of the fruits of the Spirit is joy? This joy is unlike any happiness that is produced by the world. It fills you and permeates everything you do, which is what makes you extremely attractive. Like fruit on the vine, our purpose (spiritual fruit) is to be life sustaining, life-giving, and reproductive.

Reflect on this picture of God's inside makeover and how it applies to you today.

~ God loves everyone, but probably prefers "fruits of the spirit" over "religious nuts."~

Anonymous

Day 344: The Branch and the Vine

God wants to be as close to us as a branch is to a vine. If you look closely at a tomato plant, you will see it's almost impossible to tell where one starts and the other ends. The branch is constantly drawing its nutrition from the vine. The plant continues to thrive and bear fruit as long as the gardener continues to prune it.

How does the metaphor apply to us?

We were never meant to just look pretty. We need to ask the Father to cut off the dead vines and prune back the wild branches. Our purpose is to be used by God and to model true love and joy. We are meant to stay attached to the vine—daily.

We must set ourselves free from trying to fit into our culture's way, which ultimately twists our identity. Most of us want applause, an atta-boy, or a lavish compliment. Jesus has always changed the focus to the life to come—to investing in our future. When you read Jesus' message about the kingdom of God, he is saying: "Live for God. Not other people." We must be willing to care more about what Jesus thinks about us than what others think about us.

Bearing fruit means we become others-oriented and willing to do things God's way. God's gift to us was his Son, our salvation. Our gift to God is our fruit. Depend instead on the Father, letting him take care of the personal problems and injustices that come our way. Bearing fruit means we can trust God to look after our daily needs.

Reflection: How do you need God's help even to desire to yield to his pruning? Make this a prayer this moment.

~ *At the same time, ripe, holy lives will mature and adorn the kingdom of their Father.* ~

The Apostle Matthew (Matthew 13:43, Msg)

Day 345: A Heart of Hospitality

A new pastor was visiting the homes of his parishioners. At one house it seemed obvious that someone was home, but no answer came to his repeated knocks at the door. So he took out his card, wrote Revelations 3:20 on the back, and stuck it in the door. When the offering was processed the following Sunday, he found his card had been returned. Added to it was this cryptic message, Genesis 3:10.

Reaching for his Bible to check out the verse, he broke up in gales of laughter. Revelation 3:20 begins, "Behold, I stand at the door and knock." Genesis 3:10 reads, "I heard your voice in the garden and I was afraid, for I was naked."

Luke 10:38–42 records a story about Jesus' visits to the home of close friends Lazarus, Martha, and Mary. He enjoyed their company and visited with them often. Over the years Martha's name has become synonymous with hospitality. In those days a person's reputation was largely connected to his or her hospitality. Strangers were to be treated as highly honored guests. We can imagine the pressure Martha put on herself.

Hospitality is the kindness or friendly reception and treatment of guests or strangers.[327] Today, hostesses are often haunted by the myth of a different Martha—the Martha Stewart perfection. However, most people do not expect perfection from you or your home because they don't relate to anyone with a seemingly perfect life.

Reflection: How do you feel about unexpected company?

~ *Give us true ambition—ambition to find our greatness in serving others, and the ambition to put into life more than we take out.* ~

William Barclay[328]

Day 346: God's Girls Martha and Mary

In this story (Luke 10:38–42) Jesus and the disciples were on their way to Jerusalem. They came to a village, Bethany, where Martha welcomed them into her home. No doubt she was scurrying around, preparing. She was pleased that her home had become a place of rest and friendship for Jesus and his disciples.

As soon as they got situated in the meeting room, her sister, Mary, sat at the Lord's feet, listening to what he taught. However, Martha was worrying over the big dinner she was preparing. Martha came to Jesus and said, "Lord, doesn't it seem unfair to you that my sister just sits here while I do all the work? Tell her to come and help me."

The Lord replied, "My dear Martha, you are so upset over all these details! There is really only one thing worth being concerned about. Mary has discovered it—and I won't take it away from her."

Martha was working quickly to feed over a dozen houseguests.

Thirteen hungry men and twenty-six feet to wash was not a small task. Martha was a hostess in the true biblical sense. Jesus felt at home in their house. (Jesus lived on the road, virtually homeless.)

Reflection: Why do you think Jesus faults Martha for seeking to be the competent hostess and commends Mary for sitting around doing nothing?

~ *Always set a place in your life for the unexpected guest.* ~

Anonymous

Day 347: Jesus Is the Focus

When Jesus and the men visited, they followed Lazarus into the main room, and Mary got out a basin with water to begin the ritual of foot washing. Martha noticed Mary hadn't come in to help her with kitchen detail. *Where was Mary?* Martha headed for the meeting room looking for Mary. *I can't believe it,* she must have thought. *She's sitting on the floor at Jesus' feet doing nothing but listening while I'm in here doing all the work!* It wasn't proper for women to sit with men during a meal.

However, Martha missed out on an important event: Jesus was teaching in her own home, and what a shock it must have been when he took her sister's side! She learned a lesson that would change her life—the kingdom of God was more important than a meal. Keep in mind that back in those days, hospitality was far more complicated. Foot washings and meals were challenges. Guests stayed overnight because of the great distances they had to walk. Martha was just doing what she thought was expected of her.

Mary was the sister who made the better decision. She had a deeper sense of priority. She understood why Jesus had come into the world. Jesus was not about to distract Mary from her calling to gaze upon her Lord. He was always at the center of Mary's existence. Time with Jesus takes precedence over all else.

I don't want to bruise up Martha. Later when her brother Lazarus dies, Jesus was teaching the people that he had power over life and death. Many did not believe him. Martha did (John 11:27). We see a woman of deep faith. Martha's statement of faith was the exact response Jesus was looking for.

Reflection: How is Jesus at the center of your existence today? Do you believe?

~ *We want to be a lighthouse in this neighborhood.* ~

Jennie Afman Dimkoff[29]

Day 348: Mary Plus Martha

We discover truth from both Mary and Martha. Martha is responsible, concerned about meeting the needs of others and blessed with the gift of hospitality, certainly great qualities. When we meet God someday, he won't ask us how many square feet our home was or how well decorated it was. He will ask us how many people we invited into it.

Even though Mary appears somewhat uncaring or lazy, she teaches us that it is not an easy thing to maintain the balance of our spiritual life. No woman can be spiritually healthy who does not meditate and commune with Jesus. Jesus never rebuked Martha for being a hard worker. He said only that her busyness wasn't the best thing at that moment. He did stress that Mary made the right choice. Mary had a deeper sense of priority; time with Jesus takes precedence over helping her sister.

The way each one of us loves Jesus and others will look different. God's Girl is a Mary plus a Martha. She invites a lonely coworker home for dinner and shares Jesus, or asks a new group of women from the church over for a Bible study, or invites the youth group over for a barbeque, or gives the pastor and his wife a respite from cooking for a fellowship gathering. Exercising hospitality is one more way we honor God and represent him to others.

Reflection: When guests come to your home, are they more impressed with how beautiful your home is or your genuine warmth? If you are not sure, ask a friend.

~ *What you leave behind is not what is engraved in stone monuments, but what is woven into the lives of others.* ~

Pericles

Day 349: MileStone

Steps To Overcome Negative Emotions

Move Forward

Our culture has a "do as you please" attitude. We should enjoy life and maintain a positive attitude, but that does not exempt us from following God's commandments.

Our time on earth is limited, and we are to use it wisely. The Bible says one day we all will be accountable to God for what we did on this earth; also known as judgment day, or retribution (2 Corinthians 5:10).

Paul said, "Just as man is destined to die once, and after that to face judgment" (Hebrews 9:27).

Jesus explains the coming of judgment day in Matthew 25:31–46. He uses the parable of the sheep and the goats to make a clear correlation between loving him and loving others in need.

Through Christ's payment on the cross, we have escaped eternal judgment (John 5:24); however, our actions will be judged at the seat of Christ. *Retribution means you get something for what you do—your account is settled. The moment you begin to live your new life (when you are born again), God basically says, I have an agenda for you. In the end I will do an evaluation of your life and will ask you, "Daughter, what did you do with everything I gave you? What did you do for my kingdom?"*

"Well Lord, I got four promotions and worked hard to give my kids everything they needed. We built a four thousand square foot home! I jogged every day. I was a nice person ... I gave to charities!"

No, Daughter, what did you do for My kingdom, not your kingdom?
How will you respond?

Day 350: Challenge the Old Way of Thinking

Most of us don't comprehend that everything we have belongs to God, because everything we have came from God. We must use those gifts and blessings with God's interests in mind. It is important to put God first in our life and take a stand for him. If we drift along, taking the easy, pleasant, and tolerable road, we will someday have to talk to God about that.

Don't we all want to be told when we meet God, "Well done, my good and faithful servant?" I do. We have God's promise, "What is due me is in the LORD's hand, and my reward is with my God" (Isaiah 49:4).

Warren G. Harding, twenty-ninth president of the United States said, "Service is the supreme commitment of life." Our attitude toward our guests and others reflects our relationship with God.

This week we move forward asking for a servant's heart. A heart change is often required. We begin to practice, and pray for hospitality:

> Love must be sincere. Hate what is evil; cling to what is good. Be devoted
> to one another in brotherly love. Honor one another above yourselves.
> Never be lacking in zeal, but keep your spiritual fervor, serving the Lord.
> Be joyful in hope, patient in affliction, faithful in prayer. Share with God's
> people who are in need (Romans 12:9–13).

Day 351: Taking Charge & Setting Goals

Margaret Thatcher, the first woman in Europe to be elected prime minister, said, "Look at a day when you are supremely satisfied at the end. It's not a day when you lounge around doing nothing; it's when you've had everything to do, and you've done it."

Refusing to set goals means acting without purpose. We spend time, money, and energy, but lack productivity. We have been given the privilege of planning our life according to God's will.

Charles Stanley wrote, "Throughout the Bible, the Lord directs his servants in setting goals, and then he provides the strength to achieve them. A life lacking goals is mediocre at best. Without ambitions to work toward, we have no opportunity for success. And if we never experience the thrill of achieving a long sought-after goal, we will be very disappointed with our life. No one wants a mediocre existence of waste and apathy. A believer should never settle for less than God's best. The indwelling Holy Spirit offers each of us the great potential to be a godly goal setter."[330]

You may say, sounds good, but how? I suggest we look to the encouragement of mature believers in Christ, to the power of the indwelling Holy Spirit, to his Word, and then make our decisions based on what honors God.

Reflection: How does Dr. Stanley's message change your thinking today?

~ *You miss 100 percent of the shots you never take.* ~

Wayne Gretzky

Day 352: Staying Focused on Goals

Today we'll talk about implementing more doable goals into our life.

Stay focused on your vision. Beware of a defeated attitude.

Many men in the Bible such as Moses, Elijah, and Gideon, when presented with God's plan, basically said, *God, you don't know what you're doing! I think you made a mistake.* Maybe you are saying, *I'd love to do these goals, but I'm no good at it. I don't have the energy ... I wish I could do ... But it's impossible. But, but, but ...*

God's Girl takes all the but's captive, pulls them down, throwing them out of her thoughts and vocabulary. But's only distract and disable us from being effective for the kingdom.

I have learned over the years that I have to keep an open mind and practice flexibility. If our goals don't seem to materialize, it may be because God wants us to do things a different way. What but's do you need to discard today?

Pray and Meditate

O Merciful Father, Have I today done anything to fulfill the purpose for which Thou didst cause me to be born? Have I accepted such opportunities of service as Thou in Thy wisdom hast set before my feet. ~ John Baillie[331]

Self-Soother

Make plans to go on a retreat. This may mean a day without running errands, doing fix-it projects, or shopping with a girlfriend (without the kids), or a women's church retreat—whatever your heart desires.

Day 353: A Written Game Plan

Develop a chart as a guideline to begin goal setting: Title the first page "Short-Term Goal Setting." Take out a second page and title it "Long-Term Goal Setting."
On each page list:

Goal:

Obstacle:

Game Plan:

Victory!

Author and pastor's wife Diana Hagee writes, "When you have attained your goal, do two things. First, give praise to the One who helped you attain the goal. He is well pleased with your thanksgiving offering.

"Second, set a new one. Never be without a goal in your life. Whether it is a having a special time with your family, pursuing further education, getting out of debt, buying a home, or entering retirement, never lose sight of your dreams."[332]

Be prepared for victory! Think often of the victorious women we have studied.

Reflection: List one short-term and one long-term goal. Pray about these and ask God to show you what obstacles might hinder you. What does your game plan need to look like?

~ *Don't judge each day by the harvest you reap, but by* the seeds you plant. ~

Robert Louis Stevenson (1850–1894)

Finishing this Race

Encouraged by God's Word

Many of us started this book spiritually dead... until the breath of our Lord Jesus Christ resuscitated and breathed new life and joy into us.

He asked me, "Son of man, can these bones live?" This is what the Sovereign LORD says to these bones: "I will make breath enter you, and you will come to life." The Sovereign LORD says: "Come from the four winds, O breath, and breathe into these slain, that they may live." So I prophesied as he commanded me, and breath entered them; they came to life and stood up on their feet—a vast army. I will put my Spirit in you and you will live, and I will settle you in your own land. Then you will know that I the LORD have spoken, and I have done it, declares the LORD" (Ezekiel 37:3, 5, 9–10, 14).

Day 354: Our Final God's Girl

John 4:1–42: She made her way to the well at a time of day that was too hot for most people to be outside, all in an attempt to avoid the stares and whispers. *Darn! There is a man at the well today,* she surely thought. Not just any man, but a Jew! *Perhaps he doesn't know me. I'll fill my pot quickly and leave.*

But the man spoke and asked her for a drink. Glancing around the area, she wondered, *Is he talking to me? He can't be.* Yes, he was. This was quite unusual.

This woman was a Samaritan, a member of a hated mixed race. She was also known to be living in sin, and she was in a public place. No respectable Jewish man would talk to such a woman. This man did. She said she was a despised Samaritan, unworthy of his acknowledgment. Bracing for rebuke from him, nothing came from his lips. Instead he gently said, "If you knew the gift of God and who it is that asks you for a drink, you would have asked him and he would have given you living water."

Yes, the man is Jesus. What did he mean by "living water?" In the Old Testament many verses speak of thirsting after God as one thirsts for water. God is called the fountain of life (Psalm 36:9) and the spring of living water (Jeremiah 17:13). Only Jesus could give this woman the gift that would satisfy and quench her soul's desire.

Most people never discover true life—the living water. Nonbelievers don't receive it. Believers (most of them) have it but don't experience it. You have been given the gift of the living water throughout this journey.

Reflection: How has the living water transformed you?.

~ *God wants to bless you. He gets a kick out of making His children happy.* ~

Dr. Larry Crabb[333]

Day 355: Two Kinds of Water

The woman at the well confuses the two kinds of water, most likely because no one had ever spoke to her before about spiritual hunger. We would never think of depriving our bodies of food and water, so why should we deprive our souls?

Jesus answered her, "Everyone who drinks this water will be thirsty again, but whoever drinks the water I give him will never thirst. Indeed the water I give him will become in him a spring of water welling up to eternal life."

She surely thought, *I've never heard this before. I want to hear more.* If she could just have what this man offered, she would have joy. She asks for some of that water. Jesus redirects her, "Go, call your husband and come back."

"I have no husband," she replied.

Jesus said to her, "You are right when you say you have no husband. The fact is, you have had five husbands, and the man you now have is not your husband. What you have just said is quite true."

I'm sure she was quite embarrassed. *How could he have known that? Was this a setup to shame me?* No. He was Jesus. He saw right into her soul.

Many people would call this woman a filthy sinner. I believe she was an abuse survivor. In that culture only the husband could divorce his wife. Inevitably five men rejected her, and her current love interest appeared to only want to shack up.

Reflection: When the conversation hits too close to home, we often change the subject or retreat. Her question was a smoke screen to keep Jesus away from her deepest need. How do you do the same thing?

~ *Water is the most neglected nutrient in your diet but one of the most vital.* ~

Kelly Barton[334]

Day 356: Jesus Knows!

In the story we've been studying, we see that Jesus deliberately went out of his way to meet this woman from Samaria. When he spoke to her, there was no accusation in his voice or mannerisms. She took great pains to slip in unnoticed, and now this complete stranger had the ability to expose everything about her. So she quickly changes the subject. In those days Jews did not associate with Samaritans. In fact, they avoided traveling through their region.

God does not follow man's rules or prejudices. He reaches out with a message of hope and new life to anyone who will listen and believe. Jesus knew the Samaritan woman's pain and heartache as he knows ours. Surely she felt like many of us: worthless and abandoned. Jesus understood what she needed to feel loved, valued, and accepted.

The story closes, "Many of the Samaritans from that town believed in him because of the woman's testimony..."

She immediately shared her experience with others. Despite her reputation, many came out to meet Jesus.

We all have emotional baggage that weighs us down and causes pain. Jesus drew out the details of her situation in a nonjudgmental way as a close friend does. He wanted her to be receptive to his offer of forgiveness and a relationship with God. As others see change in us they become curious, which is our opportunity to introduce them to Jesus.

Reflection: This woman knew a relationship with Jesus would fulfill her needs. Describe your relationship with Jesus today compared to when you first began this book.

~ We are better than we know. If we can be made to see it, perhaps for the rest of our lives, we will be unwilling to settle for less. ~

Anonymous

Day 357: The Last Chapter Hasn't Been Written ... Yet

Yesterday you were asked to think back to when you first began this study. What did your life look like then? Perhaps you are still facing some immovable mountains, but I hope life looks different in one way or other.

My last piece of advice is this: don't stop here. *Don't put a period where God has put a comma.* God is in the business of writing new chapters in your book of life, while closing the history chapters. The end of your story is far from finished.

Focus on what you have learned. Focus on the truth. Put on your armor and apply what you've learned every day. Until God puts down his pen and calls you home, he is still writing your story. Life may still be bumpy today, but it will look entirely different in one year. Optimism is the belief, the faith that things will get better in the future, and that God has exciting new chapters he's creating right now! Remember, God is in the business of recreating his fallen creatures.

Lastly, focus what Jesus did for you. His last prayer before leaving this earth was for you (Luke 22:41). Before his crucifixion he spoke with his Father, and you were the subject. Jesus made his decision to go to the cross, to die, for you (see Day 99). "They are God's children, since they are children of the resurrection" (Luke 20:36).

Reflection: Meditate on the chapter God is writing at this moment and give him thanks. Then try to answer, "How do I want my story to end?"

~ *Just don't give up on trying to do what you really want to do. Where there is love and inspiration, I don't think you can go wrong.* ~

Ella Fitzgerald (1917 - 1996)

Day 358: The Last MileStone
The Power of Story

Before a secret is told, often you can feel the weight of it in the air—dead weight. Moving forward means telling your story at some point, reading the chapters out loud that have been written. That doesn't mean you are being called to speak to an audience. Right now it means another step to bringing light out of darkness. If you've ever had a colossal toothache, you know the feeling of sweet relief when the dentist fixes the problem. That is how I felt when I brought my story (my secrets) to the light.

God will use your honesty and vulnerability about your experiences to not only continue the transformation process, but strengthen the faith of others. You may be thinking, *You can't imagine what I've done. I can't tell anyone.* No matter what your deep hurt or dark secret is, tell someone. Everybody feels pain. Everybody's got a secret. Hiding the pain or issue only makes it worse. Speak to someone. Just one person.

Dr. Robert McGee wrote, "Some people hide their prior conflicts better than others, but most of us have ugly stories to tell if we are honest enough to share them."[335] For some this may be an exercise of confession. You are not the only one in your particular predicament. The truth is, secrets only hold their power when they're hidden. Once revealed in the light of God's love, they lose their power. Satan's grip is broken.

Reflection: As you look back to when you first began this book, today, are you depending on God's Spirit to teach, instruct, counsel, and change you, to use you in the lives of others? Ask him to show you what your story looks and sounds like.

~ Though you cannot go back and make a brand-new start, my friend, you can start now and make a brand-new end. ~

Barbara Wilson[336]

Day 359: The Truth Will Set Me Free!

Your story may be one you are trying to forget. It would not be unusual if you feel great uncertainty about telling your story. After all, telling the story makes it real. Your thinking says, *I'm supposed to forget the past* or *shut up!* Denial is the best solution because *I won't be able to take the rejection.* Denial puts off what should be faced and is a lie from the enemy.

We have all listened to the voices of denial, deception, and evil. We've pretended everything is okay, but we're slowly dying inside. Hopefully, as a result of the work the Holy Spirit has done through this devotional study, you now see the truth or are in the process. "Even though I walk through the valley of the shadow of death, I will fear no evil, for you are with me; your rod and your staff, they comfort me" (Psalm 23:4).

It's true that we must let go of the past, *except* that which leads us to praise God and magnify his grace. I have let go of my past life of sin because I have been forgiven and my slate wiped clean. God no longer sees those sins, but I still talk about my past, as I have done in this book, to give God the glory for my healing and to encourage others. He didn't pull me out of the pit to keep his mercy and grace silent and hidden.

Everyone has a story that God desires to use. Today he wants me to use my story as in instrument in your healing, as he will use your story to help someone else, so we might know the reality of divine healing through all relationships.

Reflection: List three ways God has turned your suffering into joy.

~ One of the devil's snares is to occupy us with the past and the future, so as to take away our peace for the present. ~

Unknown

Day 360: Honestly Starting the Process

I know personally how hard it is for women to trust other women. I will guess many of you have never told your story because you have not felt safe. When looking for a trustworthy friend, seek a woman who is upfront and open about her struggles. A woman quick to listen and slow to speak, who uses the Bible as her final authority.

This is how you can start: recognize that Jesus already knows your story, and all the secrets, but that darkness will never stop his love. Secrets do have a way of creating a barrier between us and the shame-free life of freedom Jesus desires for us.

We first tell Jesus our secrets so we might find forgiveness, redemption, rescue, and ultimately eternal life. Allow the Holy Spirit to work through you and give you renewed confidence about telling your story.

Second, list several ways telling your story to a trusted friend will have a positive impact (be a real blessing) for both of you.

Now think about what you want to say in a safe way. What is your voice saying?

Start by writing out your story in a quiet, protected room. Separate your voice from the person or people in your story, and from God's voice (his Word). What is God saying to you? Now we're ready to share our story with a friend.

Only as we become convinced of the wonder and beauty of our design as God's Girl can we accept ourselves and then become truly transparent.

Reflect on each point.

> ~ *Story telling is one of the most powerful tools you and I possess. Story telling is a kind of incarnation, it gives form to what was once invisible and lends voice to what was once inaudible.* ~
>
> Jennifer Rothschild[337]

Day 361: Tomorrow is a New Day

We have met some incredible women from the Bible who were not much differ-
ent from us. I always felt the hardest part of having the blues was the aloneness.
These women were no strangers to the same kind of feelings. Let's not forget
Jesus in the garden of Gethsemane. He, too, felt isolation and alienation.

These were ordinary women with problems and pain, yet they were used by
God to do his work. For a time they walked through a dark valley like us, yet
they had one thing in common; they chose to take responsibility for their own
growth (growth begins when we accept our own weakness and obey God's stat-
utes). God used them in a powerful way, and he will use you, if you let him.

We each have a unique story about God's transformation. As you have
journeyed through this study, what were the turning points in where God has
intervened? What is he doing now? If you have children, your stories, and
passing on the stories of the women we have studied, will form the founda-
tions of your child's belief in God.

We're talking about honesty. There's a fine line between being vulnerably
honest and being just honest. When people preface whatever they're going
to say with "I'm just being honest," they're usually going to tell us what they
think. When we're vulnerably honest, our defenses are down. We're gentler,
kinder, and more open about ourselves. That is transparency. Vulnerability
and transparency come from the heart.

Reflection: Restoration does not do away with the need for continuing your
relationship with God. If you have not done so already, devise a Bible reading plan.

~ *Hope smiles on the threshold of the year to come, whispering that it will be happier.* ~

Alfred, Lord Tennyson[338]

Day 362: God is Faithful Forever!

God was faithful and just thousands of years ago, and he still is today. God never changes, and neither do his promises. There are times when you will feel sad and think that after all this work you must be doing something wrong. Sadness is just as much a part of life as joy. You may even continue to struggle with bouts of depression, but the outcome need not be dire. Marie expressed:

> In depression and dreadful suffering, I don't condemn life. On the contrary, I like it and find it good. Can you believe it? I find everything good and pleasant, even my tears, my grief. I enjoy weeping, I enjoy my despair. I enjoy being exasperated and sad. I feel as if these were so many diversions, and I love life in spite of them all. I want to live on, I cry, I grieve, and at the same time I am pleased—I know not how to express it. In the very middle of my prayers for happiness, I find myself happy at being miserable. It is not I who undergo all this—my body weeps and cries; but that inside of me which is above me is glad of it all.[339]

Just as God designed all the seasons to be part of nature, he designed all your feelings to be part of you. Would you wake up one rainy day and try to stop the rain? No. When it rains, it rains. Accept the fact that there are times when you will feel sad. Our feelings are part of God's incredible design—despair and joy.

Reflection: What is your response to what Marie expressed?

~ God is the only one who wants to be and always will be that unfailing companion and love in our journey called life. ~

Anonymous

Day 363: The Finish Line!

You have just crossed the finish line! Share in Paul's joy. "I have fought the good fight, I have finished the race, I have kept the faith" (2 Timothy 4:7).

The key to moving forward isn't adding more days to this book. There is only one book you must keep reading. In Jesus' parable of the seed and sower (Matthew 13), Jesus describes three unworthy responses to the Word of God. He reemphasizes the necessity of understanding God's Word and grasping the principles it communicates. Moving forward means maintaining a commitment to God at the deepest level. Do not allow the enemy to crowd God's Word from your mind. Being God's Girl—being filled with the knowledge of God's will and love—is resting in him, asking God to make clear his exact and precise decisions for every circumstance.

My last words are vital: our new life is about faith and humility. It is about acknowledging that we are not God. It is about acknowledging that we each need our Savior every minute of every day. It is about acknowledging that *all* our hopes are met in Jesus alone.

"Right now God is ready to welcome you. Today, he is ready to save you" (2 Corinthians 6:2, TLB). Do not wait until tomorrow. If you haven't received Jesus, do it today. Turn back to the prayer of salvation (Day 100).

Reflection: *"Be joyful always"* (1 Thessalonians 5:16). Start a "Joyful File" or box. This is a record or journal of God's simple blessings, those special moments when God winks at you. It can be a collection of cartoons or letters or poems or quotes.

~ God is our Light and our Protector. He gives us grace and glory. No good thing will he withhold from those who walk along his paths. ~

Psalm 84:11 (TLB)

Day 364: Looking Up

In his devotional titled *Grace For The Moment,* Max Lucado wrote:

> Unhappiness on earth cultivates a hunger for heaven. By gracing us with a deep dissatisfaction, God holds our attention. The only tragedy, then, is to be satisfied. To settle for earth. To be content in a strange land...
>
> We are not happy here because we are not at home here. We are not happy here because we are not supposed to be happy here. We are "like foreigners and strangers in this world" (1 Peter 2:11).
>
> And you will never be completely happy on earth simply because you were not made for earth. Oh, you will have your moments of joy. You will catch glimpses of light. You will know moments or even days of peace. But they simply do not compare with the happiness that lies ahead.

–When God Whispers Your Name[340]

I close with my prayer to you: read Ephesians 3:14–21.

This race is over, but a new adventure has just begun! God bless you.

Self-Soother

Celebrate! Schedule a one-hour massage this upcoming week.

Day 365: How Great Is Our God

Reflection

"How Great Is Our God"
Lyrics by Chris Tomlin
The splendor of the King, clothed in majesty
Let all the earth rejoice. All the earth rejoice
He wraps himself in Light, and darkness tries to hide
And trembles at His voice. Trembles at His voice
How great is our God, sing with me
How great is our God, and all will see
How great, how great is our God
Age to age He stands
And time is in His hands
Beginning and the end
The Godhead Three in One
Father Spirit Son
The Lion and the Lamb

Appendix A: Job's Depression Test

One of the most notable sufferers in the Bible is Job (the book of Job). Job lost everything: family, wealth, and health, and then he slipped into a deep pit of despair. Job's descriptions of despair are so accurate that we can use them to test our own emotional state. Charles M. Sell, a professor at Trinity Seminary, produced "Job's Depression Test."[341] You can check yourself by marking the appropriate terms.

Extreme sadness. "Why is light given to those in misery, and life to the bitter of soul" (Job 3:20). Which is true of you?

I don't feel sad.

I am somewhat sad.

I am sad all the time and can't get over it.

I am so sad that I'm not sure I can stand it anymore.

Sleep disturbance. "When I lie down I think, *How long before I get up?* The night drags on, and I toss till dawn" (Job 7:4).

I do not find myself becoming more tired than usual.

I get tired more easily than I used to.

I get tired doing almost anything.

I am too tired to do anything.

Pessimism about life. "How frail is man, how few his days, how full of trouble! He blossoms for a moment like a flower—and withers; as the shadow of a passing cloud, he quickly disappears" (Job 14:1–2, TLB).

I am not discouraged about the future.

I feel discouraged about the future.

I feel I have nothing to look forward to.

I feel the future is hopeless, and I have nothing to look forward to.

Life seems worthless. "Although I am blameless, I have no concern for myself; I despise my own life" (Job 9:21).

I get as much satisfaction out of things as I always have.

I don't enjoy things the way I used to.

I don't get real satisfaction out of anything anymore.

I am dissatisfied or bored with everything.

Helplessness. "I have no peace, no quietness; I have no rest, but only turmoil" (Job 3:26).

I don't cry any more than usual.

I cry more now than I used to.

I cry all the time.

I used to be able to cry but now can't cry, even though I want to.

Physical signs of sadness. "My eyes have grown dim with grief; my whole frame is but a shadow" (Job 17:7).

My appetite is no worse than normal.

My appetite is not as good as it used to be.

My appetite is much worse now.

I have no appetite at all.

Sexual signs.

I have not noticed any recent change in my interest in sex.

I am less interested in sex than I used to be.

I am much less interested in sex now.

I have lost interest in sex completely.

Desire for death. " ... to those who long for death that does not come, who search for it more than for hidden treasure" (Job 3:21).

I don't have thoughts of killing myself.

I have thoughts of killing myself but would not carry them out.

I would like to kill myself.

I would kill myself if I had the chance.

If you have any thoughts about taking your life, consider this an emergency and get help now! Call 1–800–273–8255 or 911 and ask for help.

Other signs of depression:

Feelings of failure

Lack of satisfaction

Irritation

Loss of interest in people.

NOTE: This is a brief self-checklist. It is not intended to be absolutely accurate. It might tell you that you need to see a professional counselor. This devotional study should not be used in place of professional counsel.

If you marked a lot of ones then depression is not on your doorstep. If you marked some twos, you are probably blue. However, if you marked a lot of threes and fours, you, like Job, have entered some sort of dark tunnel. Do any of these situations explain what has happened in your life lately?

Death of a loved one (bereavement).

Loss of a job.

Loss of a primary relationship (friend, boyfriend, mentor).

Onset of a debilitating illness or injury.

Have been attacked or wounded emotionally by someone else, resulting in anger. "Anger turned inward" once was thought to be the cause of depression. That is no longer accepted. However, when anger is turned inward, or repressed, we don't talk about our feelings because maybe a parent or a spouse or a boss has said something to make us feel guilty or angry. Then we can feel lonely, sad, guilty and blue.

(The New Testament confirms demon possession and oppression.)

Reflection: Ask yourself, "How many of the symptoms of depressions do I have?" Should I consider seeing a physician or counselor about treatment options?

Appendix B: Glossary of "Christianese" Terms

Confession: See Day 202.

Faith: Hebrews 11:1 says faith is the confident assurance that something we want is going to happen. It is the certainty that what we hope for is waiting for us, even though we cannot see it up ahead. Faith is our choice to believe that God will respond to our cries and genuine prayers (See Day 1).

The Flesh: is our inner tendency to sin or do evil; it is myself seeking its own ends in opposition to the Spirit of God. Satan works in harmony with the flesh.

Glory: is the nature and acts of God in self-manifestation, i.e., what he essentially is and does as exhibited in whatever way he reveals himself in these respects, and particularly in the person of Christ.

Holy Bible: "In the beginning was the Word, and the Word was with God, and the Word was God" (John 1:1). Over the course of history, the Bible has been banned, ridiculed, critiqued, and burned. But it has survived and continues to thrive. It is the single most popular book in all of history and has been a worldwide best-seller. Millions of people read it, interpret it, and have tested God's claims (truths). They come to the finish line grasping the same truth— the Bible is God's voice and a roadmap for our lives. The purpose of the Holy Bible is to proclaim God's plan (purpose) and passion to save his children, which is called salvation. This book, which includes Jesus' message, leads each one of us to God's highest calling—eternal life (see Days 24 and 25).

The Holy Spirit: is the presence of God in our lives carrying on the work of Jesus Christ. When we acknowledge Jesus as the Son of God and accept him as our Savior, we begin a relationship with God. He sends the Holy Spirit who takes up residence within us, guiding us down the right path. It is the Holy

Spirit that will illuminate and clarify what God wants you to see in the Bible and in this devotional study.

The Bible teaches that the Holy Spirit was alive at the creation of the world, spoke through the prophets in the Old Testament, and is alive today. The Holy Spirit helps us inwardly by working the fruit of the spirit (see Galatians 5:22–24 and Day 343). The Holy Spirit helps us to pray (Romans 8:26). Lastly, the Holy Spirit pours God's love into our hearts (Romans 5:5). We have the challenge to give the Holy Spirit the freedom to be whatever God intends him to be in our lives.

Obedience: See Day 117.

The Relationship Between Jesus Christ and God: Jesus has always been alive and is himself God. He created everything. Nothing exists that he didn't make. Eternal life is in Jesus Christ, and his life gives light to all mankind (see the Gospels of Matthew, Mark, Luke, and John).

Redemption or Redeem: To buy back from the slave market, set free, to deliver, rescue, or release on receipt of ransom (see Day 118).

Regeneration: is the renewing work of the Holy Spirit that literally makes each believer a new person the moment trust and faith is placed in Jesus Christ as Savior.

Salvation: Contrast the words of Moses in the Old Testament, "The Lord is my strength and my song; he has become my salvation" (Exodus 15:2) with John the Baptist's words in the New Testament as he prepares the way for Jesus, "And all mankind will see God's salvation" (Luke 3:6).

Salvation describes the grace of God. In the Old Testament, salvation is used of the deliverance of the Israelites from the Egyptians (see Exodus 14) and of deliverance generally from evil or danger. In the New Testament, it is specially used with reference to the great deliverance from the guilt and the pollution of sin wrought out by Jesus Christ. It is the spiritual and eternal deliverance granted immediately by God to those who accept his conditions of repentance and faith in the Lord Jesus Christ (See Days 99 and 100).

Sanctification: Sanctify means "to make holy" or "to separate," which is the Lord's plan for our lives. Romans 5:10 says we are enemies of God before we accepted Jesus. But the moment someone trusts Jesus Christ as her personal Savior, her sins are cleared away. She's adopted into the Lord's family and set apart as God's child for a *sacred purpose.* The Bible says (John 17:17; 13:17) that the way to sanctification is through God's Word becoming reality in a believer's life. We are also called saints! Not because we live sinless lives but because we live a life consistent with the one we represent. We experience spiritual peace, joy, contentment—our divine purpose.

Sin: See Days 87–90.

Trinity: is the doctrine that God is one being who exists, simultaneously and eternally, as a mutual indwelling of three persons (not to be confused by "person"): the Father, the Son (incarnate as Jesus of Nazareth), and the Holy Spirit.

The Word: most often refers to the Holy Bible and to Scripture. God's "Word" is every single Scripture verse. "All Scripture is God-breathed and is useful for teaching, rebuking, correcting, and training in righteousness, so that the man of God may be thoroughly equipped for every good work" (2 Timothy 3:16–17). The term is also synonymous with Jesus Christ. The Bible says that before anything else existed, there was Jesus Christ with God: "In the beginning was the Word, and the Word was with God, and the Word was God. He was with God in the beginning" (John 1:1).

The World: In the kingdom of God, everything is essentially different, and we tend to call everything else "the world." The world is presented in John 1:1–18 as all that is opposed to the Word, Jesus Christ. The world is the unhealthy social environment in which we live, which includes the ungodly aspects of culture, peer pressure, values, traditions, "what is in," "what is uncool," customs, philosophies, and attitudes.[342]

Endnotes

All non-referenced quotes are from: *Sales quotes by justsell.com*, www.justsell.com. "Anonymous" or "unkown" are from: Cybersalt Digest, http://www.cybersalt.org/cleanlaugh.

1   Robert McGee, *Search For Significance*, 54, Nashville: W Publishing Group, 2003

2   James Potash, M.D., *Depression ... or Just the Blues? Signs and Symptoms of Clinical Depression Can Be Hard to Self-Diagnose*, ABC News, April 9, 2007; http://abcnews.go.com/Health/Depression/story?id=3015549&page=1

3   Robert McGee, *Search For Significance*, 36, Nashville: W Publishing Group, 2003

4   Valerie E. Whiffen, *A Secret Sadness*, 1, Oakland: New Harbor Publications, 2006

5   Philip B. Kunhard Jr., Philip B. Kunhard III, Peter W. Kunhard, *Lincoln*, New York: Alfred A. Knopf, 1992

6   Les Carter, "A Dab of Depression," http://www.drlescarter.com, August 4, 2006

7   Les Carter, "Why Am I Here?," http://www.drlescarter.com, September 26, 2006

8   Florence Littauer, *Silver Linings*, 109, Birmingham: New Hope Publishers, 2006

9   Daniel G. Amen, M.D., "Healing the Hardware of the Soul," http://www.amenclinic.com/bp/articles.php?articleID=20

10   Gregory L. Jantz, *Moving Beyond Depression*, 9, Colorado Springs: Shaw, 2003

11   Today's Christian Woman, Editor's Blog, *The Sting of Rejection*, September 17, 2007

12   M. Craig Barnes, *When God Interrupts*, 75, InterVarsity Press, 1996

13   Stanley Baldwin, *What Did Jesus Say About That?* 25, Wheaton: Victor Books, 1975

14   SoulCare: New Every Morning, Nazarene.org, June 6, 2007

15   Henri J.M. Nouwen, *Life of the Beloved*, 102, New York: The Crossroad Publishing Company, 1992

16   Oswald Chambers, *My Utmost For His Highest*, August 14th

17   Martin Luther quotes: http://www.giga-usa.com/gigaweb1/quotes2/quautluthermartinx001.htm; accessed: July 30, 2007

18   Valerie E. Whiffen, *A Secret Sadness*, 10, Oakland: New Harbor Publications, 2006

19   SoulCare: New Every Morning, Nazarene.org, May 25, 2006

20   Binford W. Gilbert, *The Pastoral Care of Depression: A Guidebook*, 117, New York: Haworth Pastoral Press, 1998

21   http://www.quotesandpoem.com/quotes/listquotes/subject/faith

22   SoulCare: New Every Morning, Nazarene.org,

23   Florence Littauer, *Silver Linings*, 85, Birmingham: New Hope Publishers, 2006

24   Billy Graham, Answers To Life's Problems, 227, W. Publishing Group, 2003

25   Katherine Wollard, *Body/Mind*, "Go Ahead, Cry Yourself A River," from William Frey II, *Crying: The Mystery of Tears*

26   Christianity Today: http://www.christianitytoday.com/tcw/9w6/9w6090.html; accessed September 1, 2006

27 An Interview With Charles Stanley, http://www.beliefnet.com/story/154/story_15400_3.html, accessed August 31, 2006

28 Les Carter, "A Dab of Depression," http://www.drlescarter.com, August 4, 2006

29 C.S. Lewis Quotes: http://www.brainyquote.com/quotes/authors/c/c_s_lewis.html; assessed March, 2006

30 Reference: H. Norman Wright, *Always Daddy's Girl,* 193–195. Regal Books, 1989

31 http://www.pietyhilldesign.com/gcq/quotepages/godslove.html

32 H. Norman Wright, *Always Daddy's Girl,* 193–195. Regal Books, 1989

33 Charles Stanley, InTouch Ministries, *Life Principle Notes,* "The Power of a Personal Relationship With God," www.intouch.org

34 Source: *CNN,* 1 November 2004, http://www.general-anaesthesia.com/congenital-insensitivity/nopain.html; assessed August 7, 2006

35 SoulCare: New Every Morning, Nazarene.org

36 Vine's Expository Dictionary, Nashville: Thomas Nelson, 1996

37 Philip Yancey, *Meet The Bible,* "loving God Freely," 384

38 L. Smedes, *How Can It Be Alright When Everything is All Wrong?* 55–56, San Francisco: Harper & Row, 1982

39 Marian C. Eberly, *Christian Counseling Today,* "Resiliency: Bouncing Back From Adversity," Vol. 14, No. 4, 2006

40 Today's Gift, October 16, 2006; www.hazelden.org

41 Email Correspondence; February 17, 2007

42 Today's Turning Point with David Jeremiah, June 27, 2007

43 Cybersalt Digest, April 28, 2006

44 John White, *Excellence in Leadership,* 26, Downers Grove: InterVarsity Press, 1986

45 Henri J.M. Nouwen, *Life of the Beloved,* 76, New York: The Crossroad Publishing Company, 1992

46 Dorothy Pape, *In Search of God's Ideal Woman,* 27, Downers Grove: InterVarsity Press

47 Jim Andrews, Polishing Gd's Monuments, 81, Wapwallopen: Shepherd Press, 2007

48 SoulCare: New Every Morning, Nazarene.org

49 Chicken Soup for the Recovering Soul—Inspirations, 45, Deerfield Beach: Health Communications, 2005

50 SoulCare: New Every Morning, Nazarene.org, June 6, 2006

51 Henry Cloud, Changes That Heal, 17–18, Grand Rapids: Zondervan, 1992

52 Randy Alcorn, *The Grace and Truth Paradox,* 92, Sisters: Multonomah Publishers, 2003

53 SoulCare: New Every Morning, Nazarene.org, June 14

54 Randy Alcorn, *The Grace and Truth Paradox,* 92, Sisters: Multonomah Publishers, 2003

55 Henry Cloud, Changes That Heal, 32, Grand Rapids: Zondervan, 1992

56 Chicken Soup for the Recovering Soul—Inspirations, 59, Deerfield Beach: Health Communications, 2005

57 Carol Kent, *When I Lay My Isaac Down,* Colorado Springs: NavPress, 2004

58 http://www.singleness.org/quotes.shtml; accessed July 2, 2007

59 R. Alan Cole, *Exodus: An Introduction and Commentary,* 57, Downers Grove: InterVarsity Press, 1973

60 SoulCare: New Every Morning, Nazarene.org, April 4, 2006

61 SoulCare: New Every Morning, Nazarene.org

62 Ibid, , February 5, 2007

63 Valerie E. Whiffen, *A Secret Sadness,* 2, Oakland: New Harbor Publications, 2006

64   Soul Care, June 20, 2006

65   Nancy Stafford, *Beauty By The Book*, 129, Sisters: Multonomah, 2002

66   http://en.wikipedia.org/wiki/Lucifer; Accessed July 17, 2008

67   Oswald Chambers, *My Utmost For His Highest*, August 26th

68   Matthew Henry Quotes: http://en.thinkexist.com/quotes/matthew_
      henry; accessed July 30, 2006

69   Chicken Soup for the Recovering Soul—Inspirations, 122, Deerfield
      Beach: Health Communications, 2005

70   http://www.quotesandpoem.com/quotes/listquotes/subject/evil

71   Paul Tripp, *War of Words*, 25, Phillipsburg: P&R Publishing, 2000

72   SoulCare: New Every Morning, Nazarene.org,, October 18, 2006

73   Jeff Olson, *RBC Ministries*," When Hope Is Lost," Grand Rapids, MI, 2002

74   SoulCare: New Every Morning, Nazarene.org, July 26, 2006

75   Chicken Soup for the Recovering Soul—Inspirations, 363, Deerfield
      Beach: Health Communications, 2005

76   http://www.singleness.org/quotes.shtml accessed July 2, 2007

77   Ibid. 12

78   http://news.yahoo.com/s/ap/20070330/ap_en_mo/film_acting_
      her_age; accessed March 30, 2007

79   Stanley Baldwin, *What Did Jesus Say?* 35, Wheaton: Victor Books, 1975

80   http://thinkexist.com/quotation/sin_is_geographical/200302.html

81   SoulCare: New Every Morning, Nazarene.org

82   Molalla Church of the Nazarene, Sermon: August 13, 2006

83   Theopedia: Millard Erickson, *Christian Theology*, 578

84   C.S. Lewis Quotes: http://www.brainyquote.com/quotes/authors/c/
      c_s_lewis.html; assessed August 7, 2006

85   *The American Heritage Dictionary of the English Language, Fourth Edition,*
      Houghton Mifflin Company. 2000

86   Matthew Henry Quotes: http://en.thinkexist.com/quotes/matthew_
      henry; accessed July 30, 2006

87   Chambers, Oswald, *My Utmost For His Highest,* Repentance, December 7

88   Molalla Church of the Nazarene, Sermon: August 20, 2006

89   Cybersalt Digest, April 18, 2006

90   Gregory L. Jantz, *Moving Beyond Depression,* 45, Colorado Springs: Shaw,
      2003

91   Larry Crabb, *Shattered Dreams,* 9, Colorado Springs: Waterbrook Press,
      2001

92   Valerie E. Whiffen, *A Secret Sadness,* 23, Oakland: New Harbor
      Publications, 2006

93   *B.J. in Elim Evangel.* Walter B. Knight. 639–640, *Knight's Master Book of
      4,000 Illustrations*

94   http://www.gurze.net; accessed August 20, 2006

95   SoulCare: New Every Morning, Nazarene.org, July 4, 2007

96   http://www.singleness.org/quotes.shtml

97   Robert McGee, *Search For Significance,* 106, Nashville: W Publishing
      Group, 2003

98   Chicken Soup for the Recovering Soul—Inspirations, 93, Deerfield
      Beach: Health Communications, 2005

99   Psychology for Living, December 2007

100   http://education.yahoo.com/reference/quotations/quote/14363

101   SoulCare: New Every Morning, Nazarene.org, June 27, 2007

102   Cybersalt Digest, August 3, 2006

103   Philip Yancey, *Meet The Bible,* 23, Grand Rapids: Zondervan, 2000

104 Charles Swindoll, *Insight For Living*, March 2007

105 A.W. Tozer Quotes: http://www.worldofquotes.com/author/A.w.-Tozer/1/index.html

106 Max Lucado, *Grace For the Moment*, 87, Nashville: Thomas Nelson, 2000

107 Joel Osteen, *Your Best Life Now*, 38, New York: Time Warner Book, 2004

108 Jerry Sittser, *A Grace Disguised*, 131, Grand Rapids: Zondervan, 2004

109 Today's Gift, November 24, 2006; www.hazelden.org

110 Larry Crabb, Connecting, 31,53, Nashville: Word Pub., 1997

111 Hunter, Brenda, *In The Company of Women*, 29, Sisters: Multonomah Publishers, 1994

112 http://www.quotesandpoem.com/quotes/listquotes/subject/honor

113 Henri J.M. Nouwen, *Life of the Beloved*, 63, New York: The Crossroad Publishing Company, 1992

114 Nancy Stafford, *Beauty By The Book*, 166, Sisters: Multonomah, 2002

115 *The American Heritage Dictionary of the English Language, Fourth Edition*, Houghton Mifflin Company 2000.

116 Robert McGee, *Search For Significance*, 35, Nashville: W Publishing Group, 2003

117 Helen Keller: http://en.wikiquote.org/wiki/Helen_Keller; accessed: February 17, 2007

118 Gregory L. Jantz, *Moving Beyond Depression*, 144, Colorado Springs: Shaw, 2003

119 Jeff Olson, RBC Ministries, "When Hope Is Lost," 25

120 Chip Ingram, *God: As He Longs for You to See Him*, 92, Grand Rapids: Baker, 2006

121   Jennie Afman Dimkoff, Night Whispers, 104, Grand Rapids: Baker Books, 2002

122   Chicken Soup for the Recovering Soul—Inspirations, 339, Deerfield Beach: Health Communications, 2005

123   Rick Warren, *The Purpose Driven Life*, 18, Grand Rapids: Zondervan, 2002

124   Jerry Sittser, *A Grace Disguised,* 59, Grand Rapids: Zondervan, 2004

125   Today's Turning Point with David Jeremiah, September 1, 2007

126   Oswald Chambers, *My Utmost For His Highest,* May 14,

127   Valerie E. Whiffen, *A Secret Sadness,* "Brown and Harris 1978," 135, Oakland: New Harbor Publications, 2006

128   http://www.quotesandpoem.com/quotes/listquotes/subject/beauty

129   http://www.quotesandpoem.com/quotes/showquotes/author/Princess-Diana/13768

130   *The American Heritage Dictionary of the English Language, Fourth Edition, 2000 by Houghton Mifflin Company*

131   Robert McGee, *Search For Significance,* 11, Nashville: W Publishing Group, 2003

132   http://www.gurze.net; accessed August 20, 2006

133   http://www.quotationspage.com/quote/34418.html

134   Mother Teresa quotes: http://www.brainyquote.com/quotes/authors/m/mother_teresa.html

135   http://www.quotesandpoem.com/quotes/showquotes/author/Linda-Evans/43786

136   St. Augustine Quotes: http://www.worldofquotes.com/author/St.-Augustine/1/index.html

137   http://www.quotegarden.com/jealousy.html

138   James Dobson, In The Arms of God, Wheaton: Tyndale, 1997

139   Barbara Wilson, *The Invisible Bond,* 13, Sisters: Multnomah, 2006

140   Robert E. Rector, Kirk A. Johnson, Ph.D., and Lauren R. Noyes, *Sexually Active Teenagers Are More Likely To Be Depressed And To Attempt Suicide, Center for Data Analysis Report #03,* http://www.heritage.org/Research/Abstinence/cda0304.cfm; accessed: August 13, 2007

141   SoulCare: New Every Morning, Nazarene.org, December 6, 2006

142   Helen Keller: http://en.wikiquote.org/wiki/Helen_Keller; accessed: February 17, 2007

143   Soulcare: New Every Morning, Nazarene.org, June 27, 2007

144   Max Lucado, *Grace For the Moment,* 252, Nashville: Thomas Nelson, 2000

145   David Van Biema, Time, *Her Agony,* September 3, 2007

146   http://www.quotesandpoem.com/quotes/showquotes/author/Princess-Diana/13766

147   James Dobson, *In The Arms of God,* Wheaton: Tyndale, 1997

148   Rick Warren, *The Purpose Driven Life,* 17, grand Rapids: Zondervan, 2002

149   Remuda Ranch, *Eating Disorders Across the Lifespan: A Closer Look,* August, 2007,

150   C.S. Lewis Quotes: http://www.brainyquote.com/quotes/authors/c/c_s_lewis.html; assessed August 7, 2006

151   oulCare: New Every Morning, Nazarene.org, May 22, 2006

152   John Trent, *LifeMapping,* 30, Colorado Springs: WaterBrook Press, 1998

153   SoulCare: New Every Morning, Nazarene.org; July 13, 2006

154   Kevin Lehman, *Women Who Try Too Hard,* 151,Grand Rapids: Flemming Revell, 1987, 2001

155   *Reflecting God: Devotions for Holy Living,* 20, WordAction, June-August 2006

156   SoulCare: New Every Morning, Nazarene.org

157   *Reflecting God: Devotions for Holy Living,* 30, WordAction, June-August 2006

158   Randy Alcorn, *Heaven,* 281, Wheaton: Tyndale Publishers, 2004

159   Cybersalt Digest, May 12, 2007

160   Helen Keller Quotes: http://www.quotationspage.com/quotes/Helen_Keller

161   http://en.wikipedia.org/wiki/Vashti: *The Oxford Bible Commentary* (edited by John Barton and John Muddiman, NY: Oxford University Press, 2001, 326–327, written by Carol Meyers)

162   SoulCare: New Every Morning, Nazarene.org, June 22, 2006

163   Nancy Stafford, Beauty By The Book, 174, Sisters: Multonomah, 2002

164   Killy John and Alie Stibbe, *Bursting At The Seams*, 35, Monarch Books, 2004

165   Chicken Soup for the Recovering Soul—Inspirations, 309, Deerfield Beach: Health Communications, 2005

166   Anne Franke Quotes: http://www.brainyquote.com/quotes/authors/a/anne_frank.html

167   hicken Soup, the Recovering Soul—Inspirations, 88, Deerfield Beach: Health Communications, 2005

168   Joel Osteen, *Your Best Life Now*, 16, New York: Warner Faith, 2004

169   Today's Gift, October 30, 2006; www.hazelden.org

170   http://www.gurze.net; accessed August 20, 2006

171   SoulCare: New Every Morning, Nazarene.org, May 18, 2006

172   Cybersalt Digest, March 24, 2007

173   Today's Gift, March 31, 2007; www.hazelden.org

174   Laurence J. Peter, *The Laughter Prescription*, 88, New York: Ballantine Books, 1982

175   Dee Brestin, *Friendships of Women*, 50, Colorado Springs: Life Journey, 2005

176   Helen Keller Quotes: http://www.quotationspage.com/quotes/Helen_Keller

177   Cybersalt Digest, March 13, 2007

178 Helen Keller Quotes: http://www.quotationspage.com/quotes/ Helen_Keller

179 Chicken Soup for the Recovering Soul—Inspirations, 11, Deerfield Beach: Health Communications, 2005

180 Leila Rae Sommerfeld, *Beyond Our Control—Rape*, 34, Enumclaw: WinePress Publishing, 2006

181 http://www.quotesandpoem.com/quotes/listquotes/subject/ acceptance

182 Justsell.com, May 30, 2008

183 Today's Gift, December 25, 2006; www.hazelden.org

184 Sheri Rose Shepherd, *Fit For Excellence*, 23, Lake Mary: Creation House, 1961

185 Binford W. Gilbert, *The Pastoral Care of Depression: A Guidebook,* 115, New York: Haworth Pastoral Press, 1998

186 Max Lucado, *Answers To Life's Most Perplexing Problems,* "Struggling With Guilt and Bitterness," 18, Sisters: Multonomah, 1998

187 http://www.quotesandpoem.com/quotes/listquotes/subject/ forgiveness

188 http://www.quotesandpoem.com/quotes/listquotes/subject/anger

189 http://www.quotesandpoem.com/quotes/showquotes/author/Joan-Lunden/1722

190 Luis Palau, Answers To Life's Most Perplexing Problems, "Struggling With Forgiveness," 33, Sisters: Multonomah, 1998

191 Neil Anderson, F. Garzon, Judith King, *Released From Bondage,* 124, Nashville: Thomas Nelson, 1991

192 Sheri Rose Shepherd, *Fit For Excellence*, 23–24, Lake Mary: Creation House, 1961

193 Ibid

194   Bob George, "There's No Need To Be Depressed,"7, *Moody Monthly*, February, 1982

195   Barbara Wilson, *The Invisible Bond,* 107, Sisters: Multnomah, 2006

196   Encyclopedia of 15,000 Illustrations

197   SoulCare: New Every Morning, Nazarene.org, June 29, 2006

198   Today's Turning Point with David Jeremiah, December 5, 2007

199   SoulCare: New Every Morning, Nazarene.org, May 4, 2007

200   Chicken Soup, 41

201   *Dictionary.com Unabridged (v 1.1) Based on the Random House Unabridged Dictionary, Random House, Inc.* 2006.

202   G.O. Higgins, *Resilient Adults: Overcoming a Cruel Past,* San Francisco: Josey-Bass, 1994

203   Marian C. Eberly, *Christian Counseling Today,* "Resiliency: Bouncing Back From Adversity," Vol. 14, No. 4, 2006

204   James Dobson, In The Arms of God, Wheaton: Tyndale, 1997

205   SoulCare: New Every Morning, Nazarene.org, May 9, 2006

206   The Quotation Page, http://www.quotationspage.com/quote/2755.html, accessed July 10, 2006

207   http://www.aahistory.com/prayer.html; Accessed June 20, 2008

208   http://www.quotesandpoem.com/quotes/listquotes/subject/deception/0

209   Barbara Wilson, *The Invisible Bond,* 72, Sisters: Multnomah, 2006

210   Robert McGee, *Search For Significance,* 10, Nashville: W Publishing Group, 2003

211   Ibid

212   D. Martyn Lloyd-Jones, *Spiritual Depression,* 19, Grand Rapids: Wm. B. Eerdmans Publishing Co., 1965

213   James Dobson, *In The Arms of God,* Wheaton: Tyndale, 1997

214   *Moving Beyond Depression,* 26, Colorado Springs: Shaw, 2003

215   Joel Osteen, *Your Best Life Now,* 14, New York: Warner Faith, 2004

216   C. Peterson, *American Psychologist,* "The Future of Depression," 55:44–55, 2000

217   Keller, Rodgers, Morgan, *Hand In Hand,* Remuda Ranch Center, 1998

218   Neil Anderson, F. Garzon, Judith King, *Released From Bondage,* 21, Nashville: Thomas Nelson, 1991

219   A.W. Tozer Quotes: http://www.worldofquotes.com/author/A.w.-Tozer/1/index.html

220   Oswald Chambers, *My Utmost For His Highest,* August 26

221   Gregory L. Jantz, *October2007 Hope Newsletter*

222   Bible Illustrations; accessed October 17, 2006

223   http://jokes.christiansunite.com/Satan/Satan's_Beatitudes.shtml

224   C.S. Lewis Quotes: http://www.brainyquote.com/quotes/authors/c/c_s_lewis.html; assessed August 7, 2006

225   Barbara Wilson, *The Invisible Bond,* 37, Sisters: Multnomah, 2006

226   *Dictionary.com Unabridged, Based on the Random House Unabridged Dictionary,* Random House, Inc, 2006

227   Clinton E. Arnold, 3 *Crucial Questions About Spiritual Warfare,* 34;36, Grand Rapids: Baker Books, 1997

228   Henri J.M. Nouwen, *Life of the Beloved,* 31, New York: The Crossroad Publishing Company, 1992

229   SoulCare: New Every Morning, Nazarene.org, July 20, 2007

230   Ibid, October 6, 2006

231   http://www.singleness.org/quotes.shtml; accessed July 2, 2007

232   SoulCare: New Every Morning, Nazarene.org, June 13, 2008

233 http://www.mhsanctuary.com/Healing/auto.htm; accessed August 20, 2007

234 SoulCare: New Every Morning, Nazarene.org, June 23, 2006

235 Ibid, September 4, 2006

236 http://www.quotesandpoem.com/quotes/listquotes/subject/truth

237 Oswald Chambers, *My Utmost For His Highest,* March 23

238 Ibid.

239 http://www.singleness.org/quotes.shtml; accessed July 2, 2007

240 Cybersalt Digest, #3220, July 19, 2008

241 Helen Keller Quotes: http://www.quotationspage.com/quotes/ Helen_Keller

242 http://www.quotesandpoem.com/quotes/listquotes/subject/women

243 Today's Turning Point with David Jeremiah, August 27, 2007

244 C.S. Lewis Quotes, http://www.brainyquote.com/quotes/authors/c/ c_s_lewis.html

245 Yvonne Martinez, *From Victim To Victor,* 115–116, San Diego: RPI Publishing, 1993

246 SoulCare: New Every Morning, Nazarene.org, October 20, 2006

247 Time, *Her Agony,* 39, September 3, 2007

248 http://www.quotedb.com/categories/pride/rating

249 Today's Gift: *A Day at a Time by Anonymous,* Hazelden Foundation, 1989

250 SoulCare: New Every Morning, Nazarene.org, March 30, 2007

251 http://www.quotedb.com/categories/pride/rating

252 The American Heritage Dictionary of the English Language, Fourth Edition; *Houghton Mifflin Company,* 2006; *Random House Unabridged Dictionary,* © Random House, Inc. 2006.

253 Killy John and Alie Stibbe, *Bursting At The Seams,* 125, Monarch Books, 2004

254 *The American Heritage Dictionary of the English Language, Fourth Edition,* *Houghton Mifflin Company,* 2000

255 May 8, *The Patience Of Faith*—My Utmost For His Highest

256 Justsell.com, August 21, 2007

257 Dictionary.com Unabridged (v 1.1) Based on the *Random House Unabridged Dictionary,* Random House, Inc. 2006

258 *The Christian's Battle,* 2006, http://www.useless-knowledge. com/1234/06may/article113.html; accessed: August 21, 2007

259 http://www.quotesandpoem.com/quotes/listsubjects/Truth

260 The American Heritage Dictionary of the English Language, Fourth Edition, Houghton Mifflin Company. 2006

261 SoulCare: New Every Morning, Nazarene.org

262 Ibid

263 Jim Andrews, Polishing God's Monuments, 44–45, Wapwallopen: Shepherd Press, 2007

264 Ibid, January 31, 2007

265 Gary Smalley and John Trent, *Love Is a Decision,* 8, Dallas: Word, 1989

266 Bo Bennett Quotes, http://www.quotesandpoem.com/quotes/ listquotes/author/bo_bennett

267 Valerie E. Whiffen, *A Secret Sadness,* 49, Oakland: New Harbor Publications, 2006

268 http://www.aplaceofhope.com/newsletters/february2006.html

269 http://www.aplaceofhope.com/newsletters/february2006.html

270 Used with permission: Sherri Langton, *Today's Christian Woman,* ";" March/April 2003, Vol. 25, No. 2, p.58

271 http://www.singleness.org/quotes.shtml; accessed July 2, 2007

272 SoulCare: New Every Morning, Nazarene.org

273   Ibid, October 10, 2006

274   Cybersalt Digest, August 15, 2006

275   *The American Heritage Dictionary of the English Language, Houghton Mifflin Company,* 2000

276   SoulCare: New Every Morning, Nazarene.org, March 30, 2007

277   Charles Stanley, *In Touch Daily Devotional,* February 26, 2007

278   Helen Keller: http://en.wikiquote.org/wiki/Helen_Keller; accessed: August 17,2007

279   Laura Roberts, Psy.D., Cornerstone Clinical Services, Portland, Oregon, February 19, 2007

280   Valerie E. Whiffen, *A Secret Sadness,* 39, Oakland: New Harbor Publications, 2006

281   Selected—Encyclopedia of 15,000 Illustrations

282   Lexicon Publishing Group, LLC, www.Dictionary.com

283   Pat O'Connor *Friendships Between Women,* 17, New York: Guilford Press, 1992

284   Brenda Hunter, *In The Company of Women,* 110, Sisters: Multonomah Publishers, 1994

285   Liane Cordes, *The Reflecting Pond,* "Today's Gift," November 21, 2006: www.Hazelden.org

286   Helen Keller: http://en.wikiquote.org/wiki/Helen_Keller; accessed: February 17, 2007

287   Brenda Hunter *In The Company of Women,* 164, Sisters: Multonomah Publishers, 1994

288   C. S. Lewis Quotes: http://www.brainyquote.com/quotes/authors/c/c_s_lewis.html; assessed July 13, 2006

289   Thomas Brooks, *Precious Remedies Against Satan's Devices,* 198, Carlisle: The Banner of Truth Trust

290   Cybersalt Digest, January 14, 2006

291   http://www.singleness.org/quotes.shtml; accessed July 2, 2007

292   http://www.singleness.org/quotes.shtml

293   Today's Gift, December 22, 2006; www.hazelden.org

294   Ibid, March 25, 2007

295   Charles Swindoll, *Handbook of Preaching Resources from Literature*, 221, Nashville: Thomas Nelson, 1998

296   http://www.singleness.org/quotes.shtml; accessed July 2, 2007

297   A.W. Tozer Quotes: http://www.worldofquotes.com/author/A.w.-Tozer/1/index.html

298   SoulCare: New Every Morning, Nazarene.org, June 19, 2007

299   David McLaughlin, The Role of the Man in the Family: A Seminar For Men, 1987

300   Today's Turning Point with David Jeremiah, February 25, 2008

301   Permission granted by Lorrie Fulton to reprint, September 26, 2006

302   Focus on the Family, *God's Design for Marriage*; Gary L. Thomas is a writer and the founder and director of the Center for Evangelical Spirituality; http://www.family.org/married/growth/a0028530.cfm

303   Beverly LaHaye, *Women's Devotional Bible*, Worth Defending in Battle, 1304, Grand Rapids: Zondervan, 1994

304   http://www.singleness.org/quotes.shtml; accessed July 2, 2007

305   Ibid

306   http://www.quotesandpoem.com/quotes/listquotes/subject/beauty

307   Florence Littauer, *Silver Linings*, 75, Birmingham: New Hope Publishers, 2006

308   http://www.quotesandpoem.com/quotes/listquotes/subject/beauty

309   Kim Gaines Eckert, *Love the Skin You're In*, Today's Christian Woman, July/August 2006

310   Gregory L. Jantz, *Hope, Help, and Healing for Eating Disorders*, 96, Wheaton: Harold Shaw Publishers, 1995.

311   Gregory L. Jantz, *Moving Beyond Depression*, 117–118, 122–123, Colorado Springs: Shaw, 2003

312   Killy John and Alie Stibbe, *Bursting At The Seams*, 87, Monarch Books, 2004

313   Chicken Soup for the Recovering Soul—Inspirations, 365, Deerfield Beach: Health Communications, 2005

314   Gregory L. Jantz, *Moving Beyond Depression*, 129, Colorado Springs: Shaw, 2003

315   Henry T. Blackaby, Richard Blackaby, *Experiencing God Day-By-Day*, 215, Nashville: Broadman & Holman, 1997

316   http://www.singleness.org/quotes.shtml; accessed July 2, 2007

317   *The American Heritage Dictionary of the English Language, Fourth Edition*, 2000, *Houghton Mifflin Company.*

318   Henri J.M. Nouwen, *Life of the Beloved*, 80, New York: The Crossroad Publishing Company, 1992

319   SoulCare: New Every Morning, Nazarene.org, June 15, 2006

320   Ibid, September 25, 2006

321   Max Lucado, *Grace For The Moment*, 25, Nashville: J. Countryman, 2000

322   Larry Crabb, *Shattered Dreams*, 53, Colorado Springs: Waterbrook Press, 2001

323   Life Application Study Bible, 1055, Wheaton: Tyndale House, 2005

324   Jerry Sittser, *A Grace Disguised*, 92, Grand Rapids: Zondervan, 2004

325   James Dobson, In The Arms of God, Wheaton: Tyndale, 1997

326   A.W. Tozer Quotes: http://www.worldofquotes.com/author/A.w.-Tozer/1/index.html

327   http://dictionary.reference.com/browse/hospitality; Accessed October 4, 2006

328   SoulCare: New Every Morning, Nazarene.org, July 30, 2007

329   Jennie Afman Dimkoff, *Night Whispers*, 184

330   Charles Stanley, *In Touch Daily Devotional,* January 13, 2007

331   SoulCare: New Every Morning, Nazarene.org, *September* 20, 2006

332   Diana Hagee, *The King's Daughter*, 63, Nashville: Thomas Nelson, 2001

333   Larry Crabb, *Shattered Dreams,* 4, Colorado Springs: Waterbrook Press, 2001

334   http://www.quotesandpoem.com/quotes/listquotes/subject/food; accessed August 23, 2007

335   Robert McGee, *Father Hunger*, 147, Ann Arbor: Servant Publications, 1993

336   Barbara Wilson, *The Invisible Bond,* 147, Sisters: Multnomah, 2006

337   WomensMinistry.net Weekly, April 10, 2007

338   Today's Gift, December 30, 2006, www.hazelden.org.

339   William James, Varieties of Religious Experience, 86, Charleston: BiblioBazaar, 2007

340   Max Lucado, *Grace For The Moment,* "Made For Heaven: January 10," 25, Nashville: J. Countryman, 2000

341   Charles M. Sell, "Struggling With Depression," *Answers To Life's Most Perplexing Problems*, 146–148; Questions adapted from "Becks Inventory for Measuring Depression" (University of Pennsylvania Press, 1967)

342   Clinton E. Arnold, 3 *Crucial Questions About Spiritual Warfare*, 34, Grand Rapids: Baker Books, 1997